Trade Policies
for International
Competitiveness

A National Bureau
of Economic Research
Conference Report

Trade Policies for International Competitiveness

Edited by Robert C. Feenstra

The University of Chicago Press

Chicago and London

ROBERT C. FEENSTRA is associate professor of economics at the University of California, Davis, and a research associate of the National Bureau of Economic Research.

The University of Chicago Press, Chicago 60637
The University of Chicago Press, Ltd., London
© 1989 by the National Bureau of Economic Research
All rights reserved. Published 1989

Printed in the United States of America
98 97 96 95 94 93 92 91 90 89   5 4 3 2 1

Library of Congress Cataloging-in-Publication Data

Trade policies for international competitiveness / edited by
    Robert C. Feenstra.
        p.   cm.—(National Bureau of Economic Research conference report)
    Includes index.
        ISBN 0-226-23949-7 (alk. paper)
        1. United States—Commercial policy—Congresses. 2. Foreign
    trade promotion—United States—Congresses. 3. Investments,
    American—Congresses. 4. International competition—Congresses.
    I. Feenstra, Robert C. II. Series: Conference report (National Bureau
    of Economic Research)
    HF1455.T645 1989   89-33917
    382'.3'0973—dc20   CIP

Contents

Acknowledgments

This conference was funded by grant no. SES–8709489 from the National Science Foundation. Any opinions, findings, conclusions, or recommendations expressed in this publication are those of the authors and do not necessarily reflect the views of the National Science Foundation or the National Bureau of Economic Research.

Introduction

Robert C. Feenstra

International competitiveness has become a keyword of policy debates and indicates the ability of a country's export or import-competing industries to maintain their market share. Recent concerns that the United States is lagging in international competitiveness has led to numerous studies and policy proposals. Consider the following views, for example, drawn from different sectors of the U.S. economy. The first comes from a survey done by the *Harvard Business Review* on the question, "Do you think there is a competitiveness problem?" Nearly four thousand readers responded, and the results are summarized in the following three statements ("Competitiveness Survey" 1987, 8):

> America's competitiveness is declining—largely because of the performance of U.S. managers—and it is up to them to respond to the challenge.
>
> While the government shares part of the blame, government remedies—particularly a national economic strategy—are not solutions to the problem.
>
> Basic U.S. values—such as the work ethic, pride in quality, and deferred gratification—have slipped and must be restored if the country is to get back on track.

These statements can be taken as representative of the business sector. The views of the U.S. Congress are reflected in the Trade Bill of 1988 (*Wall Street Journal*, 22 April 1988, p. 18):

> House Ways and Means Committee Chairman Rostenkowski said the trade bill, which he called the most comprehensive ever considered by Congress, would for the first time "establish a policy that will make America a winner in international markets." House Speaker Wright declared: "We can be No. 1 again."

Robert C. Feenstra is associate professor of economics at the University of California, Davis, and a research associate of the National Bureau of Economic Research.

Finally, of course, we should consider the views of academic economists. The papers in this volume illustrate current academic research on the topic of international competitiveness. But, for a single statement from a distinguished source, we have (Samuelson 1988, 281):

> In chapter 31 Ricardo discovers what he has elsewhere gratuitously denied: that an improvement abroad can hurt Britain under free trade (or, as needs to be said today, that an improvement in Japan can hurt the American living standard).

These quotes demonstrate the wide range of opinions on international competitiveness. So too, the range of research topics in this area is diverse. The chapters in this volume explore the effects of macroeconomic and strategic trade policies on competitiveness; the recent influx of foreign direct investment to the United States, much of it from Japan; conversely, the extent to which Japanese trade barriers may have restricted imports; and the market structure of Canadian industries, with application to the U.S.-Canada free trade agreement. A brief summary of these papers will help to put them into perspective.

In the first chapter, Goulder and Eichengreen contrast the effects of "saving-promoting" and "investment-promoting" policies on exchange rates and industry output. In this case, international competitiveness is measured by the profitability and growth of U.S. export industries. The authors demonstrate how policy actions by the U.S. such as a shift from income to consumption taxes, or the restoration of investment tax credits, would have very different effects on the growth of exports. Their analysis draws a direct connection between policy actions and the competitive position of the United States.

In chapter 2, attention is shifted from *domestic* to *foreign* investment in the United States. Ray gives a comprehensive description of the pattern of foreign direct investment and its possible explanations. The recent influx of investments is indirectly a result of U.S. policies, particularly the balance of payments deficit, and poses a competitive challenge within U.S. borders. One expects that foreign direct investment will become an issue of growing importance for trade policy in future years.

The next two chapters of the volume investigate the empirical and theoretical basis for "strategic" trade policies. This phrase has come to indicate policies that may be in the national interest under an imperfectly competitive market structure (see Krugman 1986). Katz and Summers document the persistent pattern of interindustry wage differentials in the United States and other industrial countries. According to this pattern, there are some industries that consistently pay higher than average wages (even after correcting for skill differences) and that should be promoted from an efficiency viewpoint. They argue that the gains from promoting high-wage industries outweigh the potential benefits from strategic trade policy. These views are challenged, however, by the comments following chapter 3.

In chapter 4, Driskill and McCafferty directly address the modeling of strategic trade policy, particularly the use of conjectural variations. They show that the equilibrium of a dynamic duopoly game gives rise to a term similar to a conjectural variation but that this term is itself a function of policy parameters. In this sense, trade policy models that use conjectural variations are subject to the Lucas critique: that is, the model parameters change with policy.

Discussions of international competitiveness are incomplete without referring to the Japanese success story, now being repeated by other newly industrialized countries. An open question is whether the Japanese success is due to socioeconomic factors, such as the work ethic and educational system, or direct government support for industries. Saxonhouse addresses part of this question by testing whether the Japanese trade pattern, including intraindustry trade, can be explained by that country's unique factor endowments. He answers this question in the affirmative, implying that tariff and nontariff barriers do not comprehensively restrict Japanese imports. For an alternative view, the reader is referred to the comment on chapter 5 by Tyson.

The final two chapters deal with Canada's position in international markets. Schembri specifies and estimates a model of an imperfectly competitive exporter and uses it to study the effect of exchange rates on industry prices. His results support the idea of "pricing to market," under which exporters retain foreign market share by not passing through changes in exchange rates. Turning from a specific industry to the entire economy, Brown and Stern report results from a computable general equilibrium model dealing with U.S.-Canada trade. They investigate how different assumptions on market structure and product differentiation affect the outcome of a bilateral tariff elimination, as proposed with the free trade agreement. International competitiveness is indicated by entry and exit within industries and by changes in overall trade.

These chapters demonstrate the wide range of trade policies that affect international competitiveness. In the first chapter, the trade policies are macroeconomic: tax policies to affect savings and investment. In the third and fourth chapters, the trade policies are "strategic," that is, targeted at imperfectly competitive industries. More conventional policies—tariffs and nontariff barriers—are examined in the country studies of chapters 5 and 7. The remaining chapters (2 and 6) focus on topics that have important implications for the choice of trade policies: foreign direct investment and the exercise of monopolistic pricing in international markets.

In summary, these papers draw on current research to study how trade policies affect international competitiveness. While the topics covered are not exhaustive, the range of issues and research methods is impressive (for other studies of competitiveness, see Feldstein 1988 and Spence and Hazard 1988). Taken together, the chapters show the importance of macroeconomic and industry policies in determining competitiveness and, conversely, how patterns of trade and investment may influence future policies.

References

Competitiveness survey: *HBR* readers respond. 1987. *Harvard Business Review* (September–October), pp. 8–11.

Feldstein, Martin, ed. 1988. *The United States in the world economy.* Chicago: University of Chicago Press.

Krugman, Paul R., ed. 1986. *Strategic trade policy and the new international economics.* Cambridge, Mass.: MIT Press.

Samuelson, Paul Λ. 1988. Mathematical vindication of Ricardo on machinery. *Journal of Political Economy* 96(April):274–82.

Spence, A. Michael, and Heather A. Hazard, eds. 1988. *International competitiveness.* Cambridge, Mass.: Ballinger.

1 Savings Promotion, Investment Promotion, and International Competitiveness

Lawrence H. Goulder and Barry Eichengreen

Over the past two decades, international economic transactions have become increasingly important to the U.S. economy. Increased openness poses a challenge to tax policy analysts, who must now consider new channels through which policy initiatives may operate. In an open economy, it is important, for example, to distinguish policies aimed at stimulating saving from those targeted at promoting investment. The distinction gains importance to the extent that there is international mobility of financial capital; in its presence, as Summers (1988) and others have pointed out, the two types of policies are likely to have opposite effects on capital flows, exchange rates, and the performance of tradables industries.[1]

Analytic studies have been useful in identifying potential differences between savings- and investment-promoting policies in an open economy. Unfortunately, the sign as well as the magnitude of the long-run effects of these policies on many important variables (such as the current account of the balance of payments) are analytically indeterminate (see, e.g., Summers 1986). In other analytic studies, the short-term effects are indeterminate as well.[2]

Under these circumstances, numerical simulation can play an important role. Previous attempts to simulate the effects of growth-oriented tax policies within a dynamic, open-economy framework include the computable general

Lawrence H. Goulder is associate professor of economics at Harvard University and a faculty research fellow of the National Bureau of Economic Research. Barry Eichengreen is professor of economics at the University of California, Berkeley, and a research associate of the National Bureau of Economic Research.

The authors wish to thank their discussants, David W. Roland-Holst and Wing Thye Woo, as well as Lans Bovenberg, Jeffrey Frankel, Daniel Frisch, Jeffrey Sachs, Joel Slemrod, Philippe Weil, Peter Wilcoxen, and John Zysman for helpful comments. They also thank Erik Beecroft and Fernando Ramos for capable research assistance and gratefully acknowledge the financial support of the Bureau of International Labor Affairs of the U.S. Department of Labor.

equilibrium (CGE) simulations of Goulder, Shoven, and Whalley (1983), who found that the welfare effects of promoting savings through a consumption tax can be reversed when closed-economy assumptions are relaxed. Mutti and Grubert (1985) extended this analysis by introducing foreign production explicitly and by treating foreign tax systems more realistically. They confirmed that even a limited degree of international capital mobility can significantly alter results from closed-economy models. Bovenberg (1986) presented a two-country, two-good model that integrates the short- and long-run responses to tax policy changes. An attraction of Bovenberg's work is its more compelling treatment of time: Mutti and Grubert consider only steady-state results; in Goulder, Shoven, and Whalley (1983), the behavior of firms is not grounded in intertemporal optimization.

The present study combines many of the attractive features of these models. Like Bovenberg's, our model is intertemporal and characterizes not only the long-run (steady-state) effects of policy initiatives but also short-run responses and the transition to the new steady state. Decisions of consumers and producers in the United States and abroad derive from intertemporal optimization. In contrast to Bovenberg's model, but like the others above, our model is applied to actual U.S. data and contains a great deal of detail on production and taxes. We distinguish ten domestic industries, each with a different technology. Industries differ in the extent of their dependence on the export market and in the degree to which they compete with foreign producers. The model departs from previous work by treating financial behavior in considerable detail.

There is a natural complementarity between our disaggregated model of the U.S. economy and aggregated multicountry models such as that of McKibbin and Sachs (1986). While their model considers six countries (regions), it does not disaggregate industries within countries. Our model distinguishes only two countries (the United States and the rest of the world) but offers much additional industry and tax detail. Both models are based on full intertemporal optimization.

Our model preserves many features of the model of Goulder and Summers (1989), from which the present work developed, but pays far more attention to open-economy aspects. In contrast to Goulder and Summers, we derive the behavior of the foreign sector from optimizing behavior. We also introduce an international market for financial capital: domestic and foreign households each hold portfolios consisting of assets from both countries, as in Kouri (1976). Portfolio decisions give rise to capital account transactions, which are integrated with transactions on current account.

In this paper, we employ the model to assess the short- and long-run effects of savings- and investment-promoting changes in U.S. tax policy. We contrast a savings subsidy (effected through reduced income taxes and higher taxes on consumption) with investment tax credits (restored to their effective rates prior to implementation of the Tax Reform Act of 1986). Our focus is on the implications of these policies for ''international competitiveness,'' measured here by the profitability and output of U.S. export industries. We compare results under the assumption of no international capital mobility (and no international asset transactions) with those under the assumption of full international mobility (which assumes that there are no barriers to or costs of such transactions). In the case of capital mobility, we consider the importance of the degree of international asset substitutability. At one extreme is zero substitutability, where households hold domestic and foreign assets in fixed proportions. At the other is perfect substitutability, where households are indifferent between the two assets and drive the returns to equality. In general, we concentrate on intermediate cases.

Our simulation results show that the implications of these policies for international competitiveness differ radically once international capital mobility is introduced. In the absence of such mobility, investment- and savings-promoting policies each have only minor effects on U.S. export industries in the short run. In the long run, the effects of both policies are favorable since both raise the capital intensity of U.S. production, increasing productivity and incomes, reducing U.S. goods prices, and raising the overall volume of trade, all to the benefit of the export sector. Once international capital mobility is introduced, however, the effects of the two policies differ from one another in both the short and the long run. Restoring investment tax credits hurts U.S. export industries initially but helps them over the longer term. The reverse is true for the policy of exempting savings from the income tax. These differences reflect the very different implications of the two types of policies for the capital account of the balance of payments.

The rest of the paper is organized as follows. Section 1.1 offers an overview of our dynamic, open-economy CGE model. Section 1.2 lays out the structure of the model in greater detail. Section 1.3 and 1.4 describe how we solve and calibrate the model. In Section 1.5, we present our simulation results, and the final section offers conclusions.

1.1   Overview of the Model

Large CGE models are complex and all too often inaccessible. To render our model as transparent as possible, we describe here a simple heuristic model with features similar to those of the larger model used for simulations. We then describe how the larger model differs from the simple one.

1.1.1   An Illustrative Model

Behavioral Specifications

Consider a two-country model[3] in which each country's output is produced according to linearly homogenous production functions with labor and capital inputs:

(1) $$X = f(K, L),$$

(2) $$X^* = f^*(K^*, L^*).$$

The variables L and K are inputs of labor and capital in home-country production, L^* and K^* are the corresponding inputs into production in the foreign country (asterisks are used throughout to denote foreign-country variables), and X and X^* are outputs of each country. Labor supply is exogenous at each point in time. Neither labor nor physical (as distinct from financial) capital is mobile internationally.

Total domestic and foreign human wealth, TWH and TWH*, can be expressed as

(3) $$\text{TWH} = \text{PV}(wL, i),$$

(4) $$\text{TWH*} = \text{PV}(w^*L^*, i^*),$$

where w (w^*) is the wage, i (i^*) is the market interest rate, and PV $(\cdot, \cdot)$ is the present value operator, defined on flows and interest rates over all time. If investment is financed solely by retained earnings and firms must offer a rate of return to equity owners equal to the market interest rate, then total nonhuman wealth generated in each country is equal to the present value of the flow of dividends; that is,

(5) $$\text{TWK} = \text{PV}(pX - wL - pI, i),$$

(6) $$\text{TWK*} = \text{PV}(p^*X^* - w^*L^* - p^*I^*, i^*),$$

where p (p^*) is the price of domestic (foreign) output and I is the quantity of new capital goods purchases.[4] The variables TWK and TWK* are denominated in the respective currencies of the two countries. In this simple model, the produced good can be used for consumption or investment, and investment in each country is a function of the interest rate.

Income, consumption, and saving of each household are expressed in local currency. At each moment of time, total income Y (Y^*) received by the domestic (foreign) household consists of labor and capital income:

(7) $$Y = wL + \gamma\text{DIV} + (1 - \gamma^*)\text{DIV*}/e,$$

(8) $$Y^* = w^*L^* + \gamma^*\text{DIV*} + (1 - \gamma)\text{DIV} \cdot e,$$

where γ is the share of TWK owned by domestic households, γ^* is the share of TWK* owned by foreign households, $\text{DIV} = pX - wL - pI$ (similarly for DIV*), and e is the nominal exchange rate, defined as units of foreign currency per dollar. The value of consumption of each household depends on the household's total wealth and the average return on its investments:

(9) $$C = C(\text{TWH} + \gamma\text{TWK} + (1 - \gamma^*)\text{TWK*}/e, \bar{r}),$$

(10) $$C^* = C^*(\text{TWH*} + \gamma^*\text{TWK*} + (1 - \gamma)\text{TWK} \cdot e, \bar{r}^*),$$

where $\bar{r}$ ($\bar{r}^*$) is the average return on the domestic (foreign) household's portfolio, a weighted average of the returns on domestic and foreign assets.

Let α (α^*) denote the share of the domestic (foreign) household's wealth that it wishes to hold in assets located domestically (abroad). Assets from the two countries are imperfect substitutes in portfolios, with the desired portfolio shares a function of the relative rates of return (inclusive of exchange rate changes, where the dot over a variable represents its time derivative):

(11) $$\alpha = \alpha(i, i^* - \dot{e}/e),$$

(12) $$\alpha^* = \alpha^*(i + \dot{e}/e, i^*).$$

When policy shocks alter relative rates of return on domestic and foreign assets, desired portfolio shares change. At each moment in time, the capital account reflects changes in the composition of households' portfolios as well as overall increases in the value of portfolios associated with their saving. Let $S_i(= Y_i - C_i)$ represents the total saving by households resident in country i, and let S_{ij} denote the net incremental demand by household i for financial assets of country j. Households divide S_i into purchases of assets from the two countries so as to attain desired portfolio shares.

Let C_{ij} represent the expenditure by household i devoted to consumption of goods from country j. Assuming that domestic and foreign goods are imperfect substitutes in consumption, with the demands for each type of good a function of relatives prices, then

(13) $$C_{ij} = C_{ij}(C_i, pe/p^*).$$

Equilibrium Conditions

At each moment of time, equilibrium requires that the following conditions hold:

(14) $$w/p = f_L(K, L),$$

(15) $$w^*/p^* = f_L^*(K^*, L^*),$$

(16) $$C_{DD} + C_{FD}/e + pI = pX,$$

(17) $$C_{FF} + C_{DF} \cdot e + p^*I^* = p^*X^*,$$

(18) $$pI = S_{DD} + S_{FD}/e,$$

(19) $$p^*I^* = S_{FF} + S_{DF} \cdot e.$$

Here D and F subscripts denote "domestic" and "foreign." Equations (14) and (15) express the requirement that labor supply and demand balance in each country. Equations (16) and (17) show the conditions for equality of output demand and supply. The final two equations indicate the conditions for savings-investment equality in each country. Note that the balance of payments requirement,

(20)
$$C_{FD}/e + (1 - \gamma^*)\text{DIV}^*/e - C_{DF}$$
$$- (1 - \gamma)\text{DIV} = S_{DF} - S_{FD}/e,$$

is assured by equations (14)–(19) and Walras's law; it does not constitute an independent equilibrium condition.

1.1.2   The Larger Model

Behavioral Specifications

The larger model extends the simpler one in several ways. One major difference is in the degree of industry disaggregation. Our model distinguishes ten U.S. industries: agriculture and mining, crude petroleum and refining, construction, the textile and apparel complex, metals, machinery, motor vehicles, miscellaneous manufacturing, services, and housing.[5] This disaggregation enables us to address a number of topical issues relating to U.S. international competitiveness: the effects of restrictions on agricultural exports, the effects of import penetration in textiles, steel, and automobiles, and the effects of increased trade in services. The model also incorporates intermediate goods production and substitution by producers between domestic and foreign intermediate goods.

The larger model treats investment dynamics explicitly. In each industry, managers choose levels of investment to maximize the value of the firm. Because of adjustment costs associated with the installation or removal of new physical capital, firms find it optimal, in response to a change in economic conditions, to approach new long-run capital intensities gradually over time.[6]

The larger model treats corporate financial decisions in some detail. As in Goulder and Summers (1989), we model firms as financing investments through both debt and equity issues.[7]

Finally, the larger model incorporates taxes and spending by the U.S. government. It distinguishes taxes that apply to existing capital (e.g., the corporate income tax) from taxes that apply only to new capital (e.g., investment tax credits), and it accounts for the different effects of these two types of taxes on investment incentives and asset values. The spending and transfer roles of the government are modeled explicitly.

Equilibrium Conditions

In each country, four types of equilibrium conditions must be satisfied in each period. First, commodity market equilibrium requires that the supply of each good equal the sum of home and foreign demands. Second, labor market equilibrium requires that the aggregate supply and aggregate demand for labor balance. Third, savings-investment equilibrium requires that the aggregate demand for external funds by home firms equal the sum of national savings and net capital inflows. All three conditions were present in the simpler model above. Introduction of a government sector adds a fourth requirement (for each country): that total tax revenues must equal total government spending.

These equilibrium requirements are met through the adjustment of domestic and foreign wages, domestic and foreign commodity prices, domestic and foreign interest rates, the nominal exchange rate, and lump-sum adjustments to personal income taxes.[8] But, since current-period decisions depend on forward-looking expectations, the current-period prices that satisfy the market-clearing conditions in a given period depend on expectations of future prices (when agents have foresight, as is assumed here, current equilibrium prices depend on future equilibrium prices). Given this intertemporal interdependence, we solve the model by transforming the general equilibrium problem into one in which current and future prices are effectively solved separately (as described in sec. 1.3 below). This enables us to solve for the set of prices for each period that yields the intertemporal general equilibrium under perfect foresight expectations.

Dynamics

The path of the domestic and foreign economies over time depends on the adjustments of capital stocks and asset portfolios to policy initiatives and other exogenous shocks. The model has steady-state properties: in the long run, asset prices and rates of return adjust so that the rates of net accumulation of physical capital by industry and the rates of accumulation of financial capital by households equal g, the growth rate of effective labor services. This yields a steady state in which relative prices do not change and all quantities increase at the rate g.

In the short run, policy shocks generate divergences in the marginal product of capital across industries as well as in average portfolio returns to domestic and foreign residents. In the long run, firms' investment decisions ultimately equalize marginal products of capital across industries (adjusted for taxes and risk), while household portfolio decisions and savings behavior ultimately equalize overall portfolio returns. The adjustment dynamics associated with firms' investment decisions have been described by Goulder and Summers (1989). The adjustment dynamics associated with household portfolio decisions, on the other hand, are more complex in this model because of the introduction of international asset transactions. Assuming that assets issued by firms in different countries are imperfect substitutes in portfolios and that households display home-country preference, then a positive shock to domestic firms that increases the rate of return on dollar-denominated assets will raise the average rate of return on the portfolios of domestic residents relative to the average portfolio return to foreign residents. If the difference in portfolio returns were to be sustained and propensities to save were similar across countries, domestic residents would accumulate an ever-increasing share of global wealth—a result inconsistent with the existence of a steady state. What prevents this process from persisting is that the higher accumulation rate of U.S. residents, under the assumption of home-country preference, implies an increase in the share of global savings invested in the U.S.

economy. Over time, this lowers the domestic rate of return until average returns on domestic and foreign portfolios are brought to equality. The long-run equalization of returns on portfolios brought about by households' savings behavior parallels the long-run equalization of marginal products of capital brought about by firms' investment decisions.

1.2   A Detailed Description of the Model

1.2.1   Production

U.S. Industries

Production Technologies. Each of the ten domestic industries produces a single output using inputs of labor, capital, and intermediate goods. A multilevel structure governs the production of each industry output (see table 1.1). Firms choose the quantity of labor that maximizes current profits, given the current capital stock. Labor and capital combine to produce a value-added composite, VA. This composite is then combined with intermediate inputs $(\bar{x}_1, \bar{x}_2, \ldots, \bar{x}_N)$ in fixed proportions to generate output, x.

Intermediate inputs are themselves composites of foreign- and domestic-supplied intermediate goods. Treating domestic and foreign intermediates as imperfect substitutes in production endogenizes the relative prices of domestic and foreign intermediate goods. For a given intermediate good of type i, producers choose the combination of domestic and foreign inputs that minimizes costs.[9]

The producer good outputs of the ten industries have several end uses. They too serve as inputs for each industry. In addition, they satisfy the demand for final goods by government and the demand for U.S. exports by foreigners. Finally, they combine in fixed proportions to produce a representative capital good used in production and to create the seventeen consumer goods demanded by households.[10]

Producer Behavior.   Managers seek to maximize the value of the firm. Their choice variables at each point in time are employment, intermediate inputs, and investment. Labor and intermediates are chosen to maximize current

Table 1.1	**Industry Production Structure**	
Production Relation		Functional Form
X = $X(\text{VA}, \bar{x}_1, \bar{x}_2, \ldots, \bar{x}_N)$		Leontief
VA = $\text{VA}(L, \bar{K})$		CES
$\bar{x}_i$ = $\bar{x}_i(x_i, x_i^*), \quad (i = 1, 2, \ldots, N)$		CES

Note: X = gross output (exclusive of adjustment costs); VA = value added; L = labor input; $\bar{K}$ = capital input (fixed in the current period of time); $\bar{x}_i$ = composite intermediate input $(i = 1, \ldots, N)$; x_i = intermediate domestically produced input $(i = 1, \ldots, N)$; and x_i^* = intermediate foreign-produced input $(i = 1, \ldots, N)$.

profits (given the capital stock), while investment is chosen to approach optimally the long-run (profit-maximizing) capital intensity. The time required to attain the optimal capital intensity depends on adjustment costs.

A starting point for specifying the firm's behavior is the asset market equilibrium condition that risk-adjusted expected returns be equalized across domestic assets. The expected return from holding (risky) equities must be consistent with those from holding a "safe" asset such as corporate debt. The return on equity is the sum of capital gains and dividends net of tax. For every firm at each point in time,

$$(21) \qquad (1 - \kappa)\frac{\dot{V} - VN}{V} + (1 - \theta)\frac{DIV}{V} = i(1 - \theta) + \eta,$$

where V is the value of the firm, VN is new share issues, DIV is the current dividend, κ is the capital gains tax rate, θ is the marginal income tax rate, i is the normal interest rate on domestic corporate debt, and η is the equity risk premium. Imposing a transversality condition ruling out eternal speculative bubbles and integrating yield an expression equating the value of the firm with the discounted value of after-tax dividends net of share issues:

$$(22) \qquad V_t = \int_t^\infty \left[\left(\frac{1 - \theta}{1 - \kappa}\right)DIV_s - VN_s\right] exp\left[\int_t^s \frac{-r_u}{1 - \kappa}du\right]ds,$$

where r is the risk-adjusted rate of return, equal to $i(1 - \theta) + \eta$. [11]

Dividends and new share issues in each period are related through the cash-flow identity equating sources and uses of funds:

$$(23) \qquad EARN + BN + VN = DIV + IEXP,$$

where EARN represents earnings after taxes and interest payments, BN is the value of new debt issue, and IEXP is the value of investment expenditure. Earnings are given by

$$(24) \quad EARN = [pF(K, L, M) - wL - p_M M - i DEBT](1 - \tau) + \tau D,$$

where

K and L	=	inputs of capital and labor;
M	=	vector of domestic and foreign intermediate inputs;
p	=	output price (net of output taxes);
F	=	quantity of output (gross of adjustment costs);
w	=	wage rate (gross of indirect tax on labor);
P_M	=	vector of intermediate input prices (gross of tariffs and intermediate input taxes facing the industry);
$DEBT$	=	nominal debt;
τ	=	corporate tax rate; and
D	=	value of currently allowable depreciation allowances.

To determine the value of the firm, it is necessary to specify the firm's financial behavior and identify the elements BN, VN, and DIV in equation

(23). We assume that firms pay dividends equal to a constant fraction, a, of after-tax profits net of economic depreciation and that they issue new debt to maintain a constant debt-capital ratio, b. We also assume that new equity issues represent the marginal source of finance: that is, they make up the difference between EARN + BN and DIV + IEXP in (23).[12]

Investment expenditure is the sum of the "direct" costs of the new capital (net of the investment tax credit) plus adjustment costs associated with its installation:

$$(25) \qquad \text{IEXP} = (1 - \text{ITC})p_K I + (1 - \tau)p\phi I,$$

where ITC represents the investment tax credit rate, p_K is the purchase price of new capital goods, I is the quantity of investment, and $\phi(I/K)$ is adjustment costs per unit of investment. We model adjustment costs as internal to the firm: to add capital, currently available resources (labor, existing capital, and intermediate goods) must be devoted to installation.[13] Output is separable between inputs and adjustment costs:

$$(26) \qquad X = F(K, L, M) - \phi I.$$

Using the expression for the change in the capital stock,

$$(27) \qquad \dot{K} = I - \delta^R K,$$

one can derive an expression for the value of the firm in terms of I, L, M, prices, and the technology. Firms maximize this value subject to (27). As detailed in Goulder and Summers (1989), optimal investment is given by

$$(28) \quad \frac{I}{K} = h(Q) = h\left\{\left[\frac{V - B}{p_K K} - 1 + \text{ITC} + b + \omega Z\right]\left[\frac{p_K}{(1 - \tau)p}\right]\right\}$$

where $h(\cdot) = [\phi + (I/K)\phi']^{-1}$, B is the present value of depreciation allowances on existing capital, Z is the present value of depreciation allowances on a dollar of new investment, and $\omega = a(1 - \theta)/(1 - \kappa) - a + 1$. The adjustment cost function is

$$(29) \qquad \phi(I/K) = \frac{\beta/2(I/K - \zeta)^2}{I/K},$$

implying that the relation between the rate of investment and Q is simply

$$(30) \qquad \frac{I}{K} = \zeta + \frac{1}{\beta} Q,$$

where β is the adjustment cost parameter. Since they are defined in terms of discounted streams of dividends and depreciation allowances, V, B, and Z in the investment equation (28) incorporate expectations about the future. The calculation of perfect foresight expectations is discussed in section 1.3 below.

Foreign Industry

The treatment of foreign production is analogous. A representative foreign producer generates output using capital and labor inputs. The specification of investment is the same as for domestic firms, as are the foreign producer's financing rules. Total nonhuman wealth located abroad, TWK*, is the sum of foreign-located debt and equity. The value of the latter is the discounted sum of foreign dividends net of foreign share issues.

1.2.2   Household Behavior

Households are represented as forward-looking and having perfect foresight. The treatment of domestic and foreign households is similar, although more detail is provided on the domestic side.

Consumption and Asset Choices

In each country, a representative, infinitely lived household solves a multilevel decision problem (table 1.2). Consider the domestic household. Its problem is to choose a path of consumption and a path of portfolio holdings. When domestic and foreign assets are imperfect substitutes and offer different expected returns, portfolio and consumption choices need to be coordinated since the choice of portfolio affects the overall rate of return to the household. One approach to this problem would be to incorporate risk explicitly. But the integration of portfolio choice and consumption demands in the face of risk and uncertainty presents difficult, unresolved theoretical issues, particularly when there are many time periods and many consumption goods.[14] Resolving these issues is beyond the scope of this paper. Moreover, risk may only partly explain the main empirical fact of interest: that households hold diversified portfolios despite sustained differences in rates of return.[15] In this investigation, we adopt an alternative approach. Our starting point is the observation that households exhibit strong home-country preference: assets from their own country often make up the bulk of their portfolios, even when rates of return

Table 1.2   **Household Consumption Structure**

Consumption Relation			Functional Form
U	$=$	$U(\bar{C}_t, \bar{C}_{t+1}, \ldots)$	Constant intertemporal elasticity of substitution
$\bar{C}_s$	$=$	$\bar{C}_s(C_s, A_s)$	Cobb-Douglas
C_s	$=$	$C_s(\bar{c}_{1,s}, \bar{c}_{2,s}, \ldots, \bar{c}_{m,s})$	Cobb-Douglas
A_s	$=$	$A_s(\alpha_s, 1 - \alpha_s)$	CES
$\bar{c}_{i,s}$	$=$	$\bar{c}(c_{i,s}, c^*_{i,s})$	CES

Note: U = intertemporal utility; C_s = overall consumption at time s; A_s = portfolio preference index at time s; $\bar{c}_{i,s}$ = consumption of composite consumer good i at time s; $c_{i,s}$ = consumption of domestically made consumer good i at time s; and $c^*_{i,s}$ = consumption of foreign-made consumer good i at time s.

on other-country assets are comparable or higher. In keeping with this observation, we posit a portfolio preference function that is consistent with the observed home-country preference yet can be embedded within a utility-maximizing framework that allows households to adjust asset shares in accordance with differences in rates of return.[16] (Below, we also report results using an alternative specification in which consumption and asset preferences are decoupled.) In each period t, the household maximizes a utility function of the form:

$$(31) \qquad U = \sum_{s=t}^{\infty} (1 + \delta)^{t-s}(1 - \Omega)^{-1}(C_s^{\beta} A_s^{1-\beta})^{1-\Omega},$$

where δ is the rate of time performance, Ω is the inverse of the intertemporal elasticity of substitution, C is an index of overall consumption in a given period, and A is a function of the household's asset holdings. We specialize A to a constant elasticity of substitution (CES) function of α and $1 - \alpha$, the shares of the household's portfolio devoted to domestic and foreign assets:[17]

$$(32) \qquad A = k[\alpha_0^{1-\rho}\alpha^{\rho} + (1 - \alpha_0)^{1-\rho}(1 - \alpha)^{\rho}]^{1/\rho}.$$

The household maximizes utility subject to the wealth accumulation condition:

$$(33) \quad WK_{t+1} - WK_t = r_t \alpha_t WK_t + r_t^*(1 - \alpha_t)WK_t + YL_t - \bar{p}_t C_t,$$

where WK is the total nonhuman wealth owned by the household, r and r^* are the annual after-tax returns offered to the household on its holdings of domestic and foreign assets, YL is labor income net of all taxes and tranfers, and $\bar{p}$ is the price index for overall consumption.

The function $A(\cdot)$ summarizes the household's portfolio preferences: if $r = r^*$, households maximize utility by choosing the asset shares α_0 and $1 - \alpha_0$. When rates of return differ, however, maintaining the portfolio shares α_0 and $1 - \alpha_0$ has a cost in terms of a lower overall return than that which could be obtained if the household held more of the asset with the higher return. The household chooses the path of α that balances the rewards of approaching preferred shares against the costs in terms of a lower overall return on the portfolio.

The parameter ρ in the portfolio preference function is related to σ, the elasticity of substitution between asset shares ($\rho = 1 - 1/\sigma$). When $\sigma = 0$, households maintain shares α_0 and $1 - \alpha_0$ of domestic and foreign assets irrespective of differences in rates of return. As $\sigma \to \infty$, household behavior approaches the limiting case of perfect substitutability, where the slightest difference in returns leads households to hold only the asset offering the highest return.[18]

The Hamiltonian for the household's intertemporal problem is given by

$$(34) \qquad H = (1 + \delta)^{1-t}(1 - \Omega)^{-1}(C_t^\beta A_t^{1-\beta})^{1-\Omega}$$
$$+ \lambda_t(1 + \delta)^{1-t}[(r_t^* - v_t\alpha_t)WK_t + YL_t - \bar{p}_t C_t],$$

where $v_t = r_t^* - r_t$. Differentiating with respect to the control variables α and C yields the first-order conditions

$$(35) \qquad \beta(C_t^\beta A_t^{1-\beta})^{-\Omega}C_t^{\beta-1}A_t^{1-\beta} = \lambda_t\bar{p}_t ,$$

$$(36) \qquad (1 - \beta)(C_t^\beta A_t^{1-\beta})^{-\Omega}C_t^\beta A_t^{-\beta}A_t' = \lambda_t v_t WK_t .$$

Once λ, the marginal utility of wealth, is known, α and C can be identified from these two first-order conditions. Differentiating the Hamiltonian with respect to the state variable WK yields the equation of motion for λ:

$$(37) \qquad \frac{\lambda_{t+1}}{\lambda_t} = \frac{1 + \delta}{1 + \bar{r}_t} ,$$

where $\bar{r}_t$ is the average portfolio return, equal to $\alpha_t r_t + (1 - \alpha_t)r_t^*$. We identify λ in each period by first solving for its steady-state value and then applying equation (37) for transition years.

The domestic (foreign) household's total nonhuman wealth, WK (WK*), is related to industry liabilities through the following relations:

$$(38) \qquad TWK = \sum_{i=1}^{10} (V_i + DEBT_i).$$

$$(39) \qquad TWK^* = V^* + DEBT^*,$$

Where TWK and TWK* denote total nonhuman wealth located at home and abroad, denominated in the respective currencies of each resident, as in section 1.1.1 above. Total nonhuman wealth of domestic and foreign residents, WK and WK*, can be expressed as

$$(40) \qquad WK = \gamma TWK + (1 - \gamma^*)TWK^*/e,$$

$$(41) \qquad WK^* = \gamma^* TWK^* = (1 - \gamma)TWK \cdot e,$$

where γ represents the proportion of the debt and equity of domestic firms held by domestic residents and γ^* expresses the proportion of the debt and equity of foreign firms held by foreigners, as in section 1.1.1 above. If households wish to maintain current asset proportions, then $\alpha = \gamma TWK/WK$, and $\alpha^* = \gamma^* TWK^*/WK^*$. When rates of return change, however, households immediately alter the composition of their portfolios. Thus, changes in asset holdings from period to period reflect both changes in the composition of portfolios and increases in portfolio size associated with household saving.

Each asset generally yields a different return to residents of different countries; this reflects anticipated exchange rate movements and features of tax systems that impose different rates according to the residence of the taxpayer. Let $\bar{r}$ and $\bar{r}^*$ represent average returns on the portfolios of domestic and foreign residents:

$$(42) \qquad \bar{r} = \alpha r_{DD} + (1 - \alpha)r_{DF} ,$$

$$(43) \qquad \bar{r}^* = \alpha^* r_{FF} + (1 - \alpha^*)r_{FD} ,$$

where r_{DD} and r_{DF} again are the returns expected by domestic residents on assets located domestically and in the foreign country, respectively; r_{FF} and r_{FD} are defined analogously.

The Composition of Current Consumption

For domestic households,[19] overall consumption, C, in each period is a Cobb-Douglas aggregate of the seventeen consumption goods in the model, implying that consumption spending is allocated across consumption goods in fixed expenditure shares. Our model incorporates imported consumer goods by treating each good $\bar{c}_i$ as a CES composite of domestic and foreign goods of type i. Suppressing subscripts, we express the CES composite as

$$(44) \qquad \bar{c} = [\hat{\alpha}^{1-\hat{\rho}}c^{\hat{\rho}} + (1 - \hat{\alpha})^{1-\hat{\rho}}c^{*\hat{\rho}}]^{1/\hat{\rho}},$$

where c is the quantity of the domestic consumption good, c^* is the quantity of the foreign consumption good, and $\hat{\alpha}$ and $\hat{\rho}$ are parameters. The parameter $\hat{\rho}$ is related to the elasticity of the substitution, $\hat{\sigma}$, according to

$$(45) \qquad \hat{\rho} = \frac{\hat{\sigma} - 1}{\hat{\sigma}} .$$

Since $\bar{c}$ $(\cdot)$ is homothetic, the ratio of domestic and foreign goods in the composite is independent of its level. Households select the optimal mix of domestic and foreign goods to minimize the cost per unit of composite.

1.2.3   Government Sectors

The domestic economy government is the same as in Goulder and Summers (1989), to which the reader is referred for details. It has three functions: collecting taxes, distributing transfers, and purchasing goods and services.

The model incorporates each of the major taxes in the United States, as in table 1.3. It includes features of the U.S. tax code that impose different effective rates on new and old capital; the explicit treatment of profits taxes, investment tax credits, and capital gains taxes allows it to capture the effects of tax policy on investment and dividend payment decisions. The model also distinguishes economic from tax depreciation.

Table 1.3   **Model Treatment of Taxes**

Tax	Treatment in Model
1. Corporate income tax	Ad valorem tax on profits by industry; bond interest payments are expensed
2. Property tax and corporate franchise taxes	Ad valorem tax on capital stocks by industry
3. Investment tax credits	Ad valorem subsidy to investment by industry
4. Depreciation deductions	Tax credit used on the value of depreciable capital stock, tax depreciation rate, and corporate income tax rate
5. Contributions to social security, unemployment insurance, and workmen's compensation	Ad valorem tax on the use of labor services by industry
6. Motor vehicles tax	Ad valorem tax on the use of motor vehicles by industry
7. Excise taxes, other indirect business taxes, and nontax payments to government	Ad valorem taxes on output of producer goods
8. Retail sales taxes	Ad valorem tax on purchases of consumer goods
9. Personal income taxes (including state and local)	Linear function of labor and capital income
10. Social security benefits, unemployment compensation, and other transfers	Lump-sum income transfer constituting a fixed share of overall government spending

The level of government spending (transfers plus purchases) is exogenous. Transfers and purchases each represent a fixed share of overall spending. Purchases fall onto specific producer goods in fixed expenditure shares.

Since the model exhibits steady-state growth in the base case, overall real government spending must increase at that steady-state growth rate, g. In the base case, the government budget balances in each period. In revised-case simulations, real government spending is fixed at the same levels as in the base case; budget balance is maintained through lump-sum adjustments to personal income taxes.[20]

The foreign government performs the same functions and has the same tax instruments as the domestic economy government, although individual industries are not distinguished.

1.2.4   Imports and Exports

Import demands consist of the demands for imported intermediate goods by U.S. producers and for imported consumer goods by U.S. consumers. Foreign producers require the same price (after conversion to foreign currency) for goods sold in the United States as for goods sold locally. These prices adjust to clear the market for each foreign good.

Foreign demands for U.S. exports depend on the value of overall foreign output and on the price of exports relative to foreign goods:

$$(46) \qquad E_i = E_{0i} \cdot (Y^*/\bar{p}^*) \cdot \left(\frac{p_{Ei} \cdot e}{\bar{p}^*}\right)^{-\epsilon_i}.$$

Here, E_i is the quantity demanded of the ith U.S. export, E_{0i} is the original expenditure share (at prices of unity), Y^* is foreign GNP, $\bar{p}^*$ is the foreign GNP price index, P_{Ei} is the export price in dollars, and ϵ_i is the export price elasticity of demand.

1.3 Solving the Model

Equilibrium must satisfy two sets of conditions. Intratemporal equilibrium requires that, given expectations of future variables, current supplies and demands balance in each period. Intertemporal equilibrium requires that expectations conform to the values realized in later periods.

At each point in time, expectations are embedded within the current period values of "forward" variables. For the domestic economy, the forward variables are as follows:

V_i = the equity value of firm i ($i = 1, \ldots, N$);
Q_i = the tax-adjusted q for firm i ($i = 1, \ldots, N$);
Z_i = the present value of depreciation allowances on a dollar of new investment ($i = 1, \ldots, N$);
B_i = the present value of depreciation allowances on existing capital ($i = 1, \ldots, N$); and
λ = the shadow value of the domestic household's wealth.

The V_i's and B_i's can be expressed in terms of the Q_i's, Z_i's, and current values (see Goulder and Summers 1989). Hence, expectations for the domestic economy are fully summarized by the values of Q and Z for each industry and the value of λ.

The forward variables for the foreign economy are:

V^* = the equity value of the foreign firm;
Q^* = the tax-adjusted q for the foreign firm; and
λ^* = the shadow value of the foreign household's wealth.

It is possible to derive explicit relations of the form (see eq. 37; and Goulder and Summers 1989, app.):

$$(47) \qquad \begin{aligned} Q_{it} &= Q_{it}(\Psi_{1it}, V_{i,t+1}^E), \quad (i = 1, \ldots, N), \\ Z_{it} &= Z_{it}(\Psi_{2it}, Z_{i,t+1}^E), \quad (i = 1, \ldots, N), \end{aligned}$$

$$\lambda_t = \lambda_t(\Psi_{3t}, \lambda^E_{t+1}),$$
$$Q^*_t = Q^*_t(\Psi_{4t}, V^{*E}_{t+1}),$$
$$\lambda^*_t = \lambda^*_t(\Psi_{5t}, \lambda^{*E}_{t+1}),$$

where the variables Ψ_{jt} ($j = 1, \ldots, 5$) refer to prices and quantities observed in period t and V^E_{t+1}, Z^E_{t+1}, λ^E_{t+1}, V^{*E}_{t+1}, and λ^{*E}_{t+1} refer to the values, expected in period t, for V, Z, λ, V^*, and λ^* in the next period. We refer to the variables with E superscripts as "lead" variables. We also employ e^E, a lead variable for the exchange rate.

Solution proceeds in two steps. First, we posit values for the lead variables for $t = 2, 3, \ldots, T + 1$, where T is the last period simulated. The first-level, intratemporal equilibrium problem is to calculate a general equilibrium solution in every period conditional on these guesses. The second-level, intertemporal equilibrium problem is to solve for the correct values for the lead variables.

1.3.1 Intratemporal Equilibrium

Intratemporal equilibrium requires that, in each country and at each period of time, (1) the demand for labor equal its supply, (2) the demand for output from each industry equal its supply, (3) total external borrowing by firms equal total saving by residents of the given country plus the net capital inflow to that country, and (4) government revenues equal government spending. These requirements imply a total of seventeen equilibrium conditions (see table 1.4): two for the domestic and foreign labor markets, ten for the domestic product market, one for the foreign product market, two for the domestic and foreign loanable funds markets, and two for the domestic and

Table 1.4   Summary of Equilibrium Conditions

Intratemporal equilibrium conditions:

Labor demand = labor supply	In each country
Gross output demand = gross output supply	For each domestic industry and the foreign industry
Government spending = government revenue	In each country
Total industry borrowing = domestic saving + net capital inflow	In each country

Intertemporal equilibrium conditions:

$$V^E_t = V_t, \quad t = 2, 3, \ldots, T; \quad V^E_{T+1} = V_{ss}$$
$$Z^E_t = Z_t, \quad t = 2, 3, \ldots, T; \quad Z^E_{T+1} = Z_{ss}$$
$$V^{*E}_t = V^*_t, \quad t = 2, 3, \ldots, T; \quad V^{*E}_{T+1} = V^*_{ss}$$
$$\lambda^E_t = \lambda_t, \quad t = 2, 3, \ldots, T; \quad \lambda^E_{T+1} = \lambda_{ss}$$
$$\lambda^{*E}_t = \lambda^*_t, \quad t = 2, 3, \ldots, T; \quad \lambda^{*E}_{T+1} = \lambda^*_{ss}$$
$$e^E_t = e_t, \quad t = 2, 3, \ldots, T; \quad e^E_{T+1} = e_{ss}$$

foreign governments' budget balance. It suffices to solve for sixteen equilibrium conditions as the remaining one will then be satisfied by Walras's law. To obtain the intratemporal equilibrium, we employ the Powell (1970) algorithm, which tries alternative values for sixteen ''prices'': the ten domestic output prices, the foreign output price, the domestic and foreign gross interest rates, the nominal exchange rate, and the domestic and foreign tax scalars (which control the lump-sum tax adjustments necessary to bring about budget balance in each country). The nominal wage in each country (in its own currency) is exogenous and assumed to grow at a rate of 6 percent. The nominal exchange rate serves to bring nominal magnitudes at home and abroad into line (see n. 8 above).

In Appendix A, we outline the method for deriving excess demands in each period from the given set of prices tried by the intratemporal solution algorithm.

Once the intratemporal equilibrium is obtained for the first period, we augment the capital stocks of each industry on the basis of net investment and increment the total supplies of domestic and foreign labor by their growth rate, g. We then repeat the equilibrium calculations for the next period. In this manner, we solve for every period in the simulation interval.

1.3.2   Intertemporal Equilibrium

Perfect foresight requires that expectations conform to the values that ultimately obtain. To meet this requirement, we repeatedly solve the model forward, each time revising the expectations (embedded in the lead variables) that affect each intratemporal equilibrium. Appendix B describes our procedure for obtaining the perfect foresight expectations.

1.4   Data and Parameters

1.4.1   Stocks and Flows

We combine information from different sources to form a 1983 benchmark data set. Much of the benchmark data is drawn from the general equilibrium data set recently assembled by Scholz (1987). The Scholz data include information on production (final demand vectors of consumption, investment, government spending, imports, and exports by producer good; matrix of input-output transactions; vectors of labor inputs by industry; labor taxes and intermediate input taxes by industry; and production function elasticities by industry) and on consumption (matrix of expenditures on consumer goods by household; vector of savings by household; transition matrix between producer [industry] and consumer goods; and vectors of income taxes paid, sales taxes paid, marginal tax rates, and transfers received by the household).

We have supplemented these data with information on capital taxes and the financial behavior of firms, including capital gains tax rates, tax depreciation rates, dividend-payout and debt-capital ratios, and equity risk premia.[21] We have also added information on capital stocks by industry obtained from the *Survey of Current Business*. Base case values for tax rates and behavioral parameters are displayed in table 1.5. Tax rates for the foreign sector are set equal to the weighted average of the rates applying in the United States.[22]

Since domestic firms distinguish between domestic and foreign intermediate goods in production, it is necessary to employ a domestic and foreign input-output matrix describing the use of domestic and foreign-made inputs in each industry. The relations among the domestic and foreign input-output matrices, the components of final demand, and value added are indicated in figure 1.1.

Since the U.S. government does not produce a foreign input-output matrix, we constructed one. This involved categorizing imports according to their end use (intermediate use, consumption, or investment).[23]

In the benchmark data set, we impose an initial value for γ, the share of domestic nonhuman wealth owned by domestic residents, obtained from information on foreign ownership of U.S. assets and total domestically

Table 1.5   **Benchmark Values for Industry Tax and Behavioral Parameters**

Industry	Rate of Economic Depreciation (δ^R)	Rate of Tax Depreciation (δ^T)	Equity Risk Premium (η)	Debt-Capital Ratio (b)
1. Agriculture and mining	.010	.203	.139	.179
2. Crude petroleum and refining	.051	.120	.087	.181
3. Construction	.156	.220	.091	.080
4. Textiles, apparel, and leather	.078	.131	.111	.435
5. Metals	.082	.130	.084	.339
6. Machinery	.094	.140	.084	.365
7. Motor vehicles	.109	.161	.089	.255
8. Miscellaneous manufacturing	.087	.180	.083	.220
9. Services	.067	.124	.092	.527
10. Housing	.010	.070	.100	.502

Scalars:

Growth rate of effective labor services (steady-stage real growth rate)	(g)	.03
Growth rate of nominal wages (steady-state inflation rate)	(π_0)	.06
Corporate profits tax rate	(τ)	.34
Capital gains tax rate	(κ)	.05
Marginal income tax rate	(θ)	.285
Nominal interest rate	(i)	.071

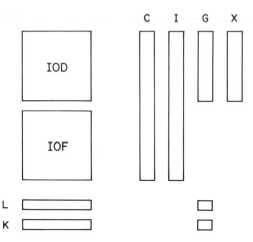

Fig. 1.1   Relations among final demand, intermediate input use,
and value added

Note: In the benchmark data set, government purchases of imports are zero, and foreign imports
are not reexported. Hence, the G and X vectors do not extend into the imports rows.

C   = Personal consumption expenditures on domestic and foreign goods
I   = Expenditures on domestic and foreign capital goods
G   = Government purchases of domestic goods, labor services, and capital services
X   = Exports of domestic goods
IOD = Domestic input-output matrix—domestic intermediate goods used by domestic in-
       dustry
IOF = Foreign input-output matrix—foreign intermediate goods used by domestic industry
L   = Labor services inputs
K   = Capital services inputs

located assets from the *Survey of Current Business* and Federal Reserve
balance sheets. We also impose a value for the U.S. share of global wealth
based on a comparison of GDP in the United States and other non-Communist
countries. With this information we derive (as discussed below) the benchmark level of foreign wealth and the benchmark portfolio shares.

1.4.2   Parameters

Parameterizing the model involves selecting certain parameters from
outside sources and deriving the remainder from restrictions posed by two
sorts of requirements:

Replication Requirement. In the base case, the model must generate
an equilibrium solution with values matching those of the benchmark
data set.

Balanced Growth Requirement. In the base case, the model must
generate a steady-state growth path.

First, we specify the exogenous growth rate of effective labor, g, and the exogenous growth rate of nominal wages, π_0. The rate g determines the steady-state real growth rate of the economy and π_0 the steady-state inflation rate. These variables take the values .03 and .06, respectively.

In our central case simulation, we employ a value of 0.06 for time preference (δ) and a value of 0.5 for the intertemporal elasticity of substitution in consumption ($1/\Omega$).

In the steady state, the rate of gross investment, I/K, in each industry must satisfy

$$(48) \qquad\qquad I/K = g + \delta^R,$$

where subscripts have been suppressed for convenience. The values for K, g, and δ^R are contained in the benchmark data set. We derive the initial level of investment in each industry from equation (48). A similar procedure determines initial values for the depreciable capital stock, KDEP.

We derive the benchmark values of firm debt (DEBT) and equity (V) from data on capital stocks, tax rates, and nominal interest rates.[24] Summing across domestic industries yields TWK, total domestically generated nonhuman wealth. Total nonhuman wealth generated abroad, TWK*, is a given multiple, m, of TWK.[25] Using TWK* and the foreign interest rate i^*, we derive foreign capital incomes.

The procedure is similar for human wealth. From data on labor incomes, taxes, and transfers, we calculate domestic human wealth, TWH, as the present value of the stream of after-tax labor and transfer income. Foreign human wealth, TWH*, is set at $m \cdot$ TWH.

From γ and the requirement of capital account balance in the base case, we derive γ^* and the initial values for the portfolio shares α and α^*.

In the benchmark equilibrium, before-tax nominal interest rates are equal at home and abroad. Those nominal interest rates must be consistent with the requirement that domestic investment equal national saving plus the net capital inflow. This condition can be evaluated only after wealth levels and portfolio shares have been determined, yet these levels and shares themselves depend on the assumed value for the interest rate. Hence, it is necessary to iterate to obtain the benchmark value for the nominal interest rate.

Table 1.6 displays the base case (calibrated) values for the principal variables of the model.

1.5 Simulation Results

The "base case" equilibrium path is the standard against which the effects of policy changes are measured. As mentioned above, the U.S. and foreign economies display steady-state growth in the base case at an annual rate of 3

Table 1.6   Benchmark Values for Income and Wealth

	U.S. Firms	Foreign Firms
Wealth:		
Human and transfer wealth	27,606	64,414
Nonhuman wealth:	8,139	18,992
Owned by U.S. households	7,407	733
Owned by foreign households	733	18,259
Income and tax payments:		
Labor income payments:	1,842	4,297
To U.S. households	1,842	0
To foreign households	0	4,297
Capital income payments:	464	1,083
To U.S. households	422	42
To foreign households	42	1,041
Indirect taxes paid	298	696
Investment expenditure and financing:		
Investment expenditure	620	1,446
Investment financing:		
Retained earnings	453	1,057
Domestic household saving	152	15
Foreign household saving	15	374

Note: All values are in billions of 1983 dollars.

percent. We perform simulations spanning an interval of seventy-five years ($T = 75$), with the equilibria spaced one year apart. Following a policy change, both economies approach the new steady state quite closely well before the seventy-fifth year, and using larger values for T does not significantly affect the simulation results.

1.5.1 Promoting Savings through a Consumption Tax

Our savings-promoting policy combines a 4 percentage point increase in taxes on consumption (sales and excise taxes, most of which are in the 5–10 percent range initially) with a compensating reduction in domestic households' marginal income tax rates from 0.285 to 0.256. The policy change is treated as unanticipated and takes effect in the first period. It is approximately revenue neutral over the long term: the present value of the stream of changes in government revenue is approximately zero.[26] It encourages saving by raising the after-tax rate of return.

No Mobility

We first examine the effects of this policy change in the absence of internationally mobile financial capital. In this scenario, the portfolios of domestic and foreign households contain only the assets of the country of residence, and thus households have no concern for rates of return offered on assets located in the other country. The effect of the policy change is to raise the after-tax return for domestic households and generate additional saving, allowing a drop in the equilibrium domestic gross interest rate. The lower interest rate implies an increase in fixed investment of 1.0 percent relative to the base case in the first period, as indicated in table 1.7. Over time, the rise in the capital intensity of the economy implies a lower marginal product of capital and a lower value of Q for any given interest rate; thus, the rate of investment falls, although the level of investment remains higher than in the base case because of the higher capital stock. In the new steady state, the rate of investment in each industry returns to its long-run value, while aggregate investment exceeds that of the base case (for corresponding years) by 1.4 percent.

In this scenario, the effects on imports and exports are minor in both the short and the long run. Since capital is internationally immobile, there is no capital account—a potentially important channel for transmitting effects on merchandise trade through its effect on the exchange rate. In the short run, real exports are not significantly affected by the policy change. Over the long term, the higher capital intensity and productiveness of the U.S. economy imply higher real output and incomes; this yields somewhat higher demands for foreign intermediate and final goods and a slightly increased volume of international trade. In the new steady state, real exports are approximately 0.4 percent higher than in the base case.

Mobility

The same initiative produces quite different effects once capital mobility is introduced. The differences are most easily seen by comparing the columns of table 1.7, which vary the substitutability of domestic and foreign assets.

We focus on the results of our central mobility case, which employs a value of 1.0 for σ. As before, the effect of the policy change is to raise the after-tax return to domestic households. We model the U.S. and foreign individual income tax systems as residence based: households pay capital income to their own governments, regardless of where the capital income originated.[27] This implies that for domestic households the new policy raises after-tax returns on savings invested at home and abroad. Thus, the policy change has no first-order effect on the international allocation of their (increased) savings. For foreign households, the change in policy does not affect the wedge between before- and after-tax returns since their marginal tax rates do not change. The asymmetry in the changes in marginal rates implies significant adjustments in the capital account.

In the central mobility case, domestic households increase their saving by 5.1 percent in the initial period. Since the largest share of domestic portfolios consists of domestic assets, and since the new policy has relatively little effect on the desired portfolio composition, the bulk of the increase in domestic household saving is directed toward domestic assets. This depresses the U.S. before-tax nominal interest rate, which falls initially from 7.1 to 6.8 percent.

Table 1.7   Effects of Savings Subsidy under Alternative Asset Mobility and Asset Substitutability Assumptions

	No Mobility			Mobility (σ = .2)			Mobility (σ = 1)			Mobility (σ = 5)		
	Period 1	Period 5	Steady State	Period 1	Period 5	Steady State	Period 1	Period 5	Steady State	Period 1	Period 5	Steady State
Nominal exchange rate (foreign currency/$)	.996	.998	1.002	.990	.997	1.006	.990	.995	1.007	.987	.988	1.014
Saving by U.S. households:	2.72	1.88	2.13	5.98	3.48	2.03	5.09	2.92	2.21	5.01	3.57	3.09
U.S. asset accumulation	2.72	1.88	2.13	5.08	2.94	2.03	3.57	2.06	2.04	1.83	1.54	2.06
Foreign asset accumulation	.00	.00	.00	15.13	8.93	2.02	20.54	11.63	3.85	44.69	24.03	13.53
Home asset accumulation share[a]	1.0	1.0	1.0	.902	.905	.910	.897	.902	.909	.878	.892	.901
Saving by foreign households:	.01	.00	.01	-1.02	-.66	-.09	-1.06	-.81	-.21	-1.46	-1.51	-.83
U.S. asset accumulation	.00	.00	.00	-10.57	-5.31	.29	-3.37	-6.41	-.52	10.13	-11.33	-4.61
Foreign asset accumulation	.01	.01	.01	-.80	-.47	-.11	-.97	-.59	-.20	-1.93	-1.12	-.68
Home asset accumulation share[a]	1.0	1.0	1.0	.965	.963	.961	.962	.964	.962	.957	.965	.963
Balance of payments (levels):[b]												
Capital account balance	0	0	0	-3,168	-2,094	-255	-3,494	-2,651	-670	-5,035	-5,213	-2,854
Trade balance	0	0	0	2,128	-14	-1,939	2,632	681	-2,689	4,295	2,739	-6,428
Net income flow	0	0	0	1,040	2,108	2,194	862	1,970	3,359	740	2,474	9,282
Real exports	.20	.33	.39	.71	.34	-.01	.75	.47	-.07	1.10	.87	-.93
Domestic investment	1.00	1.16	1.43	1.04	1.30	1.32	.75	.91	1.29	.42	.49	1.13
Domestic consumption	-.06	.06	.19	-.26	.02	.33	-.10	.10	.39	-.04	.10	.65

Note: All values express percentage changes from the base case, except in the rows corresponding to the exchange rate, accumulation shares, and balance of payments components. In the mobility scenarios, the base case values for the accumulation shares are .910 and .961 for domestic and foreign residents, respectively.

[a]Ratio of home asset accumulation to total asset accumulation. In the mobility scenarios, the base case values for the accumulation shares are .910 and .961 for domestic and foreign residents, respectively.

[b]All balance of payments items in millions of 1983 dollars. Figures are normalized to abstract from the long-run (steady-state) growth of the economy.

[c]Investment percentages may differ from personal saving percentages because of retained earnings and investment tax credits used to finance investment.

Because foreigners' marginal tax rates remain unchanged, the fall in before-tax interest rates in the United States leads to similar reductions in the after-tax returns they receive from U.S. assets. This implies a lower average return on foreigners' portfolios and lower overall foreign saving, which falls by approximately 1 percent on impact. Much of the reduction takes the form of reduced accumulation of U.S. assets; in the first year, inflows of foreign capital to the United States fall by 3.4 percent from $15.0 billion (1983 dollars) in the base case to $14.5 billion in the policy change simulation. But the increase in saving by domestic households more than offsets the decrease in capital inflows from abroad, and total saving (domestic saving plus the net capital inflow) increases, as shown in figure 1.2.

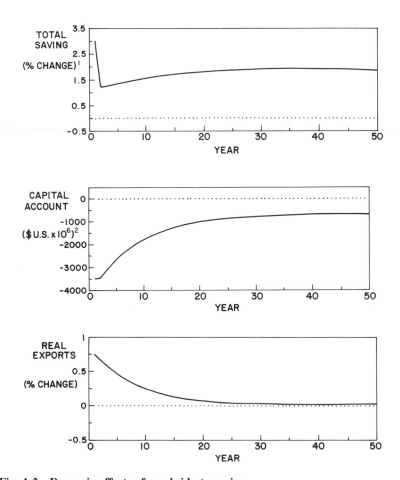

Fig. 1.2   Dynamic effects of a subsidy to saving
[1]Total saving is domestic saving plus net capital inflows.
[2]Capital account levels are normalized in each year by the factor $(1 + g)^t$, where g is the steady-state growth rate of the economy.

Increased purchases of foreign assets by domestic residents combine with reduced purchases of domestic assets by foreign residents to produce a capital account deficit since the capital account balance is zero in the base case. In the first year, the capital account balance is -3.5 billion. The capital account deficit puts downward pressure on the dollar, which depreciates by 1 percent initially. The cheaper dollar benefits export industries, whose output increases by 0.75 percent initially, and leads to a trade surplus.

Thus, the short-run effects on foreign trade of this savings-promoting initiative are different in the presence of international capital mobility. The differences stem from changes in the capital account and from subsequent effects on exchange rates.

Figure 1.2 illustrates that the long-term consequences of the savings subsidy differ substantially from the short-term effects. In the short and the medium term, domestic households enjoy a higher average return on their portfolios than do foreign households, reflecting the reduced marginal tax rates on their capital incomes. Income and savings by U.S. households grow faster than do those of foreigners. Much of the increase in saving by U.S. households is directed abroad. As a result, net income from abroad rises over time, putting upward pressure on the dollar and reducing export demands. Real exports decline (relative to the base case) over time. In the new steady state, real exports are 0.1 percent below the base case levels.

These results underscore the importance of accounting for international capital mobility in assessing the effects of savings-promoting policy on the performance of export (and import-competing) industries. Just as important, they indicate that such a policy's long-run consequences may be dramatically different from its effects in the short term.

To test the robustness of these results, we perform the same policy simulation for alternative values of σ. The essential pattern of effects is little different: whether σ equals 0.2, 1, or 5, the savings-promoting policy initially leads to increased accumulation of foreign assets by domestic households and reduced accumulation of domestic assets by foreign households. This implies a deficit on the capital account, a decline in the value of the dollar, and a rise in real exports in the short run.[28] In all three simulations, the position of exports is reversed in the long run as higher net income flows raise the value of the dollar. The magnitude of these effects increases as the value of σ grows. When σ is large, U.S. households' portfolio responses are greater: since they enjoy higher returns on assets located abroad than on those located at home, they respond to the policy change by devoting a larger share of their savings to purchases of new foreign assets.[29] As a result, the capital account deficit is larger the higher the value of σ, and exchange rate depreciation is more pronounced. Hence, export industries receive a larger initial boost.

1.5.2 Resurrecting Investment Tax Credits

We next investigate the effects of restoring investment tax credits (ITCs) to their effective rates prior to the Tax Reform Act of 1986. Since the credits apply only to equipment and not to structures, effective subsidy rates differ by industry according to the composition of each industry's physical capital in terms of structures and equipment. The ITC renewal is assumed to be unanticipated and to take effect in the first period. Where the previous policy affected incentives to save, this one affects incentives to invest.

No Mobility

The effect of implementing the ITC is to lower the effective cost of new capital to domestic industry and stimulate investment demand, as shown in table 1.8. Tax-adjusted q and investment rise everywhere except in the housing services industry, which enjoys little benefit from the policy change since its capital consists almost entirely of structures and its effective ITC rate is still zero. Heightened investment demands exert upward pressure on the domestic interest rate, which elicits an increase in saving by U.S. households of approximately 2.7 percent in the first year (see table 1.8).

The short-run effect on exports is very small. Eventually, however, real exports increase significantly relative to the base case, reflecting the fact that restoring ITCs raises the capital intensity of the economy over time, leading to higher incomes and output and a higher volume of trade. In the new steady state, real exports are approximately 2 percent higher than in the base case.

Mobility

Restoring the ITC produces quite different results in the presence of capital mobility, particularly in the short run. Again, we focus on the central mobility case ($\sigma = 1$).[30] As in the no-mobility scenario, the initial effect of the new policy is to stimulate investment demands and raise the domestic interest rate. Higher U.S. interest rates induce additional saving not only by U.S. residents but also by foreigners. Higher U.S. rates increase the relative attractiveness of assets located in the United States, leading to increased demands for these assets by U.S. and foreign residents. Total U.S. domestic saving (saving by U.S. nationals plus the net capital inflow) rises, reflecting the increase in global saving and the increase in the share of that saving devoted to the accumulation of U.S. assets. These changes in asset accumulation patterns imply a surplus on the U.S. capital account, which puts upward pressure on the dollar, making U.S. exports more expensive and reducing demand for U.S. exports by approximately 0.2 percent on impact.

Thus, restoring ITCs has different (though not exceptionally large) short-run implications for export industries once an allowance is made for international capital mobility.

In the presence of mobile capital, long-run effects differ significantly from short-run effects. The long-run effects reflect the fact that this policy change is source based, stimulating capital formation *in the United States* rather than globally (as in the savings-promotion policy). As a result, U.S. residents, who own capital located in the United States, experience faster income growth than do foreign residents. Their higher incomes bring about a rise in their

Table 1.8   Effects of Investment Tax Credits under Alternative Asset Mobility and Asset Substitutability Assumptions

	No Mobility			Mobility (σ = .2)			Mobility (σ = 1)			Mobility (σ = 5)		
	Period 1	Period 5	Steady State	Period 1	Period 5	Steady State	Period 1	Period 5	Steady State	Period 1	Period 5	Steady State
Nominal exchange rate (foreign currency/$)	1.001	1.003	1.011	1.003	1.004	1.013	1.002	1.004	1.014	1.002	1.003	1.016
Saving by U.S. households:												
U.S. asset accumulation	1.29	.41	4.56	1.11	.98	3.95	1.50	1.06	4.00	1.43	1.34	4.29
Foreign asset accumulation	1.29	.41	4.56	1.10	.90	3.98	1.12	.97	3.97	.65	.92	3.99
Foreign asset accumulation	.00	.00	.00	1.22	1.82	3.70	5.29	1.98	4.29	9.28	5.66	7.31
Home asset accumulation share[a]	1.0	1.0	1.0	.910	.909	.910	.907	.909	.910	.903	.906	.907
Saving by foreign households:												
U.S. asset accumulation	-.02	-.01	.02	.18	-.11	-.07	.04	-.13	-.11	-.05	-.32	-.30
Foreign asset accumulation	.00	.00	.00	5.24	-1.08	.29	6.75	-1.21	-.01	8.72	-2.83	-1.32
Foreign asset accumulation	-.02	-.01	.02	-.03	-.07	-.08	-.23	-.09	-.12	-.40	-.22	-.26
Home asset accumulation share[a]	1.0	1.0	1.0	.959	.962	.961	.959	.962	.961	.958	.962	.962
Balance of payments (levels):[b]												
Capital account balance	0	0	0	585	-380	-290	214	-422	-427	-78	-1,199	-1,095
Trade balance	0	0	0	-1,196	-155	-1,266	-811	-178	-1,472	-472	409	-2,559
Net income flow	0	0	0	611	535	1,556	597	600	1,899	550	790	3,654
Real exports	-.07	.35	2.00	-.32	.33	1.66	-.24	.33	1.61	-.16	.44	1.38
Domestic investment[c]	2.71	3.36	7.35	2.86	3.46	6.86	2.86	3.47	6.84	2.76	3.40	6.79
Domestic consumption	-1.21	-.98	.76	-1.21	-.99	.83	-1.23	-.99	.84	-1.20	-1.02	.92

Note: All values express percentage changes from the base case, except in the rows corresponding to the exchange rate, accumulation shares, and balance of payments components.

[a]Ratio of home asset accumulation to total asset accumulation. In the mobility scenarios, the base case values for the accumulation shares are .910 and .961 for domestic and foreign residents, respectively.

[b]All balance of payments items in millions of 1983 dollars. Figures are normalized to abstract from the long-run (steady-state) growth of the economy.

[c]Investment percentages may differ from personal saving percentages because of retained earnings and investment tax credits used to finance investment.

accumulation of foreign assets relative to foreigners' accumulation of domestic assets, causing the capital account balance to fall and ultimately become negative. The rise in net interest income from abroad also reflects the increased accumulation of foreign assets by domestic residents. These considerable income flows help push up demands for dollars and cause the exchange rate to rise over time. Finally, higher domestic incomes imply faster growth in the demands for imports by domestic consumers and domestic industry, and the trade balance worsens over time.

The negative long-run trade balance is due to higher import volumes, not lower exports: in the long run, real exports exceed base case levels. This is a consequence both of a higher volume of trade and of lower real prices for U.S. goods. The ITC raises the capital intensity of the domestic economy, making labor more productive and lowering prices of U.S. goods to foreigners. The real exchange rate falls by 0.6 percent after ten years, despite the increase in the nominal exchange rate.[31] Thus, both income and relative price changes contribute to the revival of export demands. Figure 1.3 suggests that very little time is required for the initial adverse effects of the ITCs on exports to be reversed. In the long run, the real value of U.S. exports rises by 1.6 percent over base case levels.

These results underscore the importance of distinguishing the short- and long-run effects of growth-oriented tax policy. While confirming that there may be a conflict between investment promotion and the viability of export industries, our results suggest that the conflict may materialize only briefly.

1.5.3 Differences across Industries

So far our discussion of simulation results has focused on aggregate effects. The savings- and investment-promoting policies also yield very different effects across industries, differences our model is ideally suited to bring out.

Table 1.9 displays some of these differences. The first two panels of the table show the effects of the savings subsidy in the no-mobility case and the mobility case with $\sigma = 1$. In general, the savings subsidy boosts capital goods industries (construction, metals, machinery) relative to consumer goods industries in the short run. Over the longer term, the relative advantage of capital goods industries declines as the capital intensity of the U.S. economy rises and after-tax rates of return and rates of accumulation fall. Under the savings subsidy, the differences between the no-mobility and the mobility cases are relatively minor for industries that have little dependence on the export market. In contrast, for export-oriented industries, the mobility assumptions are important, as they affect the pattern of exports over time. Thus, in the short run the export-oriented agriculture and textiles industries fare better in the presence of mobility than in its absence; the reverse is the case in the long run.

The last two panels of table 1.9 consider the effects of the ITC renewal. Here, the differences across industries reflect mainly differences in the magnitude of investment credits across industries. The petroleum refining and

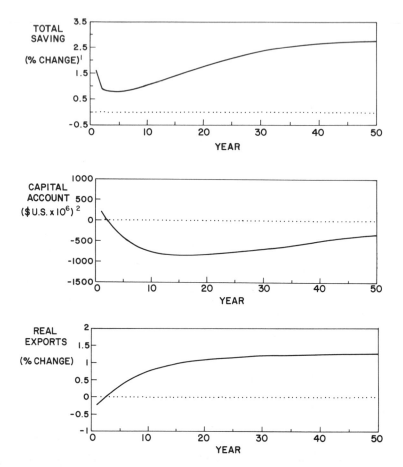

Fig. 1.3 Dynamic effects of restoring investment tax credits
[1]Total saving is domestic saving plus net capital inflows.
[2]Capital account levels are normalized in each year by the factor $(1 + g)^t$, where g is the steady-state growth rate of the economy

housing industries receive the smallest credits per unit of investment because the ratio of equipment to structures is low in these industries. In the first period, investment in housing declines slightly, and investment in petroleum refining increases by less than 3 percent, while investment in most other industries rises by between 5 and 7 percent. In the long run, investment in every industry exceeds base case levels, a consequence of the overall increase in productivity and incomes generated by the policy change.

1.5.4 Sensitivity Analysis

We test the robustness of our results further by considering the savings- and investment-promoting policies under alternative values for the parameter Ω,

Table 1.9   Effects across Industries of Saving- and Investment-promoting Tax Changes (percentage changes from base case)

	1 Agriculture and Mining			2 Crude Petroleum and Refining			3 Construction			4 Textiles, Apparel, and Leather			5 Metals		
	Period 1	Period 5	Steady State	Period 1	Period 5	Steady State	Period 1	Period 5	Steady State	Period 1	Period 5	Steady State	Period 1	Period 5	Steady State
Savings subsidy:															
1. No capital mobility:															
Investment	1.60	1.51	1.31	1.47	1.54	1.34	1.34	1.68	2.11	1.28	1.48	1.74	1.72	2.00	2.48
Employment	1.18	.19	-1.03	.74	.58	-.14	.73	.83	1.01	.37	.39	.11	.55	.55	.39
Gross output	.20	.42	.57	.24	.45	.77	.67	.81	1.07	.31	.39	.33	.41	.54	.74
Exports	-.29	.43	1.09	.01	.12	.36	.22	.22	.11	.29	.34	.27	.19	.23	.20
2. Capital mobility (σ = 1):															
Investment	1.41	1.34	1.16	1.03	1.08	.92	.98	1.37	1.89	1.02	1.20	1.50	1.39	1.62	1.97
Employment	1.42	.38	-1.07	1.23	.81	-.36	.55	.65	.91	.62	.55	.04	.78	.56	.09
Gross output	.29	.43	.46	.43	.47	.44	.51	.64	.96	.53	.51	.24	.61	.54	.41
Exports	.04	.44	.63	.23	.13	0.00	.66	.35	-.31	.91	.51	-.34	.61	.35	-.22
ITC renewal:															
1. No capital mobility:															
Investment	3.45	3.64	5.50	2.77	3.30	6.38	6.24	7.80	14.15	5.08	6.25	11.75	6.20	7.55	13.78
Employment	.61	-1.04	-2.58	-.56	-.51	-.11	2.01	2.31	5.01	-1.28	-1.06	.38	.98	1.07	2.03
Gross output	-.17	.45	2.88	-.30	.25	3.87	1.80	2.33	5.48	-1.17	-.70	1.85	.65	1.19	3.94
Exports	-.33	1.09	3.81	.12	.27	1.62	-.09	.06	.73	.03	.32	1.70	-.12	.10	1.16
2. Capital mobility (σ = 1):															
Investment	3.50	3.66	5.24	2.95	3.41	5.81	6.72	8.28	13.37	5.17	6.33	11.28	6.63	7.95	12.88
Employment	.52	-1.06	-2.53	-.73	-.56	-.15	2.14	2.39	4.66	-1.40	-1.09	.38	.94	1.08	1.75
Gross output	-.21	.46	2.74	-.36	.26	3.52	1.91	2.41	5.11	-1.28	-.72	1.80	.61	1.22	3.57
Exports	-.43	1.08	3.44	.05	.27	1.32	-.22	.04	.48	-.16	.28	1.30	-.25	.08	.89

(continued)

Table 1.9 (continued)

	6 Machinery			7 Motor Vehicles			8 Miscellaneous Manufacturing			9 Services			10 Housing		
	Period 1	Period 5	Steady State	Period 1	Period 5	Steady State	Period 1	Period 5	Steady State	Period 1	Period 5	Steady State	Period 1	Period 5	Steady State
Savings subsidy:															
1. No capital mobility:															
Investment	1.38	1.61	1.91	1.42	1.67	1.94	1.31	1.55	1.77	1.56	1.82	2.44	.45	.56	.68
Employment	.44	.43	.34	.64	.54	.16	.34	.36	.14	.29	.27	-.15	.23	.07	-.71
Gross output	.31	.43	.62	.44	.53	.56	.23	.37	.47	.18	.28	.33	-.26	-.01	.64
Exports	.28	.33	.27	.27	.32	.27	.21	.37	.44	.36	.35	.32	.00	.00	.00
2. Capital mobility ($\sigma = 1$):															
Investment	1.05	1.23	1.49	1.11	1.40	1.74	.99	1.26	1.57	1.30	1.57	2.25	.23	.34	.64
Employment	.64	.46	.10	.72	.60	.14	.41	.42	.12	.31	.33	-.08	.10	.12	-.47
Gross output	.49	.43	.35	.51	.56	.50	.30	.39	.41	.21	.31	.35	-.13	-.02	.61
Exports	.89	.50	-.33	.88	.49	-.32	.82	.52	-.17	1.03	.54	-.32	.00	.00	.00
ITC renewal:															
1. No capital mobility:															
Investment	5.69	6.87	11.73	5.13	6.35	11.64	5.77	6.90	11.70	6.64	8.21	16.30	-.60	-.60	.76
Employment	.76	.76	1.58	-.02	-.19	.41	-.18	-.16	.52	-.42	-.48	-.81	-2.01	-1.91	-1.70
Gross output	.41	.92	3.33	-.21	.27	2.86	-.31	.22	2.67	-.59	-.17	2.16	.29	-.10	.69
Exports	-.17	.20	1.70	-.08	.28	1.76	-.09	.47	2.36	.00	.25	2.24	.00	.00	.00
2. Capital mobility ($\sigma = 1$):															
Investment	5.99	7.14	11.00	5.39	6.59	11.08	6.01	7.09	11.17	6.94	8.46	15.59	-.55	-.60	.39
Employment	.72	.76	1.36	-.04	-.20	.38	-.20	-.17	.50	-.43	-.50	-.72	-2.03	-1.95	-1.40
Gross output	.37	.94	3.03	-.23	.29	2.73	-.34	.23	2.56	-.61	-.17	2.13	.27	-.08	.34
Exports	-.36	.17	1.30	-.27	.25	1.37	-.28	.45	1.94	-.20	.22	1.81	.00	.00	.00

whose inverse is the intertemporal elasticity of substitution in consumption. The simulations previously considered adopt a value of 0.5 for this elasticity ($\Omega = 2$). Table 1.10 displays results for these central case simulations as well as for simulations with values of 0.25 and 1.0 for this elasticity.

With a higher intertemporal consumption elasticity, the savings-promoting policy induces a larger increase in savings by U.S. households, a sharper drop in gross-of-tax U.S. interest rates, and a larger reduction in savings by foreign households. There is a larger increase in domestic households' accumulation of foreign assets and a larger decrease in foreign households' accumulation of domestic assets, implying larger capital account deficits initially and larger effects on exchange rates and real exports. Under all three values for the intertemporal elasticity, the pattern of effects over time is very similar: real exports rise in the short run but fall in the long run.

Restoring the ITC similarly has larger effects on domestic households' saving the larger the value of the intertemporal substitution elasticity. The pattern of effects on exports is similar across different values for this elasticity: in all simulations, the policy shock hurts exports initially but eventually leads to export volumes above base case levels.

We also consider both policies under an alternative model specification in which households' consumption and portfolio choices are independent. This alternative specification may appeal to those who prefer to leave asset preferences out of individuals' utility functions. Domestic households first choose portfolio shares according to

$$(49) \qquad d \ln[\alpha/(1 - \alpha)] = \sigma \, d \, \ln(r_{DD}/r_{DF}),$$

where σ is the elasticity of substitution between portfolio shares. They then choose consumption levels to maximize the utility function:

$$(50) \qquad U = \sum_{s=t}^{\infty} (1 + \delta)^{t-s}(1 - \Omega)^{-1}C_s^{1-\Omega},$$

where s is the current time period. The treatment of foreign households is analogous. The independence of consumption and portfolio choices in this specification is achieved at some cost: households' portfolio decisions do not stem from utility maximization but rather are based on the arbitrary rule of equation (49). Table 1.10 reveals that the pattern of results is very similar under the alternative specification: the savings-promoting policy again creates capital account deficits and stimulates exports in the short run while leading to capital account improvements and declines in real exports over the longer term. Similarly, restoring investment tax credits implies capital account surpluses and reduced export volumes in the short term and capital account deficits and higher export volumes in the long run.

Table 1.10 **Effects under Alternative Model Specification and under Alternative Values for Intertemporal Substitution Elasticity**

	.25ᵃ			.5ᵃ'ᵇ			1.0ᵃ			.5ᵃ'ᶜ		
	Period 1	Period 5	Steady State	Period 1	Period 5	Steady State	Period 1	Period 5	Steady State	Period 1	Period 5	Steady State
A. Savings Subsidy:												
Saving by U.S. households	4.25	2.72	2.61	5.09	2.92	2.21	5.24	2.83	2.10	6.86	4.35	1.97
Saving by foreign households	−.90	−.78	−.22	−1.06	−.81	−.21	−1.14	−.84	−.21	−1.39	−.97	−.22
Balance of payments (levels):ᵈ												
Capital account balance	−3,009	−2,640	−697	−3,494	−2,651	−670	−4,031	−2,991	−762	−4,695	−3,163	−704
Trade balance	2,338	923	−2,603	2,632	681	−2,689	3,094	828	−2,658	3,554	673	−2,516
Net income flow	671	1,717	3,300	862	1,970	3,359	937	2,163	3,420	1,141	2,490	3,220
Real exports	.71	.51	−.02	.75	.47	−.07	.84	.49	−.09	.94	.48	−.06
Domestic investmentᶜ	.66	.88	1.59	.75	.91	1.29	.66	.82	1.18	1.12	1.41	1.13
Domestic consumption	−.02	.10	.38	−.10	−.10	−.39	−.10	.11	.37	−.36	−.06	.34
B. Investment tax credit:												
Saving by U.S. households	.85	.78	5.76	1.50	1.06	4.00	1.88	1.12	3.33	.48	.037	4.64
Saving by foreign households	.14	−.10	−.19	.04	−.13	−.11	−.08	−.17	−.07	.16	−.11	−.14
Balance of payments (levels):ᵈ												
Capital account balance	598	−298	−691	214	−422	−427	−278	−603	−345	646	−374	−520
Trade balance	93	−170	−2,535	−811	−178	−1,472	−429	−162	−1,024	−1,088	−45	−1,955
Net income flow	505	468	3,226	597	600	1,899	707	765	1,369	442	419	2,475
Real exports	−.30	.30	1.53	−.24	.33	1.61	−.16	.34	1.65	−.29	.34	1.58
Domestic investmentᵉ	2.76	3.38	8.10	2.86	3.47	6.84	2.92	3.50	6.38	2.64	3.23	7.25
Domestic consumption	−1.18	−1.02	.86	−1.23	−.99	.84	−1.28	−.99	.80	−1.09	−.93	.91

Note: All values express percentage changes from the base case, except in rows corresponding to balance of payments components.

ᵃIntertemporal substitution elasticity.

ᵇCentral case.

ᶜIndependent consumption and portfolio choice.

ᵈBalance of payments items are in millions of 1983 dollars. Figures are normalized to abstract from the long-run (steady-state) growth of the economy.

ᵉInvestment percentages may differ from personal saving percentages because of retained earnings and investment tax credits used to finance investment.

1.6   Conclusions and Directions for Further Research

In this paper, we have presented a new framework for analyzing the effects of domestic and foreign policies on the U.S. economy. The model is unique in combining a disaggregated treatment of industry interactions, a detailed specification of personal and corporate taxes, a rigorous attention to adjustment dynamics, and an integrated treatment of current and capital account transactions. We use the model to analyze the short- and long-run effects of savings- and investment-promoting tax policies on the viability of export industries and find that in the presence of internationally mobile financial capital the effects of the two types of policies differ significantly from one another and change fundamentally over time.

In the absence of international capital mobility, investment- and savings-promoting policies each have insignificant short-run effects and favorable long-run effects on U.S. export industries. The long-run benefits reflect the fact that both policies raise the overall capital intensity of U.S. production, leading to an increase in productivity and incomes, to lower relative prices for U.S. goods, and to a higher overall volume of trade. In the presence of international capital mobility, the two types of policies differ from one another in their short- and long-term consequences. Restoring investment tax credits tends to hurt U.S. export industries in the short run but help them subsequently. The reverse is true of policies that subsidize saving. These differences reflect the very different implications of the two types of policies for the capital account of the balance of payments in the short run and the long run.

In future work, we intend to consider the normative implications of these policy alternatives; this study has concentrated on positive issues. We also plan to use the model to analyze the effects of recent changes in U.S. fiscal policy, of trade policy alternatives, and of a variety of industrial policies.

Appendix A:
Derivation of Excess Demands Based on Current Prices

Given a set of current prices, firms' optimal demands for labor and intermediate inputs can be determined. Given the interest rate and lead values for V and Z, one can derive the current values for Q and Z. From these one can derive investment, adjustment costs, demands for external funds, and the level of output of each industry.

On the consumer side, the current marginal utility of wealth λ_t (λ_t^*) can be calculated from the lead value, $\lambda_{t+1}^E(\lambda_{t+1}^{*E})$, and from the current interest rate, based on equation (37). Portfolio shares and overall consumption levels for each household can then be determined from current prices and the current value for λ, using the first-order conditions (35) and (36).

Current prices then dictate the allocation of current consumption expenditure to demands for specific consumption goods. Based on households' shares of dollar- and foreign-currency-denominated wealth and firms' dividend and interest payments, we derive households' capital incomes. Subtracting the value of consumption from households' total after-tax incomes yields household savings. Households devote their savings to the accumulation of domestic and foreign assets so as to attain the desired asset shares.

Demands by government depend only on current prices; lead variables are not employed here.

Appendix B:
Procedure for Obtaining Perfect Foresight Expectations

To solve for perfect foresight expectations, we first obtain the values for V, Z, λ, V^*, λ^*, and e that prevail in the new steady state after a policy change. In the base case, the steady-state values for these variables emerge from the calibration procedure discussed in section 1.4; in revised case simulations, a more complex simulation procedure is required.[32] We then assign the steady-state values as terminal values for the lead variables:

(B.1)
$$V^E_{T+1} = V_{ss} ,$$
$$Z^E_{T+1} = Z_{ss} ,$$
$$\lambda^E_{T+1} = \lambda_{ss} ,$$
$$V^{*E}_{T+1} = V^*_{ss} ,$$
$$\lambda^{*E}_{T+1} = \lambda^*_{ss} ,$$
$$e^E_{T+1} = e_{ss} ,$$

where T is the last simulation period and the subscript ss denotes the value for a variable in the new steady state. Next, we conjecture an initial path for the lead variables.

We then solve the model for each within-period equilibrium given the initial path of the lead variables.[33] The within-period equilibrium solution provides a sequence of derived values: $V_1, V_2, \ldots, V_T; \ldots ; e_1, e_2, \ldots, e_T$. We compare our conjectures with contemporaneous derived values updating the guesses in a Gauss-Seidel fashion. For example, we adjust the V^E path according to

(B.2)
$$V^{E(k+1)}_t = \mu V^{(k)}_t + (1 - \mu)V^{E(k)}_t,$$

where k represents the iteration and μ is a parameter between zero and one. This procedure generally brings lead and realized values within 0.01 percent of one another within fifty iterations.

In this manner, we generate paths for the forward variables that have the appropriate slope across any two consecutive periods since agents have perfect foresight and impose the appropriate relation across periods in determining a current value on the basis of the corresponding lead variable. Each equilibrium path also has the appropriate level, as determined by the terminal values for each variable.

Notes

1. Slemrod (1988) offers an excellent summary of the implications of international capital mobility for the theory of capital income taxation.

2. See, e.g., Bovenberg (1989). The direction of the effects depends on the relative magnitudes of intratemporal elasticities of substitution between domestic and foreign goods in production and intertemporal elasticities of substitution in consumption. Giovannini (1987) shows that the relative size of these elasticities also determines the welfare consequences of savings- and investment-oriented policies under ''small country'' assumptions.

3. The framework here is essentially a two-country portfolio balance model, as analyzed, e.g., by Henderson and Rogoff (1982).

4. The basis for eqs. (5) and (6) is the arbitrage condition requiring that the return to owners of firms equal the rate offered on alternative assets. This is discussed in sec. 1.2 below.

5. Thus, the model offers considerably more industry detail than the Goulder-Summers (1989) model, which distinguishes five domestic industries.

6. This is the asset price approach to investment as developed in Summers (1981).

7. There is some debate as to what constitutes the best specification of firms' financing decisions. We adopt the ''traditional'' approach, according to which the marginal source of funds for investment is new share issues. For a discussion of this and other approaches, see Poterba and Summers (1985).

8. The nominal exchange rate brings nominal magnitudes at home and abroad into line. If all prices (other than the numeraire) are endogenous, the nominal exchange rate is superfluous. This is not the case if some prices (other than the numeraire) are fixed in nominal terms, however. In the model, domestic and foreign nominal wages are specified exogenously (and increase over time at a specified rate that determines the long-run inflation rate), permitting a role for the exchange rate.

9. Thus, the demands for foreign inputs derive from optimizing behavior, with the demand elasticities directly related to the substitution elasticities embedded in the production functions.

10. This transformation of producer goods into consumer goods is necessary because the categories for outputs from production data differ from the categories for goods from consumer expenditure data.

11. For an explicit derivation of this expression for V, see Poterba and Summers (1985).

12. This specification conforms to the ''traditional'' view of dividend behavior. Some empirical support for this view is presented in Poterba and Summers (1985). Further evidence comes from the large volume of share repurchases in recent years documented in Shoven (1987).

13. An alternative is external adjustment costs, according to which the costs of adjustment are borne through payments to an agent (e.g., an enterprise providing

installation services) external to the firm. For a discussion of these different approaches, see Mussa (1978).

14. The consumption-based capital asset pricing model (see, e.g., Duffie and Zame 1987) offers a potential approach to this problem, although the difficulties of empirical implementation are formidable.

15. Mehra and Prescott (1982) and Adler and Dumas (1983), e.g., argue that exchange rate risk provides only part of the explanation as to why households maintain internationally diversified portfolios.

16. The model is agnostic as regards the specific bases for households' portfolio preferences. One explanation might invoke risk considerations. Another might refer to different liquidity services offered by domestic and foreign assets. Poterba and Rotemberg (1983) refer to such services to justify including money in individual utility functions.

17. An alternative formulation would define A in terms of asset levels rather than shares. But, since asset stocks are used to finance future consumption, adding levels of asset holdings to the utility function would introduce an element of double-counting.

18. The value of σ thus critically influences the extent to which policy shocks or other exogenous changes will generate international capital flows.

19. We do not consider the foreign household here since different consumer goods are not distinguished in the foreign country.

20. This facilitates welfare evaluations since the household utility functions do not incorporate welfare derived from government-provided goods and services.

21. Our ten-sector disaggregation is not fully compatible with the disaggregation in the Scholz (1987) data. The Scholz data include metals, machinery, and miscellaneous manufacturing as one sector, while in our model these are three different sectors. We have split out the Scholz data on the basis of the shares of value added represented by each of the three components.

We have also added information pertaining to the housing industry. The Scholz data subsume housing within a real estate sector. To use these data in our model, the real estate sector data had to be divided into housing and other real estate. The weights used to disaggregate the real estate sector data were calculated on the basis of shares of value added in the 367 × 367 input-output matrix for 1977 published by the Department of Commerce (1984).

22. Ultimately, we intend to employ tax rates that more closely reflect effective rates abroad.

23. This information was obtained from the end-use import tables of the Bureau of the Census (U.S. Department of Commerce 1983) for merchandise trade and from McCulloch (1988) for trade in services. We applied it as follows:

a) From the end-use tables we obtained consumption and investment imports by type of good. For each import, total imports for intermediate use were then calculated by subtracting consumption and investment imports from total imports (of a given type) as given by Scholz (1987).

b) Domestic intermediates were calculated by subtracting foreign intermediates from total intermediate goods.

c) The foreign (domestic) input-output matrix was then calculated by multiplying each row of the total input-output matrix by the ratio of foreign (domestic) intermediate good to total intermediate goods. Thus, we assumed that, for each type of intermediate good, the ratio of domestic to foreign inputs of that type was the same across sectors. This assumption was necessary given the absence of information on the uses of intermediate imports by sectors.

24. The procedure is described in Goulder and Summers (1989).

25. The value of m is set at the ratio of foreign to U.S. GDP.

26. As described above, government budget balance is maintained in each year through lump-sum adjustments to domestic households' individual income tax obligations. The present value of these adjustments is approximately zero.

27. The U.S. individual tax system is primarily residence based; the corporate income tax has source-based elements, however, including the foreign tax credit.

28. The difference in returns offered to U.S. savers on domestic and foreign assets is relatively small, considerably smaller than the differences in gross interest rates across countries. This reflects the appreciation of the exchange rate, which, ceteris paribus, lowers the return to U.S. households on foreign assets.

29. The case of perfect substitutability is also of interest but poses special difficulties. Under residence-based taxation, such a scenario generally implies a corner solution: for one of the residents, the after-tax return will not be the same for the two assets, and thus the resident will hold only one of the two assets. If residents' tax rates differ, then if one of the residents faces equal after-tax returns on both assets, the other will not. See Slemrod (1988).

30. We also consider the effects of this policy change under alternative values for the asset elasticity of substitution, σ. As table 1.8 shows, the general pattern of results is quite consistent with those we discuss in the text.

31. In the short run, the rate of inflation in the United States falls below the long-run rate of 6 percent. The growth of foreign prices, however, is relatively unaffected by the policy change. In the long run, rates of inflation in the United States and abroad again are equal (at 6 percent), but the ratio of price levels is different from the ratio in the old steady state.

32. The procedure involves the solution of the general equilibrium model under steady-state constraints. In the constrained system, we iterate over capital stocks and ownership shares (γ and γ^*) as well as prices. Steady-state values for capital stocks and ownership shares have been attained when (1) the derived industry Q's are equal to the steady-state values and (2) the wealth accumulation patterns of households imply no changes in the ownership shares.

33. This technique is similar to the approach of Fair and Taylor (1983).

References

Adler, M., and B. Dumas. 1983. International portfolio choice and corporation finance: A synthesis. *Journal of Finance* 38:925–84.

Board of Governors of the Federal Reserve System. 1987. Balance sheets for the U.S. economy, 1947–86.

Bovenberg, A. L. 1986. Capital income taxation in growing open economies. *Journal of Public Economics* 31:347–76.

————. 1989. The effects of investment incentives on real exchange rates and trade flows. *American Economic Review,* in press.

Duffie, D., and W. Zame. 1987. The consumption-based capital asset pricing model. Stanford University. Mimeo.

Fair, R. C., and J. B. Taylor. 1983. Solution and maximum likelihood estimation of dynamic nonlinear rational expectation models. *Econometrica* 51(4):1169–85.

Giovannini, A. 1987. International capital mobility and tax evasion. NBER Working Paper no. 2460. Cambridge, Mass.: National Bureau of Economic Research.

Goulder, L. H., J. B. Shoven, and J. Whalley. 1983. Domestic tax policy and the foreign sector. In *Behavioral simulation methods in tax policy analysis,* ed. Martin Feldstein. Chicago: University of Chicago Press.

Goulder, L. H., and L. H. Summers. 1989. Tax policy, asset prices, and growth: A general equilibrium analysis. *Journal of Public Economics,* in press.

Henderson, D., and K. Rogoff. 1982. Negative net foreign asset positions and stability in a world portfolio balance model. *Journal of International Economics* 13:85–104.

Kouri, P. J. K. 1976. The exchange rate and the balance of payments in the short run and in the long run. *Scandinavian Journal of Economics* 78:280–304.

McCulloch, R. 1988. International competition in services. In *The United States in the world economy,* ed. Martin Feldstein. Chicago: University of Chicago Press.

McKibbin, W., and J. Sachs. 1986. Coordination of monetary and fiscal policies in the OECD. NBER Working Paper no. 1800. Cambridge, Mass.: National Bureau of Economic Research.

Mehra, R., and E. Prescott. 1982. A test of the intertemporal asset pricing model. Mimeo.

Mussa, M. 1978. Dynamic adjustment in a Heckscher-Ohlin-Samuelson model. *Journal of Political Economy* 86(5):775–91.

Mutti, J., and H. Grubert. 1985. The taxation of capital income in an open economy: The importance of resident-nonresident tax treatment. *Journal of Public Economics* 31:347–76.

Poterba, J. M., and J. J. Rotemberg. 1983. Money in the utility function: An empirical implementation. Massachusetts Institute of Technology. Mimeo.

Poterba, J. M., and L. H. Summers. 1985. The economic effects of dividend taxation. In *Recent advances in corporate finance,* ed. Edward T. Altman and Martin G. Subramanyam. Homewood, Ill.: Richard D. Irwin.

Powell, M. J. D. 1970. A hybrid method for nonlinear equations. In *Numerical methods for nonlinear algebraic equations,* ed. P. Rabinowitz. London: Gordon & Greach.

Sachs, J. 1981. The current account and macroeconomic adjustment in the 1970s. *Brookings Papers on Economic Activity,* no. 2:201–68.

Scholz, K. 1987. Documentation for the 1983 general equilibrium data set. Stanford University. Typescript.

Shoven, J. B. 1987. The tax consequences of share repurchases and other non-dividend cash payments to equity owners. In *Tax policy and the economy,* ed. L. H. Summers, vol. 1. Cambridge, Mass.: MIT Press.

Slemrod, J. 1988. Effects of taxation with international capital mobility. In *Uneasy compromise: Problems of a hybrid income-consumption tax,* ed. H. J. Aaron, H. Galper, and J. Pechman, 115–48. Washington, D.C.P Brookings Institution.

Summers, L. H. 1981. Taxation and corporate investment: A *q*-theory approach. *Brookings Papers on Economic Activity* (January), pp. 67–127.

————. 1988. Tax policy and international competitiveness. In *International aspects of fiscal policies,* ed. J. A. Frenkel. Chicago: University of Chicago Press.

U.S. Department of Commerce. 1984a. *Survey of Current Business* (August).

————. 1984b. *Survey of Current Business* (February).

————. Bureau of the Census. 1983. Highlights of U.S. export and import trade. Washington, D.C., December.

————. Bureau of Economic Analysis. 1984. *Detailed structure of the U.S. economy.* Washington, D.C.:

Comment   David W. Roland-Holst

This paper makes a welcome contribution to computable general equilibrium (CGE) modeling because of its original treatment of international flow-of-funds activity. It should also be welcome in the present discussion of U.S. trade policy since a general equilibrium perspective and a more complete understanding of capital account dynamics are both essential to a comprehensive assessment of our competitive situation. My own experience is centered on modeling, so I shall focus my comments on methodology, beginning with three features of this work that I find attractive.

The authors (and Larry Summers, whose hand is apparent in part of this work) should be commended for substantially advancing the conventional treatment of savings and investment decisions. Using some recent microeconomics of savings-investment behavior as well as a set of convexifying techniques in the form of constant elasticity of substitution (CES) aggregations and Armington assumptions, the authors build a flow-of-funds component for their model that fully endogenizes interest rates and international capital flows. Not only are savings and investment more richly and rigorously specified in each period, but they are also placed in their necessary and proper context of intertemporal optimization, with some allowance for adjustment costs and uncertainty.

These innovations in flow-of-funds modeling lead to the main results of the paper. The authors experiment with different degrees of substitutability between domestic and foreign assets in domestic and foreign portfolios. The equilibria that arise with endogenous capital flows reveal a complex interplay between nominal and real influences on exchange rates. At first glance, the former are driven primarily by capital flows and the latter by demand. A closer look, however, reveals two more subtle forces at work. Capital flows lead to reverse nominal effects from profit income returning to foreign investors and to real effects from productivity changes in response to investment. The income and productivity effects of capital flows can be quite significant in the long run, and, as the authors point out, neglecting them can reverse one's conclusions about the advisability of fiscal reforms to promote domestic capital formation and competitiveness. To my mind, these results give a more refined understanding of exchange rates and capital accounts than the conventional stock-flow perspective, and they deserve further scrutiny.

Another novel feature of this model is its ingenious use of rational expectations in the solution process. Although the idea harks back to Bellman's original solution concepts for stochastic dynamic programming, explicit incorporation of rational expectations conditions in an iterative scheme provides a great expedient to solving dynamic general equilibrium models with "well-behaved" uncertainty.

David W. Roland-Holst is assistant professor of economics at Mills College.

With these and other virtues in mind, I look forward to seeing more simulation results from this model and its descendants. In the meantime, I would like to raise a few points for reflection.

This ten-sector model has been used to good advantage by the authors to study U.S. competitiveness in another paper in which they detail the composition of effects on U.S. industries of our recent trade history. However, I do wonder if the main conclusions of the present paper could have been obtained more simply and clearly from a one-sector model. The interplay between nominal and real effects is driven by financial flows, demand, and productivity changes, but I do not see an essential role here for the sectoral composition of production, consumption, or investment. By focusing these results on asset substitution elasticities in a simpler trade model, one might obtain an elegant intertemporal Marshall-Lerner condition to sort out the real and nominal exchange rate effects of capital account adjustments. Such a result is not available in the multisector case.

A final point concerns the monetary approach to the balance of payments. Computable general equilibrium model builders have tried for over a decade to incorporate monetary phonomena, without appreciable success. This represents one of the largest open problems for our field right now, and thus I do not single out the present paper for shortcomings in this respect.

In modeling economic adjustment, it would be desirable to accommodate the possibility of international payments imbalances if these are manifestations of intertemporal decisions rather than real disequilibria, that is, when they represent only differences between preferences for present and future consumption. Goulder and Eichengreen's CGE specification of asset holding and capital flows may ultimately provide a good vehicle for a neoclassical approach to the balance of payments, but its promise in this regard cannot be fulfilled, I think, without more direct treatment of monetary assets and institutions. Fortunately, a number of contributions have already been made along these lines that would be amenable to their framework. These include the lucid exposition of Dixit and Norman (1980) on this subject as well as a recent and ingenious approach to money holding by Drazen and Helpman (1987).

References

Dixit, A. K., and V. Norman. 1980. *Theory of international trade.* Cambridge: Cambridge University Press.

Drazen, A., and E. Helpman. Stabilization with exchange rate management. *Quarterly Journal of Economics* 102(4):835–55

Comment   Wing Thye Woo

This is a very high-tech paper. Given the importance of the issue of international competitiveness, the use of sophisticated techniques needs no justification. Because policymakers need to know whether strong conclusions deriving from simple models would be supported or reversed by a more complicated model, Goulder and Eichengreen's dynamic computable general equilibrium model (CGE) model is an important contribution. This high-tech model supports most of the reasoning based on simpler models.

To focus attention on trade competitiveness, I will limit my discussion to Goulder and Eichengreen's conclusions about the short-run and steady-state effects of policy changes on export volume, trade account balance, and consumption. The workings of a large and complicated model are usually hard to figure out. The virtue of the Goulder-Eichengreen model is that it can be proxied very well by a very simple model, which I will call the skeletal model. The skeletal model is essentially the GDP identity with a modicum of economic theory thrown in. The main conclusions of the high-tech model are straightforward and intuitive; they come straight out of the intertemporal allocation of consumption spending in an open-economy setting. To be specific, of the twenty-four conclusions concerning the short-run and long-run behavior of the three variables under the four policy scenarios, the skeletal model is irreconcilable with the high-tech model in only one instance. What the high-tech component really does is to add much more detail to the analysis, for example, how the size and composition of the domestic portfolio respond to shifts in savings and investment incentives. Unfortunately, these details provide no additional guidance to policymakers.

Let me now substantiate the preceding statements.

Capital Is Immobile

Equation (1) is the definition of GDP, using the usual textbook notation:

(1) $$C + S + T = Y = C + I + G + (X - M).$$

To convert the identity into a behavioral equation, I assume, as do Goulder and Eichengreen, a balanced budget,

(2) $$T = G,$$

where G is exogenous, and zero capital mobility,

(3) $$X - M = 0.$$

The policy experiments are implemented by changing the composition of a given amount of taxes (T) to distort private savings and investment behavior.

Wing Thye Woo is assistant professor of economics at the University of California, Davis.

Effect of a Savings Subsidy in the Short Run

The short run, by definition, is too short for changes in investment (I) to increase the productive capacity of the economy. The value of output (Y) is fixed. An increase in savings (S) with taxes (T) constant necessitates an equivalent fall in consumption (C). Even though the trade balance ($X - M$) is constant (zero), the components change. If consumption spending is more import intensive than investment spending, then imports would have to fall. The assumption in equation (3) would then force exports to decline by the same amount. Conversely, if consumption spending is less import intensive, then both imports and exports would rise. Hence, the skeletal model can explain why exports move in different directions in the old and new versions of the authors' table 1.7 (in the old version, which was presented at the conference but is not published in this volume, exports fell; they rise, however, in the new version).

Effect of a Savings Subsidy in the Long Run

Since the increased saving is fully translated into additional investments, the new steady state has a higher level of output. Consumption naturally rises, dragging imports up with it. Again because of the zero trade balance assumption, exports (being a residual quantity) rise too.

Effect of an Investment Tax Credit

In the short run, the rise in investment crowds out consumption given that $G, X - M$, and Y are fixed. The sign of the change in export is ambiguous, depending on the relative import intensiveness of consumption and investment spending.

The effects in the long run are the same as in the savings subsidy case because the same reasoning applies. For both the savings subsidy and the investment tax credit, the skeletal model and the high-tech model are observationally equivalent in that they both yield the same short-run and long-run response for exports, trade balance, and consumption.

Capital Is Mobile

Rewrite equation (1) as follows:

$$(4) \quad \sum_{0}^{\infty} \left(\frac{1}{1+r} \right)^i (C_{t+1} + S_{t+i} + T_{t+i}) \equiv \sum_{0}^{\infty} \left(\frac{1}{1+r} \right)^i Y_{t+i}$$

$$\equiv \sum_{0}^{\infty} \left(\frac{1}{1+r} \right)^i [C_{t+i} + I_{t+i} + G_{t+i} + (X - M)_{t+i}].$$

Using the authors' assumption

$$(5) \qquad\qquad T_{t+i} = G_{t+i},$$

where G_{t+i} is constant for all i's, we get

$$(6) \quad \sum_{0}^{\infty}\left(\frac{1}{1+r}\right)^{i} I_{t+i} + \sum_{0}^{\infty}\left(\frac{1}{1+r}\right)^{i} (X - M)_{t+i} = \sum_{0}^{\infty}\left(\frac{1}{1+r}\right)^{i} S_{t+i}.$$

Now add two dashes of economic theory to equation (6). The first is that investment and savings decisions are arrived at on quite different bases. Investments are undertaken to maximize the wealth level and hence are determined solely by the marginal product of capital (f'), the rate of return on equities (r), and the adjustment cost. Savings are determined by the intertemporal allocation of consumption for a given level of wealth.

In a discrete time formulation with all transactions occurring at the beginning of each period, the stock of foreign assets at the beginning of time $t + 1$, F_{t+1}, is given by

$$(7) \quad F_{t+1} = (1 + r)[F_t + (X - M)_t].$$

The second element of theory is to rule out Ponzi games in international borrowing, and the result is

$$(8) \quad F_t = \sum_{0}^{\infty}\left(\frac{1}{1+r}\right)^{i} (X - M)_{t+i}.$$

For ease of exposition, I will assume that $F_t = 0$, to get

$$(9) \quad (X - M)_t + \sum_{1}^{\infty}\left(\frac{1}{1+r}\right)^{i} (X - M)_{t+i} = 0.$$

Roughly speaking, equation (9) tells us that today's trade surplus is tomorrow's trade deficit. Note that, because of the discounting, the absolute size of today's trade surplus is smaller than the absolute size of tomorrow's trade deficit. Ceteris paribus, this means that the absolute size of today's real exchange rate appreciation has to be smaller than tomorrow's exchange rate depreciation.

Effects of a Savings Subsidy

Since this does not change the after-tax marginal product of capital, the immediate effect on investments is negligible. As current consumption is now more expensive than future consumption, it drops. In the short run, with Y, I, and G fixed, the decline in consumption means that the excess goods have to be sold abroad. To ensure that X will rise, the exchange rate depreciates and causes the trade balance to improve.

In the long run, yesterday's trade surplus now enables a trade deficit. To accomplish this reversal in the trade account, the exchange rate appreciates, causing exports to fall. The new steady-state trade deficit is paid for by the amortization of yesterday's loan to the foreigners.

Effects of an Investment Tax Credit

There are two ways to finance the additional investment spending. The first is to squeeze current consumption, and the second is to borrow from abroad. Given that today's investment will raise tomorrow's income, intertemporal smoothing of consumption dictates that it would not be optimal to reduce today's consumption by the same amount as the increase in investment. It is optimal to finance part of the investment with foreign savings. In the short run, with

$$(10) \qquad\qquad |\Delta C| < |\Delta I|,$$

the trade account will turn negative, requiring the exchange rate to appreciate and reduce exports.

In the long run, the skeletal model would predict that the exchange rate would depreciate in order to increase exports and therefore yield a trade surplus to repay the previous loan. The long-run sign of the trade account is the one instance, out of twenty-four, in which the skeletal model did not agree with the high-tech model. The difference comes from the existence of portfolio allocation decisions in the latter. The investment tax credit stimulates U.S. residents' desire to increase their capital holding so much that they turn their trade balance positive in the medium run in order greatly to increase their holdings of foreign assets. This massive accumulation of foreign assets turns the net income flow positive in the new steady state, causing the new steady-state trade balance to be negative.

The price for the neglect of portfolio management in the skeletal model is that, under this scenario, it is unreliable beyond a medium-run analysis. But, since the skeletal model's prediction on export and consumption levels still holds, it is inadequate for guiding policy only if the overwhelming concern is with the effect of an investment tax credit on the steady-state trade surplus.

Using the Results of This Paper for Policy-making

Let me now make three observations on why this high-tech model provides no more guidance to policy-making than the skeletal model does. The first observation is on the welfare criteria chosen. The focus of the paper is the effect of savings and investment subsidies on competitiveness, and competitiveness is defined as the volume of exports. This definition captures only one aspect of the debate over competitiveness. A large part of the relevant literature, under the heading of strategic trade policy, is more concerned about the composition than about the volume of exports. Since technical advances are more likely in some industries than others, the product mix may very well determine the future trend growth rate of the economy. In other words, to be and continue to be a "world-class economy" (to use Lester Thurow's phrase) means exporting high value added goods rather than a flood of low value added trinkets.

The analysis of investment tax credit in this paper is misleading in an important way. The important question facing policy-makers is not whether we should have an investment tax credit or a savings subsidy but whether we should have a general investment tax credit or a specific investment tax credit.

As the concern about competitiveness comes from welfare considerations, the correct indicator for economic welfare is consumption, not export volume. It is therefore surprising that the paper makes no mention of the consumption changes brought about by the investment and savings subsidy.

The second shortcoming of the analysis is that it can tell us only in which direction a variable would change in the short run and in the steady state on a policy shock. The analysis cannot be used to infer the relative efficacy of savings and investment subsidy by looking at the timing and size of the response of the endogenous variables. The fact that, under the zero capital mobility setting, consumption in the fifth period has returned to positive under the savings subsidy and is still negative under the investment credit cannot be used for welfare analysis because the authors have not provided a common scale to measure the savings and investment stimulus. The time profile of the response depends on the size of the exogenous shock, and so we cannot evaluate the relative desirability of these two policies on the basis of the simulation unless we know that the two policy shocks are of the same magnitude.

I would like to note that there is usually no unique way to scale the shocks. The scaling sometimes depends on the objective of the exercise. For example, a scaling that emphasizes capital accumulation is to set the savings subsidy at an arbitrary level, measure its effect on steady-state capital stock, and then regard the amount of investment credit needed to generate this new level of capital stock as imparting the equivalent distortion. The desirability of the two policies in inducing this capital formation is then ranked by the consumption paths generated as by-products.

In this paper, the assumption of constant total taxes rules out the usual "cost to the budget" criteria. The general point is that, until the authors can provide a scaling that is relevant to the competitiveness, we cannot choose between the different policies.

My final skepticism is about the reliability of the model. Since there are more than one set of parameters that can replicate the benchmark figures, I would have a lot more faith in the model if the authors had chosen the parameter set that yielded the best replication of the trade deficits in the last five years.

2 The Determinants of Foreign Direct Investment in the United States, 1979–85

Edward John Ray

While a great deal of theoretical work and a number of empirical pieces have dealt with the determinants of U.S. foreign direct investment (FDI) in the rest of the world, very little is known about direct investment by foreign countries in the United States.[1] My purpose in the present study is to partially redress that imbalance. I establish at the outset that, whereas U.S. foreign direct investment abroad is concentrated in manufacturing and petroleum, foreign investment in the United States is diversified across all sectors of the economy. In addition, I provide evidence that differences in relative growth in GNP across countries and movements in currency exchange rates affect the magnitude and timing of foreign direct investments in the United States.

In this paper, I develop a simple partial equilibrium model of foreign direct investment in the manufacturing sector that focuses on how contracting costs influence parent firms' decisions to invest in or to license foreign firms. The model suggests that high contracting costs are associated with goods that use firm-specific human and physical capital inputs and require substantial research and development effort in production. While this argument is hardly new or uncommon,[2] the simplicity of my contracting model and the uniqueness of the empirical work that follows from it represent novel contributions to the basic approach.

I also consider the relation between foreign firms' investments in the manufacturing sector of the U.S. economy and protectionism in the United States. Specifically, I test whether U.S. tariffs or nontariff trade barriers have

Edward John Ray is professor of economics at Ohio State University.

The author is especially grateful to Donald O. Parsons for comments on an earlier draft of the paper and to Johannes Denekamp for his able research assistance on this project. Keith Maskus, James Levinsohn, Robert Feenstra, Robert Lipsey, and anonymous referees made many valuable suggestions for revisions based on the presentation at the NBER Universities Research Conference for which this paper was prepared.

encouraged foreign firms investing in the United States either to circumvent existing trade restrictions or to neutralize the risk of future protectionist measures.[3] Furthermore, I attempt to determine the effect of intraindustry trade on foreign firms' decisions to invest in the United States.

The data consist of the values of transactions that occurred within a given industry summed to provide an industry-level value of investments at the four-digit SIC level for each year from 1979 to 1985. By pooling time-series and cross-sectional data, samples are generated that are on the order of 1,800 observations for manufacturing industries. The industry-level investment data are grouped according to the home of the parent firm and separate estimates provided of foreign direct investment in the United States for Japan, Canada, and the European Community (EC) as well as for all countries combined.

The paper has several important policy implications. First, it provides evidence that recent changes in exchange rates and relative economic growth across industrialized economies have played a role in promoting foreign direct investment in the United States. Second, it clarifies the extent to which the recent rise in nontariff trade barrier protection in the United States has induced greater foreign investment in U.S. manufacturing activities. Finally, it provides evidence regarding the extent to which foreign direct investment in the United States might create the jobs needed to reduce the structural unemployment problems that were apparent in the United States in 1979 and 1980.

2.1 Background

While most previous work on foreign direct investment has focused on the manufacturing sector, we need to have some perspective on the role that foreign investment has played in the nonmanufacturing sector. In addition to assessing the characteristics of overall foreign investment in the United States, we also need to examine the components of that investment. Therefore, I will review both overall foreign investment in the United States and the relative importance of foreign direct investment in the United States originating in Japan, the EC, and Canada.

Table 2.1 provides a summary of foreign direct investment in the United States for each year from 1979 to 1985. The data include annual investments in all sectors and in manufacturing by firms from Japan, the EC, Canada, and the rest of the world. For the period as a whole, manufacturing investment accounted for only 33.4 percent of the total foreign direct investment in the United States. Together, Japan, Canada, and the EC accounted for 79 percent of all foreign direct investment and 80.5 percent of total manufacturing foreign direct investment in the United States between 1979 and 1985.

Table 2.2 provides a summary of the largest foreign direct investments in manufacturing in the United States between 1979 and 1985 for foreign firms in general and by firms from Japan, Canada, and the EC. Table 2.3 indicates

Table 2.1   **Foreign Direct Investment Comparisons (billions of U.S. dollars)**

Year	World		Japan	
	All	Manufacturing	All	Manufacturing
1979	17.973	6.381	.723	.555
		(35.5)		(76.7)
1980	16.103	5.550	1.263	.698
		(34.5)		(55.3)
1981	31.880	9.260	1.510	.879
		(29.0)		(58.2)
1982	17.723	4.450	1.746	.477
		(25.1)		(27.3)
1983	19.388	4.286	2.226	.728
		(22.1)		(32.7)
1984	43.014	14.103	10.460	3.723
		(32.8)		(35.6)
1985	21.062	11.782	2.475	1.551
		(55.9)		(62.7)

Year	Canada		European Community	
	All	Manufacturing	All	Manufacturing
1979	3.265	1.096	12.339	3.880
		(33.6)		(31.3)
1980	4.234	1.022	8.288	3.139
		(24.1)		(37.9)
1981	12.369	4.187	11.841	3.119
		(33.8)		(26.3)
1982	4.659	.890	8.297	2.846
		(19.1)		(34.3)
1983	4.029	.698	6.739	2.531
		(17.3)		(37.6)
1984	5.451	1.122	17.531	4.901
		(20.6)		(28.0)
1985	2.577	.685	10.011	5.682
		(26.6)		(56.8)

Year	Joint Totals (Canada, EC, and Japan)		Joint Shares (Canada, EC, and Japan)	
	All	Manufacturing	All[a]	Manufacturing [a]
1979	16.327	5.531	90.8	86.7
1980	13.785	4.859	85.6	87.5
1981	25.720	8.185	80.7	88.4
1982	14.702	4.213	83.0	94.7
1983	12.994	3.957	67.0	92.3
1984	33.442	9.746	77.7	69.1
1985	15.063	7.918	71.5	67.2

Note: Percentages are given in parentheses.
[a]Values given are percentages.

Table 2.2   Top Foreign Direct Investment Transactions in U.S. Manufacturing Industries (millions of U.S. dollars)

SIC	Description	All		Japan		Canada		EC	
		Rank	FDI	Rank	FDI	Rank	FDI	Rank	FDI
2023	Condensed & evaporated milk	1	6,000.0	...		...		...	
2044	Rice milling	...		4	500.0	...		...	
2611	Pulp mills	...		...		4	562.8	...	
2621	Paper mills[a]	7	1,584.7	...		2	888.1	10	696.6
2631	Paperboard mills	...		...		...		7	837.7
2821	Plastics & resins	3	3,475.4	...		1	2,645.1	...	
2851	Paints etc.	...		...		...		4	1,037.0
2879	Agricultural chemicals NEC	5	1,779.1	...		...		2	1,774.5
2911	Petroleum refining	4	2,818.1	...		...		1	2,598.0
3241	Cement, hydrolic	...		...		...		5	991.6
3272	Concrete products NEC	...		...		8	350.9	...	
3312	Blast furnaces[b]	8	1,497.2	2	604.2	10	303.1	...	
3317	Steel pipes & tubes	...		...		6	403.0	...	
3341	Secondary smelting and refining of nonferrous metals	...		9	250.0	...		...	
3353	Aluminum sheet[c]	6	1,734.6	...		3	873.6	8	800.0
3541	Machine tools[d]	...		...		9	312.5	...	
3562	Ball & roller bearings	...		7	266.3	...		...	
3573	Electrical Computing Equipment	9	1,398.4	5	446.5	...		6	899.9
3624	Carbon & graphite products	...		...		7	378.0	...	
3634	Electrical housewares[e]	...		...		5	523.0	...	
3651	Radio & TV Sets	...		10	217.1	...		...	
3662	Radio & TV Commercial Equipment	...		6	339.4	...		...	
3674	Semiconductors	10	1,394.8	3	566.3	...		9	737.9
3711	Motor vehicles	2	3,782.1	1	2,489.5	...		3	1,208.5
3714	Motor Vehicle Parts	...		8	264.9	...		...	
Total			55,811.6		8,611.9		9,700.4		26,096.5

Note: NEC = not elsewhere considered.
[a]Except building paper.
[b]And steel mills.
[c]And plate and foils.
[d]Metal cutting types.
[e]And fans.

the values and sources of the largest foreign direct investments in the United States during the period 1979–85 and shows the relative importance of investments made by Japanese, Canadian, and EC firms. The ten largest EC firm investments are among the top twenty investments that were undertaken during the period. In contrast, the second through the tenth largest Japanese

Table 2.3   **Top Foreign Direct Investment Transactions (all industries in millions of U.S. dollars)**

Rank	SIC Code	Description	Transaction Value	Japan	Canada	EC	Other
1	4899	Communications	5,099	1			
2	1311	Crude petroleum & natural gas	5,000			1	
3	5172	Petroleum products	3,650			2	
4	2023	Cond. & evap. milk	3,000				Switzerland
5	2023	Cond. & evap. milk	3,000				Switzerland
6	2821	Plastics	2,580		1		
7	1381	Oil & gas drilling	2,500				Kuwait
8	1021	Copper ores	2,500			3	
9	1211	Bituminous coal & lignite	2,400				Australia
10	1211	Bituminous coal & lignite	2,000				Australia
11	1311	Crude petroleum & natural gas	1,062			4	
12	1311	Crude petroleum & natural gas	1,000				Australia
13	2851	Paints etc.	1,000			5	
14	1381	Oil & gas drilling	967			6	
15	1021	Copper ores	938			7	
16	6020	Commercial banks	820			8	
17	6020	Commercial banks	820			9	
18	6300	Insurance	780			10	
19	1382	Oil & gas exploration	750				Australia
20	3353	Aluminum sheet & foil	750		2		
29	1311	Crude petroleum & natural gas	630		3		
30	. . .	. . .	600		4		
33	4011	Operating railroads	571		5		
34	4011	Operating railroads	571		6		
35	4011	Operating railroads	571		7		
38	6000	Banking	547		8		
41	3634	Electric housewares	523		9		
42	. . .	. . .	500		10		
47	3711	Motor vehicles	500	2			
51	2044	Rice milling	500	3			
56	3711	Motor vehicles	450	4			
60	6100	Credit agencies	425	5			
67	1061	Ferroalloy ores	400	6			
91	3711	Motor vehicles	338	7			
92	. . .	. . .	330	8			
93	6000	Banking	325	9			
111	3312	Blast furnaces	292	10			

[a]The investment was not identified.

investments ranked between forty-seventh and one hundred eleventh overall. The second through the tenth largest Canadian investments ranked between twentieth and forty-second overall.

As we pursue the relevance of previous theoretical and empirical work to U.S. experience, it is worth remembering that in-bound investment is not concentrated in manufacturing. It is also worth noting that, for the period under consideration, the share of foreign direct investment in the United States originating in the EC was 44.9 percent while the shares originating in Canada and Japan were 21.9 percent and 12.2 percent respectively.

2.2 Contract Costs and Foreign Direct Investment

This section provides a partial analysis of the decision to undertake foreign direct investment that focuses on how contracting costs influence direct investment decisions. Specifically, I begin with the assumption that a firm has decided to enter a foreign market directly rather than rely on exports. Given that decision, the firm must then decide whether to enter that market through an affiliate or through a licensee. The process of explaining how a firm chooses between direct investment and licensing provides insight into firm and market characteristics that are conducive to foreign direct investment.

While my focus here is on the decision-making process of a single firm, that process can be placed in context by assuming that the market setting within which the investment decision is made is that of a firm producing a differentiated product in an industry characterized by Chamberlinian-type monopolistic competition. Assuming either Dixit-Stiglitz (1977) or Lancaster (1979) type preferences for the differentiated goods by consumers abroad will permit us to derive foreign market demand curves for the product of each firm, including our single producer.

In simplest terms, the choice between foreign direct investment and licensing of a foreign firm will depend on the expected present value of the discounted profit stream accruing to the firm from investing compared to licensing. Empirical evidence on U.S. direct investment abroad in manufacturing and on foreign direct investment in manufacturing in the United States in recent years reflects a strong preference for majority-owned and, almost as often, wholly owned foreign subsidiaries rather than licensing arrangements to take advantage of opportunities to earn profits in foreign markets.[4] Therefore, the model must be able to explain market, production, and/or contracting conditions that generate a general preference for direct investment over licensing and for substantial majority control when foreign direct investment takes place.

2.2.1 Foreign Direct Investment versus Licensing

Let P_F and Q_F represent the foreign price of the product and the output by a foreign subsidiary in a given market period. In addition, assume that production can be characterized as follows:

(1) $$Q_F = F\left(L_F, K_F, H_F, K_F^s\right),$$

where L_F and K_F are basic labor and capital inputs and H_F and K_F^s are specialized human and physical capital assets associated with the production of the firm's differentiated product. The process of deciding whether to invest or to license is essentially one of determining which method of operating in the foreign market will maximize the expected discounted value of appropriable rents that the firm can get from the use of H_F and K_F^s. The term H_F represents managerial and marketing know-how as well as technical expertise that can be conveyed to the foreign subsidiary directly from the home office or provided to a licensing firm through consulting arrangements. I presume that the specialized capital inputs, K_F^s, are constructed in the foreign country under the scrutiny of the parent firm or subject to contractual restraints in the case of licensing. Abstracting from issues of production and/or consumption smoothing over time, I assume that all the current output is sold.

Costs in each production period include factor input costs, C_F, plus marketing costs associated with the foreign market, M_F. Marketing costs are assumed to be a positive and increasing function of sales and of the degree of adaptation that the firm has to make to market its product abroad, d. Adaptation could include anything from a modest differentiation of an existing product sold in the home market, in which case d would be small, to the development of totally unrelated products for sale abroad, in which case d would be large. I assume that d is a positive and increasing function of the degree of nonsubstitutability between parent firm and subsidiary firm products.

The profitability of investment abroad at any point in time, π_t, is simply

$$(2) \qquad \pi_t = R_{Ft} - C_{Ft} - M_{Ft} \, ,$$

where R_{Ft} represents current revenue and the discounted present value of expected profits from foreign direct investment can be written as π_I. The assumption that the firm is concerned only with the discounted present value of its foreign operations presumes that the firm is risk neutral and that there are no bankruptcy risks.

The alternative possibility facing the firm would be to license the use of specialized human and physical assets to a foreign producer, who would provide royalty payments to the firm in return for the use of the specialized assets. The returns to the licensing firm will be equal to the value of the licensed services less the costs of defining and enforcing the terms of the contract. The value of the firm's specialized assets in any period is equal to the sum of the implicit value of specialized human and physical capital assets, $w_h H_{Ft} + r_s K_{Ft}^s$, where w_h and r_s are specialized asset prices per unit time.

The cost of contracting with the licensee can be thought of as simply the sum of the costs of monitoring and enforcing the terms of the agreement by which the licensee has access to the use of the specialized human and physical capital assets of the home-country firm. The licensing firm incurs positive contracting costs either because there exists the possibility of opportunistic behavior by the licensed firm in the use of specialized assets or because it is difficult to assess the implicit value of the use of the specialized assets that are licensed. I assume that licensing contract costs, C_L, are positively related to the use of both kinds of specialized assets and to the ratio of specialized physical capital to human capital required in production. This last argument will be denoted by $k_{F_t} = K_{F_t}^s / H_{F_t}$. Therefore, the value of the licensing arrangement to the licensing firm, π_{L_t}, in any period, should be equal to the net revenues accruing from licensing,

(3) $$\pi_{L_t} = w_h H_{F_t} + r_s K_{F_t}^s - C_{L_t}(H_{F_t}, K_{F_t}^s, k_{F_t}) ,$$

and the discounted present value of a licensing agreement to the licensing firm can be written as π_L. The firm in possession of the specialized assets will choose to invest abroad when

(4) $$\pi_I - \pi_L > 0.$$

Therefore, the desire to invest abroad rather than license a foreign producer will be positively related to licensing contracting costs and negatively related to the marketing costs of the investing firm.

To this point, I have not discussed the conditions under which anyone would be interested in buying a license abroad. Assuming that marketing costs associated with selling abroad, M_F, are not relevant to a host-country producer,[5] we can denote the discounted expected profitability of a license to a buyer as π_B. The profit from licensing a firm in any given period, π_{L_t}, represents a cost to the licensee. If contracting costs are high enough, it will never pay to offer to sell licenses abroad. If licensing costs, π_L, are high enough, it will never pay to purchase a license. In the case in which licensing and investing abroad are both feasible, direct investment abroad will be preferred when

(5a) $$\pi_I - \pi_L > 0,$$

and

(5b) $$\pi_B - \pi_L > 0.$$

In effect, the likelihood that a firm will choose to invest abroad, and therefore the value of foreign direct investment within an industry in any given period of time, will be negatively related to the cost of marketing the product abroad and positively related to the costs of defining and enforcing licensing agreements (i.e., contracting costs). More formally, the value of industry investment abroad, FDI, can be written as a function of marketing and contracting costs as follows:

(6) $$\text{FDI} = f(M_F, C_L)$$
$$<0, \ >0$$

where the inequality signs reflect the derivatives of $f(\cdot)$ with respect to M_F and C_L. Marketing costs increase as the degree of substitutability between the parent firm's product and the subsidiary firm's product decreases or as the diversity, d, between the two products increases. I assume that product diversity and therefore M_F will be smallest and FDI greatest when the foreign direct investment is in production in the same industry as the one in which the parent is already operating. In the empirical work in section 2.3 below, I use the percentage of investment within an industry for which the parent and subsidiary firms have the same four-digit SIC code as a direct measure of the substitutability between parent and affiliate products. Therefore, I expect the within-parent industry index to be positively related to foreign direct investment in the United States.

Contracting costs are directly related to the requirements of specialized human and physical capital inputs per unit of output. In the empirical work that follows, I use the research and development intensity of production (R&D) as an indicator of the need for specialized asset inputs per unit of output.

I also assume that specialized asset values are more easily appropriable by the owner over time through licenses if they are embodied in human capital than if they are embodied in physical capital, which can be disassembled, copied, and therefore stolen by a licensee. Therefore, foreign direct investment would be more likely the greater the share of physical capital in the specialized asset mix of the parent company. Holding scale phenomena constant, as measured by midpoint plant shipments in an industry, MPS, I use the capital-labor ratio to measure the ratio of firm-specific specialized physical capital to specialized human capital.

In the empirical section, I use industry investment, which is the sum of investment decisions across representative firms in our monopolistically competitive framework, as the unit of analysis. These points can be summarized as follows:

$$(7) \qquad \text{FDI} = g(\underset{<0,}{d}, \quad \underset{>0,}{\text{R\&D}}, \quad \underset{>0,}{K/L}; \text{MPS}),$$

where the inequalities below the variables reflect the expected effect of each right-hand-side variable on the value of industry foreign direct investment.

The analysis I have presented presumes that the parent firm behaves like a Chamberlinian monopolistic competitor in the foreign market. That assumption permitted me to focus on the relative attractiveness of licensing and investing to the parent firm without regard to the choices made by producers of other variants of the product and to think about industry behavior as the simple sum of decisions by individually and independently acting parent firms. To the extent that the market is dominated by a few firms in oligopolistic competition, the choices facing our single producer are much more complex.

The original Gruber, Mehta, and Vernon (1967) argument that foreign direct investment could be interpreted as a defensive strategy to maintain market shares abroad by oligopolistic producers of differentiated consumer goods could lead to very different relations among the key variables under discussion here. I include a consumer goods measure and a measure of industry concentration in the estimated investment equations in section 2.3 with the expectation that neither will be positively related to foreign direct investment decisions. Along those same lines, we would expect midpoint plant size within industries in which direct investment occurs to be insignif-icant, which is consistent with easy entry into the industry.

The functional relation tested in the next section is based on the discussion here but includes consideration of two other factors that tend to promote both foreign direct investment and licensing of foreign firms by a parent company. First, I include a measure of growth within individual industries as well as a measure of growth in the foreign country relative to growth in the parent-company country. Finally, I assume that, given the decision to invest abroad, a firm will be more likely to time that investment when the foreign currency is cheap than when it is expensive. That timing makes sense only if a decline in the value of the foreign currency is assumed to be temporary.

2.3   Empirical Evidence

While the regressions summarized in table 2.4 are directly related to the partial equilibrium model of section 2.2, the empirical work summarized in tables 2.5–2.8 below is more exploratory. Those results represent an effort to provide preliminary evidence of the relevance of factors that were not part of the model but have been suggested in previous work as potentially important determinants of foreign direct investment activity.

Referring to table 2.4, I proceeded with the analysis of firm-specific foreign direct investment activity in the context of a model of monopolistic compe-tition. A priori, there is no reason to presume that markets are not highly concentrated and difficult to enter and that oligopolistic interactions are not at the heart of an explanation of foreign direct investment decisions in manufacturing. The evidence in table 2.4 indicates that in fact industries in which foreign direct investment is likely to occur and in which large transactions will be realized tend to be industries in which plant size is likely to be relatively small (except for Japan) and market concentration is insignificant or a negative factor. In addition, there is no particular bias in foreign direct investment activity in the United States toward consumer goods, which are often thought of as possible targets for oligopolistic competition.

As expected, the value of foreign direct investment in the United States is positively related to whether the subsidiary is producing goods that belong to the same four-digit SIC category as those of the parent firm. That relation reflects a minimum of diversification between the parent and the subsidiary firms.

I argued that foreign direct investment would be positively related to the research and development intensity of production and/or the capital-labor ratio holding plant size constant (reflecting the ratio of firm-specific physical capital to human capital). The research and development factor is significant as a determinant of the value and likelihood of foreign direct investment from each area into the United States (except for Japan and Canada in terms of value). Foreign direct investment in the United States is positively related to the capital-labor ratio, holding plant size constant, except in the case of Japan (and Canada in terms of likelihood).

Industry-specific growth and relative growth in GNP in the United States were positively related to foreign direct investment from each of the major areas considered. Industry growth was significant with respect to the value of foreign direct investment by Japan and all investors as a group. Industry growth was significant with respect to the likelihood of foreign direct investment in the United States for the EC and for investors in general. Relative GNP growth in the United States was significant in explaining the value of Japanese and general investment.

The exchange rate effect indicates that a relatively cheap U.S. dollar served as a significant stimulus to foreign direct investment into the United States from each of the major investing areas except Japan. Such opportunism presumes that a cheap U.S. dollar is a temporary phenomenon, which was not the case relative to the yen.

The regressions also include industry size (the log value of industry shipments in the United States in 1982). That variable is intended to reflect the possible significance of measurement errors associated with the use of industry rather than firm data to explain the probability and magnitude of foreign direct investments. As indicated in table 2.4, measurement problems may be relevant.

The results obtained in table 2.4 suggest that manufacturing sectors in which foreign direct investment has been significant in the United States during the early 1980s can be characterized as relatively unconcentrated research- and specific-factor-intensive industries. There is no particular bias toward consumer or intermediate goods production and generally no evidence of scale economies in production, except in the case of Japanese investments. To the extent that individual market expansion and macroeconomic factors have influenced foreign decisions to undertake direct investments in the United States, they have worked in predictable fashion. Relative real economic growth in the United States during the 1980s and industry-specific growth encouraged foreign direct investment from abroad, and foreigners took advantage of periods when the U.S. dollar was relatively cheap to undertake U.S. investment projects.

2.3.1   Alternative Explanations of Foreign Direct Investment

Early efforts to explain the phenomenon of U.S. foreign direct investment around the world after World War II took two forms.[6] On the one hand, it was

Table 2.4   Foreign Direct Investment in the United States: Production Characteristics

Dependent Variable	Constant	Consumer Goods[a]	Midpoint Plant Size[b]	R&D Intensity[c]	Capital-Labor Ratio[d]	Market Concentration[e]	Within Parent Industry[f]	Industry Size[g]	Industry Growth[h]	U.S. Growth Trend[i]	Exchange Rate[j]	R^2	No. of Observations
Industry-level FDI:													
All countries	-5.00	-.03	.0003	1.93	.0001	-.01	1.29	.31	.001	.03	3.47	.118	1,806
	(6.15)	(.30)	(.61)	(2.42)	(5.07)	(2.49)	(12.54)	(7.89)	(2.59)	(2.50)	(2.02)		
Japan	-2.16	.03	.003	1.86	-2.8×10^{-5}	-.001	2.03	.20	7.0×10^{-4}	.24	-3.41	.353	1,806
	(1.66)	(.25)	(3.68)	(1.63)	(.84)	(.35)	(13.61)	(3.22)	(1.68)	(2.96)	(1.23)		
EC	-4.39	-.09	2.5×10^{-5}	3.07	1.1×10^{-4}	-.01	1.27	.33	.001	.01	.01	.165	1,806
	(10.26)	(.78)	(.04)	(3.51)	(4.68)	(2.21)	(10.20)	(7.38)	(4.00)	(1.80)	(2.28)		
Canada	-6.69	-.22	-.002	-.45	.0001	-.003	1.47	.30	.0002	.11	.03	.006	1,806
	(4.54)	(1.14)	(1.77)	(.33)	(3.56)	(.84)	(5.42)	(4.47)	(.42)	(.57)	(2.03)		

Probability of industry-level FDI:

All countries	−7.50	.09	−.002	3.61	.0001	−.006	56.26	.41	.001	.007	7.87	.409	1,806
	(7.70)	(.75)	(1.91)	(3.63)	(3.92)	(2.50)	(.003)	(8.63)	(2.52)	(.47)	(3.87)		
Japan	−3.64	.15	−.0003	4.98	$−1.4 \times 10^{-5}$	−.002	66.49	.22	.0004	.11	−.36	.481	1,806
	(2.57)	(1.02)	(.32)	(3.79)	(.38)	(.62)	(.01)	(3.21)	(.83)	(1.29)	(.12)		
EC	−5.55	−.17	−.002	4.49	1.5×10^{-5}	−.004	40.36	.43	.001	.01	.02	.399	1,806
	(11.02)	(1.32)	(2.03)	(4.37)	(.48)	(1.54)	(.002)	(8.18)	(2.73)	(1.60)	(4.64)		
Canada	−7.23	−.21	−.002	−1.79	9.3×10^{-5}	−.003	12.51	.33	6.0×10^{-4}	.25	.03	.220	1,806
	(4.80)	(1.12)	(1.60)	(1.24)	(2.92)	(.82)	(.06)	(4.69)	(1.30)	(1.29)	(2.21)		

Note: The first four regressions in the table are estimated using tobit since the dependent variables are bounded below by 0.00 and there are a substantial number of limit observations. Each of the last four regressions is estimated using probit since the dependent variable is a 1.0 or 0.0 dummy value, depending on whether there was any investment in a given industry in a given year in the United States. Absolute *t*-ratios appear in parentheses below the coefficients. Dependent variable observations are at the four-digit industry level for each of the years 1979–85.

[a]This is a 1972 measure of the proportion of industry sales for final consumption purposes.

[b]Midpoint plant size is measured by the midpoint plant shipment value for each industry using 1972 data.

[c]Research and development is measured by the ratio of total research and development expenditures to total costs across industries in 1972.

[d]The capital-labor ratio is the average value in 1972 for each industry.

[e]This is the industry four-firm concentration ratio in 1982.

[f]This is a constructed variable that represents the percentage of individual investments within an industry in a given year that are in the same four-digit SIC category as the parent firm's four-digit SIC.

[g]Industry size is measured by the log of the value of industry shipments in 1982.

[h]Industry growth is measured by the percentage change in the value of shipments within each given four-digit SIC industry between 1972 and 1982.

[i]U.S. growth trend in the all industry regressions is measured by real GNP changes in the current year. U.S. growth trends are measured by real GNP growth in the United States relative to real GNP growth in Japan, the EC, and Canada for the corresponding regressions. The measures are for the current year.

[j]The exchange rate trend in the all industry regressions is measured by the average of the U.S. dollar/yen exchange rate during the current year. The EC and Canadian regressions use the deutsche mark and the Canadian dollar in place of the yen as appropriate in the exchange rate.

presumed that the formation of the EC and the separate European free trade area in the early 1950s created trade barriers to U.S. exports to Europe that could be circumvented by the creation of U.S. production subsidiaries in Europe. On the other hand, it was argued that foreign direct investment might be one method by which producers in oligopolistic industries could maintain their market positions abroad as their exports became less competitive. This defensive investment hypothesis is most congenially identified with industries that are dominated by a few relatively large producers of differentiated consumer products.

The regressions reported in table 2.5 are intended to provide crude evidence on the applicability of the defensive investment hypothesis as an explanation of recent foreign direct investment in the United States. As indicated, neither the likelihood nor the value of foreign direct investments in the United States by industry was found to be positively related to market concentration (except the value of foreign direct investment for Japan) or the production of consumer goods.[7] That evidence does not exclude the possibility that a more complicated version of the defensive investment hypothesis can be sustained but it does shift the burden of proof to those who would argue that defensive investment strategies might explain foreign direct investment in U.S. manufacturing industries.

The argument that foreign direct investment can be viewed as a tariff-jumping technique has current appeal given the rise in protectionist sentiments in the United States since the early 1970s. Furthermore, a literature has developed that suggests the use of foreign direct investment to establish a market presence within a country to prevent future trade restrictions from being implemented (see Wong 1987, and the references cited therein).

Tables 2.6 and 2.7 report efforts to estimate the relation between tariff and nontariff trade barriers in the United States and decisions to undertake foreign direct investments in the United States. Recent studies suggest that the most highly protected industries in the United States enjoy both tariff and nontariff trade barrier protection (e.g., Marvel and Ray 1983; Ray and Marvel 1984; and the references cited in both). The interactive terms in tables 2.6 and 2.7 reflect industries with high overall protection. The issue is whether foreign direct investment has been induced by protectionist measures. The results presented in table 2.6 rely on the use of post–Tokyo Round nominal tariff rates for 1986, while the estimates in table 2.7 are generated using post–Kennedy Round effective protective rates. The results in table 2.6, which are sustained in table 2.7, suggest that investments in the United States from abroad have not been stimulated by U.S. protectionism. It is hoped that these preliminary results will inspire those who believe in the importance of strategic foreign direct investment to influence trade policy to attempt more systematic efforts in this direction.

Recent theoretical and empirical work has suggested that foreign direct investment may either cause or be caused by intraindustry trade (see, e.g.,

Table 2.5   **Foreign Direct Investment in the United States: Defensive Investment**

	Independent Variables								
Dependent Variable	Constant	Consumer Goods	Market Concentration	Within Parent Industry	Industry Size	U.S. Growth Trend	Exchange Rate	R^2	No. of Observations
Industry-level FDI:									
All countries	-5.47	-.15	-.001	1.25	.40	.03	3.42	0.098	1,806
	(7.01)	(1.64)	(.52)	(12.35)	(14.88)	(2.47)	(2.00)		
Japan	-3.69	.05	.006	2.08	.38	.22	-3.23	0.290	1,806
	(2.99)	(.36)	(2.60)	(14.30)	(9.26)	(2.83)	(1.18)		
EC	-4.82	-.24	-.001	1.21	.43	.01	.01	0.092	1,806
	(14.48)	(2.18)	(.41)	(9.98)	(14.32)	(1.74)	(2.21)		
Canada	-6.29	-.30	-.004	1.34	.28	.11	.03	0.003	1,806
	(4.59)	(1.65)	(1.62)	(5.05)	(6.53)	(.61)	(2.01)		
Probability of industry-level FDI:									
All countries	-7.39	-.27	-.003	56.80	.45	.008	7.60	0.389	1,806
	(7.97)	(2.46)	(1.65)	(.003)	(12.95)	(.54)	(3.80)		
Japan	-3.94	-.07	.001	63.82	.30	.11	-.40	0.472	1,806
	(2.97)	(.48)	(.27)	(.01)	(6.49)	(1.27)	(.14)		
EC	-5.34	-.27	-.003	40.37	.45	.01	.02	0.378	1,806
	(13.28)	(2.23)	(1.55)	(.003)	(12.18)	(1.57)	(4.55)		
Canada	-6.78	-.25	-.005	12.91	.30	.24	.03	0.207	1,806
	(4.82)	(1.42)	(1.67)	(.04)	(6.68)	(1.30)	(2.19)		

Note: See notes to table 2.4.

Table 2.6   Foreign Direct Investment in the United States: Nominal Tariff and Nontariff Barrier (NTB) Jumping

Dependent Variable	Constant	Nominal Tariff[a]	NTBs[b]	Nominal Tariff-NTB Interaction[c]	Within Parent Industry	Industry Size	U.S. Growth Trend	Exchange Rate	R^2	No. of Observations
Industry-level FDI:										
All countries	−5.54	−.01	−.12	.01	1.24	.41	.03	3.45	.100	1,806
	(7.12)	(.90)	(1.16)	(.94)	(12.36)	(14.92)	(2.43)	(2.02)		
Japan	−3.31	−.01	−.64	.03	2.07	.40	.23	−5.55	.268	1,806
	(2.65)	(.74)	(3.49)	(1.18)	(14.18)	(9.24)	(2.87)	(1.28)		
EC	−5.07	−.01	−.22	.01	1.21	.46	.01	.01	.092	1,806
	(15.49)	(.54)	(1.96)	(1.08)	(9.98)	(14.81)	(1.73)	(2.27)		
Canada	−6.32	−.06	−.08	−.06	1.43	.27	.13	.03	.002	1,806
	(4.61)	(2.27)	(.49)	(1.98)	(5.38)	(6.37)	(.68)	(2.02)		
Probability of industry-level FDI:										
All countries	−7.75	−.01	−.32	.02	56.25	.49	.01	7.66	.385	1,806
	(8.38)	(.78)	(2.74)	(.97)	(.003)	(13.75)	(.45)	(3.83)		
Japan	−3.87	−.01	−.55	.03	62.01	.32	.12	−.61	.479	1,806
	(2.89)	(.77)	(2.86)	(1.17)	(.01)	(6.74)	(1.34)	(.20)		
EC	−5.84	.01	−.33	.02	41.13	.49	.01	.02	.376	1,806
	(14.88)	(.64)	(2.60)	(1.01)	(.002)	(13.14)	(1.54)	(4.67)		
Canada	−6.84	−.06	−.05	.05	12.88	.29	.25	.03	.203	1,806
	(4.86)	(2.22)	(.30)	(1.59)	(.06)	(6.55)	(1.34)	(2.22)		

Note: See notes to table 2.4.

[a]This measure equals post–Tokyo Round, 1986, nominal tariff rates.

[b]NTBs are measured by a dummy variable that takes on a value of 1.0 if nontariff trade restrictions are present in an industry in the post–Kennedy Round period and 0.0 otherwise.

[c]This is an interactive term reflecting the presence of both nominal tariff and NTB protection across industries in the post–Kennedy Round period. While the interactive term uses post–Kennedy Round NTB protection out of necessity, the term would accurately reflect high tariff and NTB-protected industries in the post–Tokyo Round period too except for those cases of high tariff industries that would have received NTB protection for the first time after 1975. There are few if any likely cases among the 327 four-digit SIC industries.

Table 2.7   Foreign Direct Investment in the United States: Effective Tariff and Nontariff Barrier (NTB) Jumping

Dependent Variable	Constant	Effective Tariff[a]	NTBs	Effective Tariff-NTB Interaction[b]	Within Parent Industry	Industry Size	U.S. Growth Trend	Exchange Rate	R^2	No. of Observations
Industry level FDI:										
All countries	-5.63	.003	.003	-.01	1.25	.41	.03	3.46	.100	1,806
	(7.18)	(.52)	(.03)	(.74)	(12.40)	(14.58)	(2.42)	(2.03)		
Japan	-3.50	.01	-.40	-.01	2.07	.41	.23	-3.50	.264	1,806
	(2.78)	(.63)	(2.10)	(.65)	(14.21)	(9.17)	(2.88)	(1.26)		
EC	-5.30	.01	-.15	-.002	1.21	.47	.01	.01	.103	1,806
	(15.38)	(2.21)	(1.28)	(.26)	(10.01)	(14.76)	(1.74)	(2.29)		
Canada	-6.30	-.01	.19	-.0003	1.43	.26	.12	.03	.002	1,806
	(4.59)	(1.05)	(1.14)	(.02)	(5.35)	(6.07)	(.63)	(1.98)		
Probability of industry-level FDI:										
All countries	-7.89	.01	-.13	-.01	56.15	.49	.01	7.67	.387	1,806
	(8.46)	(1.06)	(1.03)	(1.32)	(.003)	(13.38)	(.45)	(3.84)		
Japan	-4.14	.01	-.29	-.01	62.49	.34	.12	-.54	.479	1,806
	(3.07)	(1.13)	(1.46)	(.86)	(.01)	(6.79)	(1.32)	(.18)		
EC	-6.09	.01	-.15	-.01	40.88	.51	.01	.02	.379	1,806
	(14.66)	(2.50)	(1.07)	(1.24)	(.002)	(12.92)	(1.56)	(4.68)		
Canada	-6.83	-.01	.19	-.003	12.75	.28	.25	.03	.201	1,806
	(4.85)	(1.00)	(1.09)	(.20)	(.06)	(6.31)	(1.31)	(2.17)		

Notes: See notes to tables 2.4 and 2.6.

[a]Effective protection is measured by U.S. post–Kennedy Round effective protection rates at the four-digit level.

[b]This is an interactive term that reflects the presence of both effective protection and NTBs in an industry.

Ethier 1986; Helpman 1984; and Marvel and Ray 1987). Table 2.8 contains estimated relations that treat intraindustry trade in 1972 as a determinant of foreign direct investment in the United States between 1979 and 1985. In brief, there is no evidence that the existence of intraindustry trade within a manufacturing sector serves as an inducement for future foreign direct investment in that industry.

2.4 Conclusions

The evidence presented in this study makes it clear that foreign direct investments in the United States in recent years have been much less concentrated in the manufacturing sector than was true of U.S. foreign direct investments in the rest of the world during the first three decades after World War II. Investments in manufacturing in the United States have been predominantly from Canada, Europe, and Japan. Those industries that have attracted the most interest and investment inflows from foreign firms were both consumer and producer goods manufacturers. Neither scale economies nor market concentration is significant in general in investment target industries. But affiliate production is intensive in the use of firm-specific human and physical capital, reflecting the difficulties of contracting for the use of such factors through arm's-length licensing contracts. Parent and subsidiary firms tend to produce similar products, reflecting the tendency to create subsidiaries abroad to produce goods with which the parent firms are already most familiar.

Relative gains in real economic growth in the United States as well as industry-specific growth appear to have had some positive effect on decisions to invest in the United States by foreign firms, and investments appear to have been timed to take advantage of a relatively cheap U.S. dollar when possible. There is no clear evidence in this study to support either the defensive investment hypothesis or the tariff-jumping argument.

This last observation is consistent with the view that foreign investors were no more interested than domestic investors were in putting money into declining industries in the United States, which traditionally have been the major beneficiaries of protectionist measures. The much-needed structural shifts in manufacturing in the United States that began in the late 1970s were reenforced by a massive inflow of capital from abroad. The structural unemployment problems that developed as a by-product of market shifts during the early 1980s were not offset by an inflow of direct investment funds from abroad into declining industries. Rather, foreign direct investments in the United States appear to have contributed to the expansion of existing industries and the creation of newer ones that have provided new jobs.

Table 2.8   Foreign Direct Investment in the United States: Intraindustry Trade Effects

Dependent Variable	Constant	Intraindustry Trade[a]	Within Parent Industry	Industry Size	U.S. Growth Trend	Exchange Rate	R^2	No. of Observations
Industry-level FDI:								
All countries	−5.56	-4.0×10^{-4}	1.25	.40	.03	3.44	.102	1,806
	(7.18)	(.38)	(12.40)	(15.30)	(2.43)	(2.02)		
Japan	−3.31	−.001	2.09	.36	.22	−3.13	.238	1,806
	(2.69)	(.38)	(14.35)	(8.96)	(2.84)	(1.14)		
EC	−4.86	−.001	1.20	.44	.01	.01	.099	1,806
	(15.23)	(1.18)	(9.97)	(14.74)	(1.73)	(2.23)		
Canada	−6.67	.002	1.40	.30	.11	.03	.001	1,806
	(4.88)	(.95)	(5.29)	(6.95)	(.61)	(1.99)		
Probability of Industry-level FDI:								
All countries	−7.80	.002	56.89	.47	.01	7.60	.383	1,806
	(8.48)	(1.47)	(.003)	(13.70)	(.49)	(3.81)		
Japan	−3.86	−.0003	64.04	.29	.11	−.37	.473	1,806
	(2.92)	(.16)	(.01)	(6.52)	(1.27)	(1.27)		
EC	−5.71	.001	40.38	.47	.01	.02	.372	1,806
	(14.80)	(.76)	(.003)	(12.85)	(1.53)	(4.61)		
Canada	−7.25	.003	12.55	.31	.24	.03	.200	1,806
	(5.17)	(1.49)	(.06)	(7.17)	(1.28)	(2.18)		

Note: See notes to table 2.4.

[a]Intraindustry trade is measured using 1972 four-digit SIC data and consists of an index scaled from 0.0 to 100 percent with higher values corresponding to greater trade overlap. The precise measure used equals:

$$2 \min \frac{(\text{IMPORTS, EXPORTS})}{\text{IMPORTS} + \text{EXPORTS}} \times 100.$$

Appendix
Variable Sources and Definitions

Dependent Variable Name	Description
Industry-level foreign direct investment	Foreign direct investment into the United States by industry in millions of U.S. dollars. (Unless otherwise specified, the observations include those from the 469 Manufacturing four-digit SIC codes.) *Source:* "Foreign Direct Investment in the United States: Completed Transactions, 1974–1983 Volume II: Industry Sector" (Washington, D.C.: U.S. Department of Commerce, International Trade Administration [ITA], June 1985). (Two additional years from the ITA on tape were also used.)
Probability of industry foreign direct investment	A dummy variable that takes on the value one if the value of the transactions by industry is greater than zero and zero otherwise. *Source:* "Foreign Direct Investment in the United States."

Independent Variable Name	Description
U.S. growth trend:	
All country regressions	Annual real percentage change in the U.S. GNP from 1979 to 1985. *Source: 1987 Economic Report of the President* (Washington, D.C.: U.S. Government Printing Office, 1987), table B-5, col. 2, p. 251.
Japan regressions	Ratio of real U.S. GNP growth to Japanese real GNP growth from 1979 to 1985. *Source: European Economy* (Committee of European Communities), no. 29, table 8, p. 144.

EC regressions	Ratio of real U.S. GNP growth to an average of EC member countries' real GNP growth from 1979 to 1985. *Source: 1987 Economic Report of the President,* table B-106, p. 366; and *1981 Economic Report of the President* (Washington, D.C.: U.S. Government Printing Office, 1981), table B-107, p. 353.
Canada regressions	Ratio of real U.S. GNP growth to the Canadian real GNP growth from 1979 to 1985. *Source:* Same as EC regressions.
All country regressions	Annual rate of exchange between the U.S. dollar and the Japanese yen ($/yen) from 1979 to 1985. *Source: 1987 Economic Report of the President,* table B-105, p. 365.
Japan regressions	Annual rate of exchange between the U.S. dollar and the Japanese yen ($/yen) from 1979 to 1985. *Source: 1987 Economic Report of the President,* table B-105, p. 365.
EC regressions	Annual rate of exchange between the U.S. dollar and the West German mark ($/DM) from 1979 to 1985. *Source: 1987 Economic Report of the President,* table B-105, p. 365.
Canada regressions	Annual rate of exchange between the U.S. dollar and the Canadian dollar ($US/$CAN) from 1979 to 1985. *Source: 1987 Economic Report of the President,* table B-105, p. 365.
Consumer goods	Output attributed to personal consumption expenditures divided by total output. *Source: USITC's Industrial Characteristics and Trade Performance Data Bank* (Washington, D.C.: U.S. International Trade Commission [USITC], Office of Economic Research, June, 1975).
Market concentration	The percentage of sales accounted for by the four largest firms in an industry. *Source: 1982 Census of Manufactures.*

Within parent industry	This is a dummy variable that takes on a value from 0 to 100 percent, reflecting the extent to which parent and affiliate firms have the same four-digit SIC code for transactions in an industry. *Source:* "Foreign Direct Investment in the United States."
Industry size	Natural log of the value of shipments by industry in 1982. *Source: 1982 Census of Manufactures.*
Nominal tariff	Post–Tokyo Round, 1986, nominal U.S. tariff rates. *Source:* Computer tape (Washington, D.C.: USITC, Office of Economic Research, May 1988).
Nontariff barrier dummy	A dummy variable that takes on the value of one if there exists a nontariff barrier for that industry and zero otherwise. *Source: USITC's Industrial Characteristics and Trade Performance Data Bank.*
Nominal tariff–nontariff barrier interaction	Nontariff barrier dummy × Post–Tokyo Round tariffs in the United States *Source:* See individual variables listed.
Effective protection	The effective protection rates were estimated by the USITC assuming fixed intermediate input-output coefficients. *Source:* USITC, *Protection in Major Trading Countries,* Publication no. 737 (Washington, D.C.: USITC, August 1975).
Effective protection–nontariff barrier interaction	Nontariff barrier dummy × U.S. effective tariff protection. *Source:* See individual variables listed.
Agriculture industry dummy	This is a dummy variable that takes on a value of one for four-digit SIC industries 2000–2199 and zero otherwise.
Textiles industry dummy	This is a dummy variable that takes on a value of one for four-digit SIC industries 2200–2399 and zero otherwise.
Intraindustry trade measure for 1972	A measure equal to: $(\{2 \cdot [\text{Min}(\text{IMPORT72, EXPORT72})]\} / (\text{IMPORT72} + \text{EXPORT72})) \cdot 100$. *Source:* Data tape (Washington, D.C.:

	USITC, Office of Economic Research, 1972).
Midpoint plant size	This variable is constructed from data reported in the *1972 Census of Manufactures*. (A detailed description is available from the author on request.)
Research and development intensity	Percentage of scientists and engineers in the work force of an industry. *Source: 1972 Census of Manufactures*.
Capital-labor ratio	Gross book value 1972 divided by labor employment 1972. *Source:* U.S. Bureau of the Census, *Annual Survey of Manufactures, 1974*, M74(A5)-1 (Washington, D.C.: U.S. Government Printing Office, 1977).

Notes

1. Recent empirical work on outbound U.S. foreign direct investment includes Baldwin (1979), Grubaugh (1987), Kravis and Lipsey (1982), Lipsey and Weiss (1981), and Williamson (1986). Recent theoretical pieces more appropriately applied to outbound investments include Batra (1986), Chen (1985), Krugman (1979), and Wong (1987).

2. Earlier work focusing on the use of foreign direct investment to extract rents that would be difficult to capture through licenses includes Aliber (1970), Caves (1971), McGee (1966), and Vernon (1966). More recent work on contracting costs and the appropriability of rents includes Brecher (1982), Ethier (1986), Grossman and Hart (1986), Helpman (1984), Horstmann and Markusen (1987), Rugman (1980), and Williamson (1981).

3. The possibility that trade restrictions may induce foreign direct investments is explored more fully in recent papers by Brander and Spencer (1987), Chen (1985), Williamson (1986), and Wong (1987).

4. The mean values of ownership control associated with foreign direct investments in manufacturing in the United States for the regions considered here throughout the sample period were as follows: all countries, 86.34 percent; Japan, 86.57 percent; the EC, 87.85 percent; and Canada, 80.49 percent.

5. In effect, I assume that M_F reflects additional costs to the parent firm of selling its product in a distant market that is less well known to the parent firm than its domestic market. Foreign license candidates are presumed to have idiosyncratic information about their own markets.

6. Early work that focused on the tariff-jumping aspects of foreign direct investment included Horst (1971, 1972a, 1972b). Papers that raised the possibility of defensive investment included Aliber (1970), Caves (1971), Gruber, Mehta, and Vernon (1967), Hymer (1976), Ray (1977), and Vernon (1966).

7. Monopoly and oligopoly models are embodied in papers dealing with foreign direct investment by Brander and Spencer (1987), Horstmann and Markusen (1987), and Levinsohn (1987), among others.

References

Aliber, Robert Z. 1970. A theory of direct foreign investment. In *The international corporation*, ed. Charles Kindleberger, 17–34. Cambridge, Mass.: MIT Press.

Baldwin, Robert E. 1979. Determinants of trade and foreign investment: Further evidence. *Review of Economics and Statistics* 61(1):40–48.

Batra, Raveendra N. 1986. A general equilibrium model of multinational corporations in developing economics. *Oxford Economic Papers* 35(2):342–53.

Brander, James, and Barbara Spencer. 1987. Foreign direct investment with unemployment and endogenous taxes and tariffs. *Journal of International Economics* 22(3/4):257–79.

Brecher, Richard A. 1982. Optimal policy in the presence of licensed technology from abroad. *Journal of Political Economy* 90(5):1070–78.

Caves, R. E. 1971. International corporations: The industrial economics of foreign investment. *Economica* 38(149):1–27.

Chen, Tain-Jy. 1985. Alternative policies for foreign investment in the presence of tariff distortions. *Australian Economic Papers* 24(45):394–403.

Dixit, Avinash, K., and Joseph E. Stiglitz. 1977. Monopolistic competition and optimum product diversity. *American Economic Review* 67(4):297–308.

Ethier, Wilfred J. 1986. The multinational firm. *Quarterly Journal of Economics* 101(4):805–33.

Feenstra, Robert, and Kenneth Judd. 1982. Tariffs, technology transfer and welfare. *Journal of Political Economy* 90(6):1142–65.

Grossman, Sanford J., and Oliver D. Hart. 1986. The costs and benefits of ownership: A theory of vertical and lateral integration. *Journal of Political Economy* 94(4):691–719.

Grubaugh, Stephen G. 1987. Determinants of direct investment. *Review of Economics and Statistics* 69(1):149–52.

Gruber, W., D. Mehta, and R. Vernon. 1967. The R&D factor in international trade and the international investment of United States industries. *Journal of Political Economy* 75(1):20–37.

Helpman, Elhanan. 1984. A simple theory of international trade with multinational corporations. *Journal of Political Economy* 92(3):451–71.

Horst, T. 1971. The theory of the multinational firm: Optimal behavior under different tariff and tax rates. *Journal of Political Economy* 79(5):1059–72.

————. 1972a. Firm and industry determinants of the decision to invest abroad: An empirical study. *Review of Economics and Statistics* 54(3):258–66.

————. 1972b. The industrial composition of U.S. exports and subsidiary sales to the Canadian market. *American Economic Review* 62(1):37–45.

Horstmann, Ignatius, and James Markusen. 1987. Licensing versus direct investment: A model of internalization by the multinational enterprise. *Canadian Journal of Economics* 20(3):464–81.

Hymer, Stephen. 1976. *The international operations of national firms: A study of direct foreign investment.* Cambridge, Mass.: MIT Press.

Kravis, Irving B., and Robert E. Lipsey. 1982. The location of overseas production and production for export by U.S. multinational firms. *Journal of International Economics* 12(3/4):201–23.

Krugman, Paul. 1979. A model of innovation technology transfer and the world distribution of income. *Journal of Political Economy* 87(2):253–66.

Lancaster, Kelvin. 1979. *Variety, equity, and efficiency.* New York: Columbia University Press.

Levinsohn, James. 1987. Strategic trade policy and direct foreign investment: Tariffs versus quotas. Discussion Paper no. 210. University of Michigan.

Lipsey, Robert E., and Merle Yahr Weiss. 1981. Foreign production and exports in manufacturing industries. *Review of Economics and Statistics* 63(6):488–94.

Marvel, Howard P., and Edward John Ray. 1983. The Kennedy Round: Evidence on the regulation of international trade in the United States. *American Economic Review* 73(3):190–97.

———. 1987. Intraindustry trade: Sources and effects on protection. *Journal of Political Economy* 95(6):1278–91.

McGee, John S. 1966. Patent exploitation: Some economic and legal problems. *Journal of Law and Economics* 9(2):135–62.

Ray, Edward John. 1977. Foreign direct investment in manufacturing. *Journal of Political Economy* 85(2):283–97.

Ray, Edward John, and Howard P. Marvel. 1984. The pattern of protection in the industrialized world. *Review of Economics and Statistics* 66(3):452–58.

Rugman, Alan M. 1980. *Multinationals in Canada: Theory, performance and economic impact.* Boston: Martinus Nijhoff.

Vernon, Raymond. 1966. International investment and international trade in the product cycle. *Quarterly Journal of Economics* 80(2):190–207.

Williamson, Oliver E. 1981. The modern corporation: Origins, evolution, attributes. *Journal of Economic Literature* 19(4):1537–68.

Williamson, Peter J. 1986. Multinational enterprise behavior and domestic industry adjustment under import threat. *Review of Economics and Statistics* 68(3):359–68.

Wong, Kar-yiu. 1987. The protectionist threat and *quid pro quo* foreign investment: Theory and policy implications. University of Washington. Mimeo.

Comment   Keith E. Maskus

This paper on foreign investment in the United States is ambitious in what it tries to do and in what it succeeds in doing. Ray has assembled a huge data base on individual foreign firms' investment decisions in the United States over the period 1979–85 and related those decisions, aggregated to the industry level, to a large set of U.S. industry characteristics, many of which will be familiar to those who have read his papers on protection and intraindustry trade. Ray's intent is to characterize the various motives for foreign direct investment in the United States across a broad range of manufacturing and nonmanufacturing industries, though his focus is clearly on manufacturing. He has unearthed some interesting regularities in the data set, the most striking of which are that foreign direct investment (FDI) is concentrated in U.S. industries with a high research and development content and evidently is unrelated to heavy industry concentration. Further, more FDI is induced by a cheap dollar. These findings are useful and will help shape our understanding of motivations for FDI coming into the United States.

I wish to raise several questions about the analysis in the paper. The first issue is Ray's motivation in undertaking this research. What might be

Keith E. Maskus is associate professor of economics at the University of Colorado, Boulder.

different about FDI in the United States that would distinguish this paper from the enormous volume of literature on other FDI flows, mainly those flowing out of this country? To the extent that investment flows into the United States come from other developed countries (and clearly the overwhelmingly majority do), it is difficult to see what might be expected to characterize incentives for them distinctly from those driving investment in other directions. A related issue is whether the situation in the United States has really changed in the 1980s in such a way as to attract not only more FDI but also a distinctive pattern of FDI, which, after all, has been coming into the United States in various degrees for a long time.

These points do not suggest that an analysis of FDI entering the United States is unimportant. There is much valuable information to be learned from such an exercise. It seems, though, that the paper would be strengthened by some consideration of what might be unique about the current U.S. market for absorbing FDI. The paper hints at a proximate answer by pointing out that FDI in the United States is diversified across several sectors and is certainly not dominated by manufactures. This fact is especially true of Japanese FDI, which is predominantly in wholesale trade or distribution and banking and finance. Are we to conclude from this that the U.S. service sector is peculiarly open to FDI? If so, perhaps foreign investors are positioning themselves to exploit a clear U.S.-based comparative advantage in supplying U.S. and foreign markets? But I suppose one might as easily ask whether manufacturing is peculiarly closed to FDI in comparison with other countries. And, more generally, some reference could be made to specific characteristics of the U.S. economy in the aggregate—its large size and proximity to another major market, Canada, come to mind, along with putatively more flexible approaches to labor-market adjustments, environmental regulation, and the like—that might attract or repel FDI in the United States differently from FDI elsewhere. A final intriguing possibility might be that burgeoning FDI in the United States in the 1980s may reflect not only exchange rate changes and growth rates, as indicated in the paper, but also a readjustment to the postwar disequilibrium distribution of the global capital stock. The view that international firms are accumulating their desired capital distributions in the United States, if accurate, would have rather distinctive implications for the ongoing, somewhat paranoid debate about the future status of this country as a net debtor.

A second issue concerns aspects of the model that Ray puts forward to explain the investment/licensing decision. All economists have their favored arguments to insert into objective functions or optimization problems, and so it is perhaps unfair to complain about any particular omission here. However, I was surprised to see essentially no discussion of FDI as a risk-management technique, something that is presumably central to the investment decision. We know, for example, that currency risks can either expand or curtail FDI. Increases in such risks might well underlie some of the greater FDI flows in the 1980s. It would be difficult to measure industry-specific currency risks (let alone other international risks) for the empirical work, so this exclusion is understandable. However, it is feasible to develop some aggregate measures of risk to use in conjunction with the other variables of an aggregate nature, such as economic growth. Several measures of bilateral real and nominal exchange-rate volatility have been established in the literature.

A further modeling issue relates to the assumption of monopolistic competition, implying a high degree of competition and reasonably free entry. This is done essentially for convenience, forgoing the need to worry about strategic interactions among domestic and foreign competitors. But strategic rivalry may be precisely the issue in explaining much FDI. What prior evidence we have is that firms that become multinational tend to be large firms at home and abroad. It can be argued that FDI may require significant departures from competition to generate sufficient profits to overcome the disadvantages of operating a subsidiary in a foreign market. The issue then becomes an empirical one. Ray finds that the consumer-goods nature of an industry is unrelated to FDI. Perhaps more significant is his discovery that industry concentration within the United States apparently provides no independent motivation for FDI, or perhaps even a negative one, arguing against the strategic-rivalry hypothesis. These results are sufficiently strong as to give pause to enthusiasts of oligopoly-based theories of FDI. However, I doubt their conclusiveness. For example, concentration is a barrier to all entry, including FDI, so it is unsurprising to find no relation between them. Such a finding does not necessarily mean that there are no subtle strategic interactions surrounding the entry decision itself or even that industry concentration within the United States is the best way to approach that question empirically. Further work might consider this issue more completely.

I turn finally to some of the empirical issues in the paper. First, because all the industry-specific explanatory variables are measured with U.S. data, FDI is related to U.S. industry characteristics alone. This effort is important because we are interested in the particulars of local competition that may attract or repel foreign investment. But, by not considering also the characteristics of the home-country environment, we may be missing a substantial part of the description of determinants of FDI. Of course, this latter approach would require the assembly of industry characteristics in other countries as well, an enormous task that might be feasible only on a much more limited set of data. Furthermore, I note the significant finding in the paper that FDI is stronger within industries than across industries, so the omission of foreign data may not be serious to the extent that parent-country characteristics mirror those in the United States.

A second empirical question relates to Ray's efforts to investigate the links between FDI and trade barriers in order to examine the various hypotheses surrounding those links: tariff jumping and quid pro quo investment, for example. I doubt that these questions have been given a fair hearing here, simply because the timing of the data used is suspect. Though tariff rates are from 1986, the effective protection rates and nontariff barriers are taken from the International Trade Commission's data bank, which lists trade barriers from 1970 or the post–Kennedy Round era. The FDI flows, however, are for a much more recent period, meaning that more recent measures of effective protection and nontariff trade barriers (abstracting from the prior issue of how even to measure such barriers) would be more appropriate. It strains things somewhat to claim that the obvious rise in nontariff trade barriers in the 1980s is unrelated to FDI when the data on trade barriers are so old. The difficulty is perhaps especially relevant for assessing the extent of quid pro quo investment, in which FDI is supposed to come before policy decisions regarding trade interventions (and to deter such interventions), so that the timing is, in a crucial sense, just opposite that in the empirical work. And, evidently, issues of simultaneity would arise as well in considering more fully the link between trade barriers and investment flows.

Finally, I conclude with two observations about empirical results that I find intriguing. First, there appears to be some difference between the manufacturing industries in which Japanese FDI is concentrated and other countries' FDI. The Japanese are less interested in capital-intensive industries (suggesting, under Ray's conception, that Japanese FDI embodies lower amounts of specialized physical-capital assets, though, strictly from an empirical view, I wonder how well proxied that variable is by a simple capital-labor ratio) and are insensitive to exchange-rate changes in pursuing FDI (though in that regard there may well be lags that might usefully be identified in a time-series analysis). This unique Japanese performance seems potentially interesting in the face of widespread concern in the United States over incoming investment and might usefully be explored further.

Second, I note that Ray finds no relation between intraindustry trade and incoming FDI. Still open, however, is the question of intraindustry investment. Are there any unique determinants of such investment (which cannot be explored with this data set) that have not been captured in existing models of FDI, and how can they be pursued empirically?

Comment   James Levinsohn

The paper is a much-needed attempt to get some empirical handle on just what causes inward foreign direct investment (FDI). The author has used a rich data source—FDI by firms at the four-digit SIC level to address an important and current real-world policy concern. This sort of work is often time consuming,

James Levinsohn is assistant professor in the Economics Department at the University of Michigan, Ann Arbor.

and it is nice to see someone dig in and search for what answers may lie out there in the data. In preparing my comments, I have tried to keep in mind what I think is the primary goal of the paper—to shed some light on what is behind inward FDI. My comments, then, are primarily directed at what the *results* of the paper may or may not tell us.

The comments on the paper fall into three categories. I will first briefly discuss the theory presented in the paper. Second, I will raise some concerns about the data used for the estimation section of the paper. Third, I will mention a few issues related to the estimation procedure itself.

The paper begins with a model of FDI in manufacturing. I have two fairly broad comments on this section of the paper. The first may just be a matter of semantics. I think of an economic model as an analytic setup in which, in this case, firms maximize profits subject to various constraints imposed by the economic environment in which they operate. Standard operating procedure is to characterize the optimum and then perform some sort of comparative statics exercises to see how firms adapt to a small change in their economic environment. With luck, one can sign these changes—which are frequently the net effect of many interacting variables—and derive predictions about the signs of coefficients in an estimating equation. An example along these lines with respect to FDI in a very different and much simpler context is a paper eleven years ago by Ray in the *Journal of Political Economy* (Ray 1977).

The model in the paper is not like this. There is no explicit optimization, nor is the interaction of myriad economic influences on FDI explicitly laid out. Rather, the reader is presented with what amounts to reduced-form equations in which the expected signs on various arguments are stated as intuition. That intuition, I want to stress, usually seems right to me. One issue raised by formalizing intuition about *net* results rather than laying out the structure behind the intuition is that it is hard to know what the policy implications of the results actually are. On occasion, though, the author's intuition is not obvious to me. An example here is the assumption that specialized capital and labor are more easily appropriable by the owner over time through licenses than if they are embodied in physical capital (i.e., FDI). Maybe, and maybe not. It is not obvious to me and would seem to depend on agency issues.

My other comment about the model concerns its relevance to the empirical work that is intended to motivate. The discussion in this section of the paper is directed at whether a foreign firm decides to compete in the home market via FDI or via a licensing arrangement. It is assumed that for some reason the foreign firm cannot compete in the home market by just exporting. My hunch is that this is indeed how most international competition takes place. Still, the assumption may be right if there are prohibitive trade taxes. Yet, although such taxes show up in the estimating equation, they are assumed away in the model itself. Other potentially key variables that show up in estimated equations but that are absent from the discussion of the model are proxies for market structure. Another variable that is in the estimating equation but not in the model is the exchange rate. The intuition expressed here is that the foreign firm will be more likely to take the plunge and invest via FDI when there is a known to be temporary decline in the domestic exchange rate. The only role exchange rates play in the discussion is that they act like a large sign reading "bargain days this month." It may be that exchange rates should enter a model of FDI, but it is not clear that this is the only way. If firms know that an exchange rate is temporarily undervalued, it would seem that they could gain from this information by buying the cheap currency and later selling it for a higher price, and this story is independent of FDI. (Indeed, with well-functioning financial futures and options markets in foreign exchange, it is unclear what FDI can accomplish that arbitrage cannot.) The point of this is that *how* exchange rates enter the picture depends on the structure of the problem, and this is not presented in the paper.

The punchline here is that I think most readers, as the author does, believe that variables such as market structure and exchange rates matter, but, without some sort of economic model of how they matter, it is difficult to interpret the results.

I would like next to raise a few questions about how to interpret the results, given the data used.

I have one fairly minor and one less minor qualm about the relation between the data set used and the economic questions addressed. To raise the less major point first, the discussion in the modeling section of the paper clearly implies that the transactions that did not occur (which are represented by zeros in the probit regressions) were instead licensing arrangements. Is this the case? If not (as one might suspect), perhaps either the modeling section of the paper should be amended or more appropriate data should be utilized.

More important, the variables for research and development, nontariff trade barriers, effective rates of protection, plant size, and capital-to-labor ratios play a key role in the story that the author discusses. It is only natural, then, that they should be in an estimated equation investigating foreign direct investment from 1979 to 1985. Yet the variables for research and development intensity, the capital-to-labor ratio, and plant size are from 1972, according to table notes. The nontariff trade barrier variable is from 1975. Explaining a firm's investment decision by the economic environment it in part faced four to thirteen years ago, if the firm was even in business then, creates some problems when we try to interpret the results.

If these variables do not change over time or change proportionately across industries and over time, then this is not likely to be a problem. But implicit in using a time-series cross section is that the variables do vary over time. How important is this issue likely to be?

For the case of nontariff trade barriers, using the correct data would, I suspect, perhaps make a big difference. Use of nontariff trade barriers is widely thought to have increased dramatically over the last fifteen years. It also seems that, while aggregate capital-to-labor ratios may not have moved a lot, at the four-digit level they probably did. The same story applies to the research and development variable.

I am left wondering how to interpret the results of equations that examine how today's investment decision is affected by economic conditions of, on the average, a decade earlier.

The last set of issues that I want to raise has to do with how some econometric concerns may affect our interpretation of the paper.

Let us assume that the data set is a panel and that therefore there is variation over time in addition to variation over firms. It seems reasonable that some of the variables that are not in the estimating equation may be quite correlated with time. This would argue for inclusion of fixed effects in the model. This could be done by just including year dummies in the estimated equations when Tobit was used. It is a simple procedure and would use only five degrees of freedom. It may, though, change the results. It seems worth trying. This simple procedure is not going to work for the probit regressions, though, as the estimates would be inconsistent.

Another point concerns sensitivity analysis. There is none. Especially since the functional form and choice of which variables to include are fairly ad hoc, it would be nice to convince the reader that the results are robust to the choices actually made. There is a side benefit to this that relates to the interpretation of results. The paper does not attempt to say anything about the *magnitude* of the results. The reader is left wondering whether the effects of various influences on the FDI decision are quantitatively important and how they compare with one another. If the Tobit regressions were estimated without using the zero observations using a log-linear functional form, we could interpret the coefficients as elasticities and would avoid the problem of not being able to compare effects measured in different units. This might help our interpretation of the results.

To summarize, the paper addresses an important policy issue. It is heartening to see empirical research on this timely topic. In the end, though, I was left wondering about the interpretation of some of the results.

Reference

Ray, Edward John. 1977. Foreign direct investment in manufacturing. *Journal of Political Economy* 85:283–97.

3 Can Interindustry Wage Differentials Justify Strategic Trade Policy?

Lawrence F. Katz and Lawrence H. Summers

Industrial policies have been a major source of economic and political debate in the United States and other nations in recent years. Advocates of industrial policies assert that, since all public policies inevitably influence the composition of output and some industries are "better" for a national economy than others, it is appropriate for governments to manage their influence on the economy to promote such goals as growth and competitiveness. Industrial policy advocates often cite Japan as an example of a nation that has benefited from sound industrial policies. Critics of industrial policy have generally cited standard economic arguments against such policies, suggesting that, in competitive or nearly competitive markets, there are no gains to be had from altering the composition of output.

In tandem with political debates over industrial policy, a burgeoning academic literature on strategic trade policy, initiated by Brander and Spencer (1983, 1984) and surveyed in Krugman (1986) and Dixit (1987), has examined policy measures that can shift monopoly rents from one nation to another when product markets are imperfectly competitive.[1] A central focus in this literature has been on imperfections in product markets, especially

Lawrence F. Katz is assistant professor of economics at Harvard University and a faculty research fellow of the National Bureau of Economic Research. Lawrence H. Summers is professor of economics at Harvard University and a research associate of the National Bureau of Economic Research.

The authors thank William Dickens and Alan Krueger for many helpful discussions. They are grateful to Robert Stern for generously providing trade flow data, to Richard Baldwin for providing data on Airbus, and to Joe Cooper, David Cutler, and Daniel Kessler for expert research assistance.

markets with large learning curve effects. While this literature has yielded intriguing counterexamples to some widely believed propositions, we believe that its emphasis on product market imperfections as the potential rationale for industrial policies is somewhat misplaced.[2]

We suspect that deviations from competitive labor markets that give rise to significant interindustry wage differentials are at least equally important for industrial policy as product market imperfections are. Industrial policy advocates such as Robert Reich and Lester Thurow, who encourage subsidies for "high value added production," appear to be referring not to especially profitable industries but to industries that pay high wages. Certainly, the international pervasiveness of subsidies to steel industries is probably more easily understood on the basis of the very high-wage jobs they provide than on the basis of the profits earned by steel companies.

The observation that rents accruing to labor are much more significant than monopoly rents received by firms is a very general one. For the American nonfinancial corporate sector in 1987, employee compensation represented 82 percent of value added, while operating profits represented only 18 percent, with the bulk of the latter figure being the return to capital rather than monopoly rents. It follows that the labor rents associated with industry wage differentials of even 10 percent bulk very large when compared with plausible estimates of firms' monopoly rents.[3] In fact, Katz and Summers (1989) find that variations in labor rents across industries are at least two to three times as important as variations in the rents accruing to shareholders.

This paper explores both theoretically and empirically the implications of labor market imperfections for trade policies, focusing on the situation of the United States in the 1980s. We begin in section 3.1 by demonstrating that, contrary to competitive labor market theories, there are substantial differences between industries in the compensation received by workers with similar characteristics working under apparently similar conditions. The industrial wage structure is remarkably stable across time and space. While unions are a partial source of these wage differentials, wage differentials are large for nonunion workers and in settings like the American South, where union threats are not very important. The differentials appear to arise from the differential importance of motivating, retaining, and recruiting workers, as suggested by the efficiency wage theories surveyed in Katz (1986) and from the rent-sharing considerations considered in more detail in Katz and Summers (1989).

Section 3.2 considers theoretically the implications of noncompetitive wage differentials for trade and industrial policies. We find that interindustry wage differences provide a rationale for policies quite similar to those that have been advanced by industrial policy advocates. While it is difficult to justify subsidizing industries that achieve high value added per worker by relying on abnormally skilled workers or by using a great deal of capital or other inputs, there is a rationale for subsidizing industries that have high value added per worker because of noncompetitive wage differentials. If firms hire labor to the point where its marginal product equals the wage, the marginal productivity of an additional worker is greater in sectors paying premium wages than in competitive wage sectors. In this case, policy measures that expand employment in high-wage sectors may be desirable. Of course, the basic thrust of this theoretical argument is not new. The role of factor market distortions in the design of optimal trade policies has played a prominent role in trade theory at least since the work of Hagen (1958) and Bhagwati and Ramaswami (1963). Furthermore, both stylized calculations and consideration of actual examples suggest that these effects may well be quantitatively important.

Section 3.3 combines data on industry wage premiums with data on trade flows to assess the importance of wage differentials for trade policies. We reach three primary conclusions. First, wage differentials cause the United States to reap extra gains from trade, at least within the manufacturing sector. Manufacturing exports in the United States come disproportionately from industries that pay premium wages, while manufacturing imports generally come from low-wage sectors. Second, exporting high-wage goods while importing lower-wage goods is a characteristic common to other developed countries. Third, despite concerns about undesirable changes in the structure of the U.S. economy, it does not appear (at least through 1984) that changing trade patterns have disproportionately hurt the high-wage portion of the U.S. manufacturing sector. Instead, increased import competition has had its greatest effect on employment in low-wage parts of the U.S. manufacturing sector.

Section 3.4 concludes the paper by offering a tentative assessment of the implications of our results for actual trade, industrial, and tax policies. Our general view is that policies directed at reducing imports are likely to have extremely adverse effects on economic welfare, whereas certain measures aimed at expanding employment in export sectors may increase welfare. Any economic case for activist policy must be tempered by a recognition that theoretically optimal policies are extremely unlikely to be implemented in practice.

3.1   The Importance of Interindustry Wage Differentials

Several recent studies have documented large and persistent wage differentials among industries, even after controlling for a wide variety of worker and job characteristics (Dickens and Katz 1987a, 1987b; Krueger and Summers 1987, 1988; and Murphy and Topel 1987).[4] The pattern of these differentials is remarkably parallel in looking at data for different countries and time periods and suggests that workers in some sectors earn substantial rents. This section summarizes the available evidence on the interindustry wage structure and discusses the consistency with the evidence of alternative models of wage determination. We conclude that competitive labor market explanations stressing unmeasured labor quality and compensating differentials do not provide a plausible explanation for a substantial component of interindustry wage variations, even for nonunion workers. Instead, industry wage differentials largely reflect firms' differing needs to use high wages to motivate, retain, and recruit their workers and rent-sharing considerations.

3.1.1 The Magnitude of Interindustry Wage Differences

We analyze industry wage differences in the United States using cross-sectional data on individuals from the 1984 Current Population Surveys (CPS). All twelve CPS surveys from 1984 were combined to generate a sample large enough to estimate accurately wage differentials for detailed industry categories.[5] Our sample consists of nonagricultural employees sixteen years old or older and excludes workers employed in public administration. The earnings variable is usual weekly earnings divided by usual weekly hours.[6] The procedures utilized are described in Krueger and Summers (1988). In particular, we normalize the estimated wage differentials as deviations from the (employment-weighted) mean differential.

The first column in table 3.1 reports the proportionate difference in wages between the average worker in a two-digit census industry and the weighted average worker in all industries. The second column reports the normalized industry wage differences after controlling for education, age, occupation, gender, race, marital status, standard metropolitan statistical area, full-time work, and student status and allowing many of the coefficients to differ for males and females. Controlling for available worker characteristics has little effect on the rankings of different industries; the correlation of the industry wage differentials estimated with and without controls is 0.96. This finding suggests that comparisons of average industry wages over time and across countries may be useful since it is unlikely that controls would change one's inferences about the relative rankings of industries in the wage structure.

Table 3.1   **Estimated Industry Log Wage Differentials—Full Year 1984 CPS**

Industry	(1) All without Controls	(2) All with Controls[a]	(3) All—Total Compensation with Controls[a]	(4) Nonunion with Controls[a]
Mining	.396	.268	.280	.273
Construction	.163	.113	.100	.068
Lumber	−.118	−.030	.007	.007
Furniture	−.120	−.035	−.014	.005
Stone, clay, & glass	.084	.070	.124	.066
Primary metals	.269	.169	.270	.166
Fabricated metals	.128	.077	.138	.082
Machinery excluding electrical	.299	.149	.186	.177

Table 3.1   (continued)

Industry	(1) All without Controls	(2) All with Controls[a]	(3) All—Total Compensation with Controls[a]	(4) Nonunion with Controls[a]
Electrical machinery	.177	.085	.114	.107
Transport equipment	.375	.211	.288	.194
Instruments	.247	.110	.139	.158
Miscellaneous manufacturing	−.102	−.062	−.041	−.015
Food	.039	.052	.105	.041
Tobacco	.248	.236	.424	.213
Textile	−.146	−.002	.010	.048
Apparel	−.358	−.153	−.149	−.111
Paper	.220	.168	.205	.149
Printing	.055	.033	.037	.034
Chemical	.343	.192	.237	.223
Petroleum	.490	.294	.543	.292
Rubber	.090	.101	.146	.132
Leather	−.294	−.134	−.113	−.090
Other transport	.245	.179	.208	.092
Communications	.385	.250	.373	.215
Public utilities	.349	.201	.278	.192
Wholesale trade	.108	.040	.018	.058
Eating & drinking	−.605	−.244	−.274	−.228
Other retail trade	−.267	−.139	−.169	−.138
Banking	.098	.048	.077	.066
Insurance	.101	.049	.053	.069
Private household	−.809	−.339	−.490	−.312
Business services	−.010	−.015	−.046	.004
Repair services	−.076	−.085	−.115	−.053
Personal services	−.384	−.180	−.219	−.161
Entertainment	−.211	−.130	−.151	−.144
Medical services	−.152	−.034	−.030	−.014
Hospitals	.096	.060	.064	.077
Welfare services	−.187	−.203	−.286	−.207
Education services	.078	−.078	−.099	−.105
Professional services	.271	.091	.052	.105
Sample size	135,595	135,595	135,595	106,599
Weighted adjusted SD of differentials[b]	.270	.144	.185	.141

Note: [a]Standard errors are not reported to save space. In all cases, the standard errors are between .004 and .020, except for tobacco, which has standard errors ranging from .039 to .049.

[a]Controls include education and its square; six age dummies; eight occupation dummies; female dummy; race dummy; standard metropolitan statistical area dummy; three region dummies; full-time work dummy; full- and part-time student dummies; interactions of the female dummy with marriage, education, education squared, and the six age dummies; and a constant. Each column was estimated from a separate cross-sectional regression.

[b]Weights are employment shares for the entire sample (union and nonunion).

The controls do substantially reduce the estimated interindustry dispersion of wages. The standard deviation of the estimated wage differentials falls from 27 percent without controls to 14 percent when controls are added. Almost all this decline is attributable to holding occupation and sex constant. Industry affiliation has a large effect on relative wages even allowing for observed differences in occupation, human capital variables, and demographic background. Industry differentials range from a high of 29 percent above the mean in petroleum to 34 percent below the mean in private household services. Durable goods manufacturing, mining, and chemicals industries pay wages well above those for workers in retail trade and service industries, all else constant. Substantial wage differentials are also apparent within the traded-goods (manufacturing) sector.

One possibility is that these differentials largely serve to offset differences in nonwage compensation. One nonwage aspect of compensation that we can control for using our data is fringe benefits. Fringe benefits account for as much as 50 percent of compensation in some industries. To adjust for variation in fringes across industries, we multiplied our CPS hourly wage data for each worker in the sample by the ratio of total labor costs to wages in the corresponding industry in 1984.[7] The third column of table 3.1 presents estimates of industry wage differentials with the dependent variable adjusted to reflect both wage and nonwage compensation.[8] The estimated standard deviation of industry differentials actually increases by more than one-fourth, from 14.4 to 18.5 percent. Thus, the consideration of fringe benefits reinforces, rather than reduces, industry compensation differences.

Discussions of industry wage differences frequently emphasize the importance of unions in wage setting. The inclusion of union membership and union coverage dummy variables in the specification reported in the second column of table 3.1, however, has little effect on the estimated industry differentials. The standard deviation of the differentials falls from 14.4 to 13.9 percent. Since unions are likely to have different effects on wages in industries with different product market structures and costs of strikes, a better approach is to assess the importance of industry differentials for a sample containing only nonunion workers.[9] Column 4 of table 3.1 presents these. The industry wage premia are quite substantial for nonunion workers. We also estimated differentials for the union workers in our sample and found the standard deviation of the differentials to be slightly larger for nonunion workers (14.1 as opposed to 13.3 percent). The correlation of the differentials for the union and nonunion samples is 0.80. There appears to be little difference in the process generating industry relative wages in the union and nonunion sectors. Further evidence that unions are not the primary factor accounting for wage differentials comes from Krueger and Summers's (1988) finding that the wage structure in the southern part of the United States looks very similar to that in the rest of the country, despite much lower rates of unionization.

3.1.2   Regularities in the Interindustry Wage Structure

Industry wage differences appear to be quite stable across time and space. Krueger and Summers (1987) examine evidence on the industry wage structure in the United States from 1900 to 1984. They find that the correlation between relative wages in nine major industries is 0.62 between 1900 and 1984 and 0.91 between 1970 and 1984. Krueger and Summers further document that the relative rankings of industry average wages in detailed manufacturing industries are also extremely stable over time. Figure 3.1 plots industry wage differentials for nineteen two-digit manufacturing industries estimated from the May 1974 CPS against analogous differentials estimated from the May 1984 CPS.[10] Despite widespread concern about the effect of trade on affected industries, the figure illustrates that the industry wage structure in manufacturing has been very stable over the last decade. Freeman and Katz (1987) study the effects of import competition on wages in U.S. manufacturing and find that a 10 percent decrease in industry revenues from increased import penetration reduces an industry's relative wage for production workers by only 0.5 percent.[11]

Industry wage patterns are remarkably similar among countries with diverse labor market institutions. Table 3.2 presents evidence on the remarkable similarity of relative wages in manufacturing among nine countries in 1983.

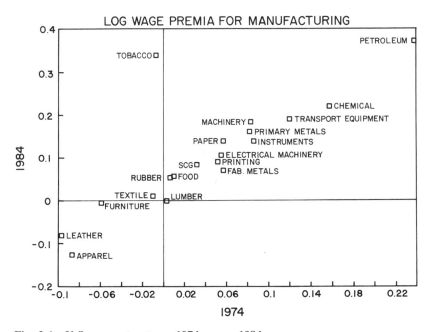

Fig. 3.1   U.S. wage structure: 1974 versus 1984

Table 3.2   **Correlations of Log Manufacturing Wages among Countries in 1983**

	Country								
	Australia (yr.)	Chile (yr.)	France (hr.)	Germany (hr.)	Japan (yr.)	Korea (hr.)	Sweden (yr.)	United Kingdom (yr.)	United States (hr.)
Australia	1.00	.66	.80	.81	.84	.67	.77	.78	.92
Chile		1.00	.60	.60	.69	.46	.67	.56	.67
France			1.00	.89	.80	.53	.64	.77	.85
Germany				1.00	.94	.62	.75	.93	.95
Japan					1.00	.59	.80	.95	.92
Korea						1.00	.68	.59	.66
Sweden							1.00	.79	.79
United Kingdom								1.00	.86
United States									1.00

Note: In the column headings, "yr." denotes yearly wages, and "hr." denotes hourly wages. Wages are for operatives, except for France, where the wage is the average wage of all workers. The data cover nineteen manufacturing industries. Data are available for only eighteen industries for Korea and Australia, seventeen industries for Germany, and fifteen industries for France. Each pairwise correlation uses the maximum number of industries possible.

Source: Industrial Statistics Yearbook, 1984, vol. 1 (New York: United Nations, Department of International Economic and Social Affairs, Statistical Office, 1986).

The use of a single occupational group (operatives) allows us to control for skill mix differences across countries. The cross-country correlations of relative wages are quite high, typically between 0.6 and 0.9. For example, the correlation between the relative wages of operatives in the United States and Japan is 0.95. We illustrate this similarity in the wage structures of the United States and Japan in figure 3.2. Krueger and Summers (1987) also find strong positive correlations in relative average industry wages among a larger group of countries. The stability in differentials across time periods and countries strongly suggests that these wage differences result from factors fundamental to the operation of industrial economies and are not the artifact of particular collective bargaining systems or government interventions in the labor market.

The industry wage structure also appears to be very similar for different types of workers. Dickens and Katz (1987b) find that interindustry wage differentials are highly correlated across occupations: in industries where one occupation is highly paid, all occupations tend to be highly paid. For example, they find that the correlation in industry average wages for managers and laborers is 0.83, even after controlling for worker characteristics. Furthermore, Krueger and Summers (1988) show that the pattern of differentials is quite similar for young and old workers and for workers with short and long job tenure.

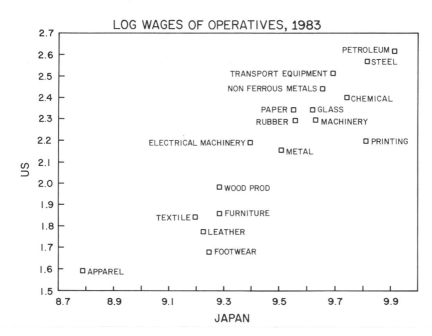

Fig. 3.2   **Wage structure: United States versus Japan**

3.1.3   The Characteristics of High- and Low-Wage Industries

The evidence summarized above indicates that there exists a pattern of wage differentials in which all workers in some industries are paid more than similar workers in other industries. This raises the question of what are the attributes of high- and low-wage industries. Dickens and Katz (1987a) review the literature on the relations among industry characteristics and industry wages. They find that, even after controlling for observed human capital, geographic, and demographic variables, both union and nonunion wages are positively correlated with capital intensity, measures of product market power and ability to pay, union density, average education level, and firm and establishment size. High-wage industries also have much lower quit rates than low-wage industries.

The characteristics of high-wage and low-wage industries in U.S. manufacturing are illustrated in figure 3.3. The tendency of capital intensive industries (and those with a low labor share) to pay high wages is apparent. The relation between research and development spending and wages is less clear cut. Unfortunately, as Dickens and Katz note, it is not possible to disentangle the independent effects of these factors on wages reliably.

3.1.4   Do Industry Wage Differentials Reflect Labor Rents?

The competitive labor market model offers two types of explanations for persistent interindustry wage differentials. These differentials may compensate

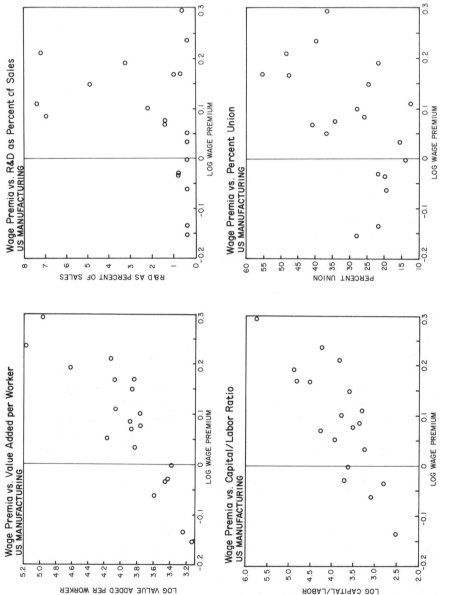

Fig. 3.3

for nonpecuniary differences in job attributes, or they may reflect differences in unmeasured labor quality. If compensating differentials and unobserved ability adequately explain the bulk of measured industry wage differences, then the presence of large industry wage differentials should not be an important consideration in the evaluation of trade policies.

Interindustry wage differences do not appear to be easily explained by compensating differentials, for several reasons. First, Krueger and Summers (1988) find that the inclusion of controls for observable differences in working conditions tends to increase rather than decrease estimates of the extent of interindustry wage variation. Furthermore, the estimates in table 3.1 indicate that the consideration of fringe benefits leads to substantially larger estimates of industry compensation differences. Thus, the consideration of observed nonwage compensation exacerbates the industry differentials.

Second, the strong correlation in interindustry wage differences across occupations is also difficult to explain through equalizing differences since it is unlikely that whenever working conditions are poor for production workers they are also poor for managers, secretaries, and salesmen. Third, Pencavel (1970) and many others have shown that there is a strong negative correlation between industry wage differentials and quit rates. Furthermore, Holzer, Katz, and Krueger (1988) find that high-wage industries attract a greater number of job applicants per opening than do low-wage industries. These findings strongly suggest that workers in high-wage industries earn rents.

An alternative competitive explanation of these wage differences is that they largely reflect differences in workers' productive abilities that are not captured by the variables available in individual level data sets. While it is almost certain that unobserved quality differences account for much of the variation in the wages that workers with similar observed characteristics receive, this does not necessarily imply that differences in the average wage paid in different industries are the result of differences in the average level of unobserved ability. Four types of evidence suggest that it is unlikely that a large part of measured interindustry wage differences can be accounted for by unmeasured ability.

First, Krueger and Summers (1988) find that, after controlling for sex and occupation, controlling for other skill variables such as education and experience has only a very small effect on the dispersion of industry wages. This is because there are only minor differences in educational attainment and in experience across industries after controlling for differences in occupational composition. Given the absence of a high degree of industrial sorting on the basis of observed labor quality proxies, a high degree of sorting on unobserved characteristics would be surprising.

Second, Krueger and Summers (1988) present longitudinal evidence that when individual workers move between industries, either because of displacement or because of normal labor market processes, their wages change by amounts similar to the industry differentials estimated in cross-sectional regressions.[12] This finding casts some doubt on the hypothesis that measured interindustry wage differences are largely attributable to unobserved productive ability.

Third, much evidence indicates that more profitable industries—those with more monopoly power and those where labor's share is smaller—pay higher wages. These regularities hold in different times and places and explain a sizable fraction of interindustry wage variation. There is no obvious reason why these product market characteristics should be strongly correlated with unmeasured ability.

Fourth, the strong similarity in wage differences for different types of workers is also problematic for the unmeasured ability view. Why should industry technologies almost always have such strong skill complementarities that those requiring unusually good operatives require unusually good managers and clerical workers? Furthermore, industry differences in observed quality measures for different occupational groups do not appear to be nearly as strongly correlated as do their industry wage differentials. Dickens and Katz (1988) find that industry average education levels are only weakly positively correlated for many occupations and are negatively correlated for some groups.

Our reading of the evidence is that it is difficult to account convincingly for the industry wage structure on the basis of unobserved ability differences or equalizing differences. Instead, it appears that workers in high-wage industries earn rents.

3.1.5   Alternative Explanations for Labor Market Rents

The natural economic approach to explaining why firms in high-wage industries fail to cut wages in the absence of any legal compulsion is to isolate reasons why reducing wages would be unprofitable for a firm. This is the approach taken in the large and growing efficiency wage literature. This literature, surveyed from a theoretical perspective in Stiglitz (1987) and from an empirical perspective in Katz (1986), has put forth a number of possible explanations for firms' failure to cut wages in the face of an excess supply of labor and their willingness to confer rents on incumbent workers.

A first explanation, emphasized by Shapiro and Stiglitz (1984) in the context of unemployment and Bulow and Summers (1986) in the context of wage differentials, emphasizes the firms' need to deter their workers from shirking. Conferring rents on them, which will be forfeited if they are caught shirking, may be an efficient alternative to more extensive monitoring costs. This theory may rationalize the observation that capital intensive firms and those offering more job autonomy pay higher wages because the cost of shirking is higher in these firms. Krueger (1987) provides some supporting evidence by documenting that fast food firms appear to trade off wages and monitoring effort.

A second explanation revolves around firms' desire to avoid turnover because of fixed hiring and training costs. This explanation, elegantly modeled by Stiglitz (1985), is consistent with the observation that wage premia appear to be somewhat larger for experienced than for inexperienced workers. It is also supported by frequent references to the need to monitor turnover in personnel books. A third related explanation for firms' willingness to confer rents involves adverse selection considerations (Weiss 1980). If more able workers have higher reservation wages than their less able counterparts, firms that reduce wages may find that the average ability of their work force declines so rapidly that unit labor costs increase. This explanation is consistent with the complaints of some managers that the "wrong" workers quit in good times.

While each of these explanations can be formalized, they appear insufficient to account fully for the observed pattern of wage differentials. A striking feature of this pattern is the similarity in industry wage patterns for different occupational groups. It is difficult to see why industries with an especially great need to motivate and retain operatives should also have an especially great need to motivate and retain clerical workers. The similarity of wage patterns in different occupations, along with the observation that monopoly power appears to influence wages, suggests that firms for which production interferences are especially costly may pay abnormally high wages even in nonunion settings.

This type of behavior can be justified on the grounds of "gift exchange" theories of the type advanced by Akerlof (1984). In these models, a worker's effort depends on his or her perception of how fairly he or she is being treated. Perceived fairness in turn depends on how profitable the firm is. A related argument might hold that firms pay high wages to "buy the peace," avoiding unions or collective visible shirking of the kind that Mathewson (1969) and Mars (1982) find in many industrial settings. The "peace" may be worth more to some firms than to others. A final explanation invokes expense preference behavior on the part of managers, who may feel more loyalty to employees than to shareholders, particularly at low levels. If the efficiency effects of wage increases described in previous paragraphs are important, it may not be very costly for firms to raise wages.

3.1.6   Conclusions

The evidence in this section suggests that industry wage differentials for similar workers are substantial. It appears that these wage differentials largely reflect rents earned by workers in high-wage industries. No doubt, industry wage differences result from a number of sources. Fortunately, as we argue in the next section, the implications of noncompetitive wage differentials for trade policies are similar for a variety of underlying causes of the differentials as long as firms choose employment levels on their labor demand curves.

3.2   Wage Differentials and Trade Policies

The basic argument linking labor market imperfections and trade policies has long been recognized by trade theorists (see, e.g., Bhagwati and Srinivasan 1983; and Magee 1976). It has been echoed, though in a less clear fashion, in the American debate over industrial policies. If competitive forces do not equalize wages in different sectors, and if firms operate on their labor demand curves, then the marginal product of labor in different sectors will not be equated, resulting in allocative inefficiencies. Policies that raise employment in high-wage sectors at the expense of employment in low-wage sectors will therefore increase allocative efficiency. This line of argument captures the thrust of industrial policy arguments suggesting that countries can raise their workers' standards of living by encouraging the growth of "high value added industries."

We begin by demonstrating that the interaction of trade policies with wage differentials has welfare consequences that are likely to be more important than the profit-shifting effects that have been the focus of recent discussions of strategic trade policy. Then we examine arguments against subsidies to employment in high-wage sectors based on rent-seeking and equity considerations. We conclude that on economic grounds there is a reasonably strong welfare argument for measures that promote production in high-wage industries, though any policy judgment must depend on an assessment of how skillfully the government would manage its interventions.

3.2.1   Wage Differentials in a Closed Economy

For simplicity, consider a stylized economy with two sectors.[13] Following the terminology of Doeringer and Piore (1971), we label these sectors "secondary" and "primary." As we discuss below, the primary sector pays higher wages and offers workers more responsible jobs than the secondary sector. Secondary-sector output, taken as the numeraire, is given by $Y^n = w_0 L^n$. The secondary-sector labor market is competitive, so workers employed in the secondary sector receive a wage equal to their marginal product, w_0. Primary-sector output is given by the constant returns to scale production function $Y^p = F(K^p, L^p)$. The demand for primary-sector output is a decreasing function of its price, $p = p(Y^p)$, $p' < 0$. We assume that the wage differential, d, in the primary sector is a nondecreasing function of employment, $d = d(L^p)$, $d' \geq 0$.[14] It may depend positively on the level of employment because workers' ability to extract rents is increased when the demand for labor increases or because the cost of leaving a high-wage job is reduced when there are more high-wage jobs in the economy.

Assume initially that the economy is closed and that the capital stock is fixed. Firms in the primary- and secondary-sector product markets are assumed to act competitively. Then the first-order condition,

(1) $$p(Y^P)F_L(K^P, L^P) = w_0(1 + d),$$

determines the level of primary-sector employment. This level of primary-sector employment is inefficiently low. As figure 3.4 illustrates, a subsidy to employment in the primary sector at a rate just sufficient to offset the wage differential $(1/[1 + d])$ would permit the economy to attain the first-best allocation of labor.[15] Note that such a subsidy increases efficiency, even though it may lead to a widening of interindustry wage differentials. We return below to the question of whether it represents a Pareto improvement.

So far we have maintained the assumption of perfect competition in product markets and the assumption that the capital stock in each industry is fixed. Relaxing these assumptions tends to strengthen the case for policies directed at expanding the primary sector. If firms in the primary sector have market power, this is another reason apart from wage premia why the social marginal product of labor in the primary sector exceeds the social marginal product of labor in the secondary sector. Put more straightforwardly, there is an efficiency case for subsidizing the variable inputs of a monopolist.

Allowing for variable capital input strengthens the case for subsidies to high-wage industries. If wage differentials do not depend on the capital intensity of the primary sector, then the appropriate policy instrument in the presence of noncompetitive wage differentials is a wage subsidy. If wage differentials are an increasing function of capital intensity, as some rent-sharing theories would suggest, then there is a case for capital investment subsidies to offset the "tax" levied by labor on capital investments.

How substantial are the potential gains from public policies directed at offsetting the effects of interindustry wage differentials? One way of answering this question is by comparing the efficiency costs of interindustry wage differentials with other distortions that have received more attention

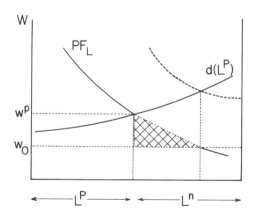

Fig. 3.4 Subsidies and economic efficiency

from economists. Section 3.1 showed that the standard deviation of nonunion industry compensation differences, after correcting for measured ability differences, was about 18 percent. About 15 percent of private-sector American workers are covered by trade union agreements, and it is generally estimated that their compensation is about 20 percent above that of other workers. If this were the only source of wage inequality, the standard deviation of wages would be approximately 7 percent. This suggests that the allocative inefficiency attributable to industry wage effects is at least comparable to the efficiency costs arising from union wage differentials.

A different standard of comparison is the distortionary consequence of taxation. Assuming that labor's share in output is about three-quarters—a 20 percent difference in labor costs between two sectors—will affect the product mix in the same way as a 60 percent capital income tax or a 15 percent sales tax. The former figure is more than what is at stake in the much-discussed distortion between corporate capital and owner-occupied housing. Much smaller differentials in effective tax rates played a prominent role in the recent U.S. tax reform debate. Discussions of sales taxes invariably treat differences of only a few percentage points in the rates on included and excluded items as a serious problem.

Interindustry wage differences appear to cause allocative distortions greater than those resulting from trade unions or the corporate income tax. A different way of demonstrating their importance is by evaluating the marginal social product of capital in the primary sector in their presence. The value of output measured at preintervention prices in our stylized economy is given by

$$(2) \qquad Y = pF(K^p, L^p) + w_0 L^n,$$

where $L^n + L^p = L$ and L is the fixed stock of labor in the economy. Differentiating (2) with respect to K^p, the primary-sector capital stock, and then using both the first-order condition (1) and the assumption that the primary-sector production function displays constant returns to scale, we obtain the result

$$(3) \qquad dY/dK^p = r\{1 + [\alpha d/(1 - \alpha)(1 + d)]\}$$

where Y represents the total value of national income, r is the return received by the suppliers of capital, and α represents labor's share in the primary sector. Taking labor's share to be three-quarters and the wage differential to be 20 percent, this implies that the marginal product of additional capital in the primary sector is inflated by half because of the preexisting wage differential. This suggests that substantial gains may be achievable by targeting investment incentives toward high-wage sectors.

3.2.2   Wage Differentials in a Small Open Economy

In the case of a small open economy, illustrated in figure 3.5, the relative price of primary-sector output is determined on international markets and is

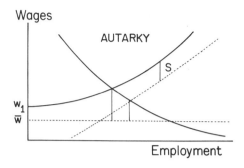

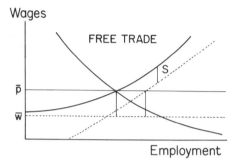

Fig. 3.5   Subsidies in closed and open economies

assumed to be unaffected by the domestic production mix. The demand function $p(Y^p)$ becomes perfectly elastic. This does not change the first-order condition (1) or the desirability of employment subsidies for the primary sector. Opening up the economy does, however, strengthen the case for large subsidies. In a closed economy, subsidies to the primary sector encounter diminishing returns as its output declines in value with increased production. This does not happen when the price of output is set on world markets and is insensitive to the level of domestic production.[16]

There is a further point to be made. As figure 3.5 illustrates, the marginal welfare gained per dollar of subsidy will be greater the greater is the world price of primary-sector output. As the world price of primary-sector output expands, and as domestic production therefore expands, the wage differential increases, raising the social gain to inducing further expansion of the primary sector. This observation resonates somewhat with discussions of industrial policy that claim that governments should support "sunrise" export industries rather than "sunset" import-competing industries.

We have focused on the desirability of employment or production subsidies for the high-wage sector. An obvious alternative is protection, through the exclusion of foreign competition. As illustrated in figure 3.6, protection has the virtue of expanding the primary sector but the disadvantage of raising the consumer price of the primary-sector good. It is clear from the figure that the former effect is first order while the latter effect is second order. It follows that

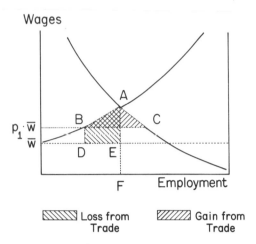

Fig. 3.6   **The gains and losses from protection**

at least small movements toward protection will be welfare enhancing, though they will be less desirable than primary-sector employment subsidies. This is an illustration of the general principle discussed by Bhagwati and Srinivasan (1983), that, in the presence of distortions, policies can be ranked, with instruments that most directly address distortions being preferred.

Discussions of activist trade policies typically stress the potential defect that they invite retaliation, which offsets any initial benefits. This argument does not apply when policy options are limited to subsidies directed at capturing labor market rents. In the model considered here, it is true that countries would prefer that their subsidies to primary-sector output not meet retaliation. In our model, however, subsidies that are retaliated against by similar subsidies are nonetheless likely to raise the welfare of both countries.[17] This is because they will drive the world economy to a situation such as subsidized first-best optimum, depicted in figure 3.4. Note further that subsidies beyond the point where the marginal product of labor in the primary sector and the marginal product of labor in the secondary sector are equated are inefficient in both open and closed economies.

3.2.3   Gauging the Importance of Labor Rents

Under most plausible estimates, the wage differential effects stressed here are of greater importance for trade policy than the product market monopoly rent-shifting effects discussed in recent work on strategic trade policy. The social return to increased investment in the presence of wage differentials can easily be as much as 50 percent greater than the private gain. The point may be illustrated more strongly by considering two recent studies of strategic trade policies—Baldwin and Krugman's (1987a, 1987b) study of European subsidies to Airbus Industrie for the development of the A300 jet and Dixit's (1988) study of trade in automobiles.

Baldwin and Krugman construct a simple simulation model incorporating both learning curve effects and strategic interactions in aircraft industry. Their data indicate that the subsidy had very substantial effects on the allocation of airplane production between the United States and Europe. It also reduced prices in the industry considerably. The Baldwin-Krugman analysis suggests that the subsidy program cost $1.47 billion in profits for the European airline industry and increased the consumer surplus of European customers by $1.43 billion, leading to only a negligible change in economic welfare. Their analysis takes no account of the rents gained by labor as it moved from lower-wage industries into the high-wage airplane industry, however. A policy analysis should not treat the rent component of the wage bill as a social cost of production but as a component of the social surplus generated by the industry.[18]

To estimate the "labor rent" effects of the Airbus program, we assumed alternatively that compensation in the entire product chain of airplanes was 25 percent higher than the economy average and that it was 25 percent higher in only the final stage of production—airline assembly. Combining these figures with Baldwin and Krugman's estimates of the diversion of sales toward the Airbus consortium and information on labor's share in airplane production permits a rough estimate of the labor rent–shifting effect of the Airbus subsidy of the A300.

The results in table 3.3 indicate that, once labor rent considerations are recognized, the overall assessment of the Airbus program for European welfare turns from marginally negative to strongly positive. Even in the less favorable case, the subsidy generates a welfare gain representing about half its cost. The estimated gain would be far greater, recognizing the high level of unemployment in Europe, if we assumed that some of those hired by Airbus would otherwise have been unemployed.

A similar conclusion is suggested by Dixit's recent study of the automobile industry. He finds that allowing for labor rents in the American automobile industry dramatically alters the results of his analysis based on imperfect competition in the product market. Policies promoting domestic production that appear undesirable without taking account of labor market imperfections yield large gains once the existence of these imperfections is acknowledged.

More careful empirical analysis of more specific incidents is needed before firm judgments about the potential importance of labor rent shifting can be made. The examples here were selected by other authors because of potentially important product market imperfections. It would be valuable to examine industries, such as steel, that are noted for large labor market imperfections.

3.2.4 Some Possible Objections

Our analysis so far has assumed away rent-seeking behavior. At least two types of rent seeking need to be considered. First, it is possible that wage differentials generate wait unemployment of the sort envisioned by Harris and

Table 3.3   Labor Market Rents and the Effects of the Airbus A300 Program
                   on European Welfare

	Scenario		
	(1)	(2)	(3)
		20% Labor Rents	20% Labor Rents
	No Labor	at Final Stage	at All Stages
	Rents	of Production[a]	of Production[b]
Change in present discounted value of:			
Consumer surplus	1.43	1.43	1.43
Profits	−1.47	−1.47	−1.47
Labor rents	.00	.90	1.84
Net change in welfare	−.04	.86	1.80

Note: All figures are in billions of dollars. The computations assume a 5 percent discount rate and cumulative production of 398 units over a twenty-year product cycle.

Sources: Adapted from table 5 of Baldwin and Krugman (1987b). The changes in present discounted value of labor rents are based on the authors' own calculations. Information on employee compensation, value of shipments, and value added for the U.S. aircraft industry (SIC 3721) are from the 1985 Annual Survey of Manufactures (Bureau of Census, *Statistics for Industry Groups and Industries* [Washington, D.C.: U.S. Government Printing Office]).

[a]The change in labor rents is computed as the change in the present discounted value of shipments for Airbus calculated from the Baldwin-Krugman simulation ($15.41 billion) times the ratio of employee compensation to value of shipments in the U.S. aircraft industry in 1985 (0.291) times the share of rents in employee compensation (0.20).

[b]The change in labor rents is computed in a manner analogous to that described in n. a above with the share of employee compensation in value added in the U.S. aircraft industry in 1985 (0.596) replacing the share of employee compensation in value of shipments

Todaro (1970). In the extreme case where the primary sector hires randomly each period from a pool of waiting applicants, $w^p(1 - u) = w^0$, where u is the unemployment rate in the primary sector. In this case, there is no gain to increasing primary-sector employment since, for each job created in the primary sector, $u/(1 - u)$ workers move from the low-wage sector into unemployment (Harberger 1971).[19] A more plausible formulation of wait unemployment would recognize that incumbent employees typically retain the rights to their jobs each period so that only new openings and those jobs where the incumbent worker has quit or been terminated are available to be allocated to the unemployed. Under this scenario, if workers have positive discount rates and enter the primary-sector queue to the point where the utility of being in the queue equals the utility of being employed in the low-wage sector, extra employment in the primary sector will generate less induced unemployment than in the initial case considered. Thus, a small subsidy to the primary sector will still be desirable.[20] Furthermore, if workers are able to queue for high-wage jobs from low-wage jobs, rent seeking through wait unemployment may not be an important problem.

The second type of rent-seeking behavior involves efforts to create wage differentials. Union organizing drives are an obvious example. If larger wage differentials lead to larger employment subsidies, such rent-seeking activity will be encouraged. In this case, subsidies to high-wage industries, while increasing efficiency ex post, may create large ex ante inefficiencies if they lead to more resources being devoted to trying to push up wages. We doubt that this point is of vast practical importance. Union organizing budgets and employer resistance expenditures are trivial compared to the rents earned by union workers. Taking 20 percent of the work force to be unionized and a 20 percent union compensation effect implies that 4 percent of wages, or about $75 billion a year, represents rents. Union organizing budgets in the United States certainly total far less than $1 billion. Furthermore, the evidence surveyed in the previous section suggests that most wage differentials do not arise from organizing activity.

A different line of argument against policies directed at subsidizing the primary sector stresses their antiegalitarian consequences. The essence of such policies is, after all, subsidizing workers who are receiving relatively high wages. The argument is more subtle, however, than it at first appears. Subsidies to the primary sector enlarge it, thereby raising the probability of secondary-sector workers being able to move into the primary sector. Bulow and Summers (1986) demonstrate that small subsidies to the primary sector are Pareto improvements relative to laissez faire in the special case where all workers are homogeneous, movements between sectors can be characterized by a Markov process, and efficiency wage considerations lead to constant lifetime utility differences between workers in the two sectors. More generally, efficiency-enhancing subsidies will not produce Pareto improvements, particularly if there are some secondary-sector workers who have no chance of getting primary-sector jobs because of their lack of skill. It is of course possible to argue that optimal subsidies should be given to improve the allocation of output, and then income redistribution measures should be used to offset any perverse distributional consequences.[21]

On balance, the arguments in this section suggest that there is a legitimate economic argument in support of policies directed at encouraging production in high-wage sectors of the economy. Even though such measures are likely to increase wage differentials, they nevertheless may increase economic welfare. Especially in nonunion contexts, it appears unlikely that rent-seeking losses will outweigh the gains achievable through increasing high-wage employment.

3.3   Wage Differentials and American Trade Policies

The belief that international competition is profoundly changing the economic landscape and leading to the deindustrialization of America is often expressed in debates over American industrial policy. The crude argument that the United States is losing its manufacturing base to international competitors is often put forward as a justification for policies directed at limiting imports or spurring exports. In George Meany's picturesque phrase, "You cannot have a healthy economy based on everyone doing everyone else's laundry."

The claim that the United States might lose its ability to compete in all industries rests on confusion. As long as foreigners are unwilling to accumulate claims on American assets indefinitely, the United States must ultimately run a surplus. The interesting question for structural trade policy is therefore whether trade balance with a high level of both exports and imports or with a low level of both exports and imports is preferable.

To shed light on this issue, tables 3.4 and 3.5 present information on the characteristics of American manufacturing industries, distinguishing between "import" and "export" industries. We focus only on manufacturing because of data limitations regarding other sectors and because manufacturing accounts for the lion's share (about two-thirds) of American trade.[22] The data refer to three-digit census industries. The number of import or export workers in each industry is estimated as the product of the industry's total number of employees and the fraction of total industry shipments represented by imports or exports.

Table 3.4 lists the manufacturing industries with the highest import and export shares. Most of the export industries rely heavily on high technology, aircraft being a prominent example. The import industries are more mixed, ranging from footwear to office machines to motor vehicles. Particularly in the case of export industries, it is striking that durable and capital goods play an important role in merchandise trade.

Intraindustry trade is very important even at the three-digit level; the correlation between import and export shares was 0.06 in 1983. To highlight the differences between import and export workers, the first three columns of table 3.5 compare the average characteristics of the most import- and the most export-intensive industries with those of the entire manufacturing sector.

A clear pattern emerges from the table. Relative to the entire manufacturing sector, export industries look much more like the primary-sector firms described by Doeringer and Piore (1971), while import industries look much more like secondary-sector firms. Wages in export-intensive industries are 12 percent above average after adjusting for skill differences, while wages in import-intensive industries are 16 percent below average. Roughly similar differentials are observed for both union and nonunion workers. The widely cited examples of automobiles and steel, where very high-wage industries face substantial import penetration and are almost completely unable to export, appear to be atypical. The general pattern is that export-intensive industries are the ones with substantial wage premia.

Reflecting patterns of American comparative advantage, export-intensive industries in the United States also employ more skilled workers and do more

Table 3.4 **High Import Penetration and Export Supply Ratio Three-Digit Census Industries in U.S. Manufacturing, 1983**

		Industries Employing Top 10% of Workers by Import Penetration Ratio[a]			
CIC	Industry	$M/(M + S)$	X/S	Log Wage Premium[b]	Employment (1,000s)
381	Watches, clocks, and watchcases	.511	.085	−.242	14.6
221	Footwear, except rubber	.511	.024	−.174	119.6
222	Leather products	.371	.041	−.166	49.7
391	Jewelry and miscellaneous manufacturing	.335	.084	−.120	278.6
261	Pottery	.332	.108	−.142	37.5
321	Office and accounting machines	.283	.148	.069	66.3
390	Toys, amusements, and sporting goods	.260	.113	−.095	96.4
151	Apparel and accessories	.214	.016	−.216	1,014.9
351	Motor vehicles	.204	.087	.174	658.6

		Industries Employing Top 10% of Workers by Export Supply Ratio[c]			
		X/S	$M/(M + S)$	Log Wage Premium[b]	Employment (1,000s)
352	Aircraft and aircraft parts	.438	.051	.153	527.0
312	Construction machinery	.318	.059	.110	346.7
322	Electronic computing equipment	.263	.115	.083	354.4
310	Engines and turbines	.252	.053	.227	95.6
371	Scientific instruments	.235	.111	.020	264.4
361	Railroad equipment	.208	.070	.194	25.0
191	Agricultural chemicals	.183	.055	.035	45.9
192	Industrial chemicals	.173	.081	.169	322.6

Source: NBER trade–immigration–labor market data set (available from the labor studies group of the National Bureau of Economic Research, Cambridge, Mass.); and Dickens-Katz (1987a) industry data set.

[a]The employment weights used in calculations for the top 10 percent import workers are actual employment for the top eight industries and 67,200 for motor vehicles.

[b]Log wage premiums are calculated from separate regressions on union and nonunion samples from the full year 1983 CPS. The log wage premium for an industry equals $\{[(UD + 0.192) \cdot UCOV] + NUD \cdot (1 - UCOV)\}$, where UD is the estimated industry wage premium for union workers, NUD is the premium for nonunion workers, UCOV is the fraction of workers in the industry covered by union agreements, and 0.192 is the estimated union-nonunion wage differential for the full-year 1983 CPS from Katz (1986).

[c]The employment weights used in calculations for the top 10 percent export workers are actual employment for the top seven industries and 185,800 for industrial chemicals.

Table 3.5   **Characteristics of Typical Import and Export Workers in U.S. Manufacturing Industries, 1983**

	(1) Typical Manufacturing Worker	(2) Top 10% Imports	(3) Top 10% Exports	(4) Typical Import Worker	(5) Typical Export Worker
Average hourly wage for production workers	8.88 (1.93)	6.03	10.37	8.36	9.60
Log wage premium for all workers	.00 (.115)	−.163	.116	−.022	.054
Log wage premium for nonunion workers	.00 (.10)	−.135	.128	−.015	.059
Log wage premium for union workers	.00 (.12)	−.214	.071	−.051	.035
Percentage female	33.7 (18.5)	68.5	24.8	40.3	28.2
Percentage immigrants	8.1 (4.3)	17.0	6.6	10.0	7.3
Percentage black	10.3 (3.6)	12.3	7.1	10.7	8.7
Percentage unionized	29.8 (13.9)	27.4	28.0	30.1	29.7
Research and development expenditures as a percentage of sales	2.9 (3.5)	1.1	8.7	3.1	5.5
Percentage production workers	68.2 (13.1)	79.8	52.1	70.9	62.4
Average years of schooling	13.1 (.8)	12.0	14.1	12.9	13.5
Value added per worker (thousands of dollars)	50.5 (22.6)	28.8	59.3	45.4	54.2
$M/(M + S)$ (in percentages)	9.7 (8.2)	27.0	7.8	18.5	10.0
X/S (in percentages)	9.0 (9.2)	4.4	30.6	9.0	18.5

Note: Columns 1, 2, and 3 are three-digit census industry averages weighted by industry employment. Import and export rankings are based on 1983 trade data. Columns 2 and 3 present average characteristics of the top 10 percent of workers by industry $M/(M + S)$ and X/S respectively. Column 4 presents three-digit census industries weighted by industry employment times M/S. Column 5 presents three-digit census industries weighted by industry employment times X/S. The numbers in parentheses are standard deviations.

Sources: Dickens-Katz 1983 industry data set described in Dickens and Katz (1987a); and NBER trade–immigration–labor market industry data set.

research and development than import-intensive industries. Export-intensive industries devote 8.7 percent of sales to research and development, compared to 1.1 percent for import-intensive industries. The average worker in export-intensive industry has fourteen years of schooling, compared with 12 years for the average worker in import-intensive industry. Import-intensive industries also disproportionately employ women, blacks, and immigrants, whereas export industries employ these workers to less than the average extent.

The comparisons in columns 4 and 5 of the characteristics of the industries employing typical export and import workers suggest all the same qualitative conclusions as the more extreme comparisons of export- and import-intensive industries. Industry differences are attenuated because, in many cases, export- and import-intensive industries coincide as a result of the importance of intraindustry trade. Nonetheless, the wage differential between the typical worker in import- and export-intensive industry is about 8 percent.

These results suggest that, for the United States, policies that succeed in promoting trade and increasing the volume of both exports and imports will tend to raise welfare by moving workers from lower- to higher-wage industries. The gains are potentially significant. For example, the estimates here suggest that eliminating a manufacturing trade deficit of $150 billion by raising exports rather than by reducing imports would increase labor rents by at least $12 billion. If export-intensive industries were expanded relative to import-intensive industries, the gains could be up to three times as great.

3.3.1 International Comparisons

We have already documented that the wage structure is very similar in all countries. It follows that there is no way in which all countries can dispro-portionately export goods produced with high-wage labor. A reasonable con-jecture is that one concomitant of increased economic development is increased comparative advantage in the production of primary-sector goods. To examine this possibility, table 3.6 presents evidence on the American wage premium of import- and export-intensive industries for a number of countries along with information on the American wage premium associated with the industries employing typical export and import workers.

The data provide initial support for our conjecture about patterns of economic development. Korea imports goods produced by high-wage indus-tries and exports goods produced by low-wage industries. This is not simply a consequence of their abundance of low-skilled labor. The wage premia used in these comparisons are estimated controlling for measured labor quality, and the evidence cited in section 3.1 above suggests that they do not primarily reflect unobserved aspects of skill. Most of the developed countries appear to export relatively high-wage premium goods while importing relatively low-wage goods. It is interesting that the difference in wage premiums between high- and low-net-export industries is particularly pronounced in Germany and Japan.

The observation that specialization in high-wage industries is correlated with per-capita income might be taken as evidence in favor of policies encouraging the growth of these industries. Such an inference would be premature, however. It seems plausible that improved technology, manage-ment, or worker skills would lead countries to shift toward capital intensive industries requiring investment in job-specific human capital and highly

Table 3.6   **U.S. Log Wage Premia of Typical Import and Export Workers in Manufacturing in Nine Countries, 1983**

Country	(1) Typical Manufacturing Worker[a]	(2) Typical Import Worker[b]	(3) Typical Export Worker[c]	(4) Top 10% Net Export Worker	(5) Bottom 10% Net Export Worker
Australia	.006	.019	.063	.132	.034
Chile	− .024	− .000	.017	.013	.055
France	.016	.037	.053	.110	.020
Germany	.045	.021	.051	.145	− .106
Japan	.002	− .012	.030	.134	− .113
South Korea	− .039	.020	− .089	− .216	.077
Sweden	.030	.001	.035	.053	− .045
United Kingdom	.014	.013	.027	.082	− .128
United States	.000	− .004	.033	.051	− .170

Note: This table utilizes data from eighteen ISIC manufacturing industries: 321, 322, 323, 324, 331, 332, 341, 342, 351, 355, 361, 362, 371, 372, 381, 382, 383, 384.

Sources: Trade flow data on an ISIC basis were provided by Robert Stern of the University of Michigan. The U.S. industry log wage premium variable aggregates using employment weights the variable described in n. b below of table 4 from three-digit census industries to ISIC industries. Employment data are from *Industrial Statistics Yearbook, 1984,* vol. 1 (New York: United Nations, Department of International Economic and Social Affairs, Statistical Office, 1986).

[a]Three-digit ISIC U.S. industry log wage premia weighted by each country's industry employment.

[b]Three-digit ISIC U.S. industry log wage premia weighted by each country's industry employment times M/S.

[c]Three-digit ISIC U.S. industry log wage premia weighted by each country's industry employment times X/S.

motivated workers. Moving workers from low- to high-wage industries is likely to lead to increases in static allocative efficiency. Whether it would lead to increases in rates of growth is more problematic.

3.3.2   Trends in American Trade

Discussions of American competitiveness have differed on whether the changing trade patterns of recent years are simply the consequence of aberrant exchange rate movements brought about by macroeconomic policies and speculative forces or are instead the result of long-term structural deterioration. A central issue in the deindustrialization debate is whether the United States has suffered particularly severe competitive losses in "good industries," variously defined as those that emphasize technology or have high value added per worker. The analysis in the preceding section suggests that examining the relative performance of high- and low-wage industries probably provides the best way of getting at this issue.

Assuming fixed ratios of employment to shipments, table 3.7 indicates how changing trade patterns have affected employment in high- and low-wage

Table 3.7   **The Direct Effect of International Trade on Employment by Wage Class, U.S. Manufacturing, 1960–84**

	Change in Employment (in thousands) From[b]:		
Wage Premium Class[a]	Imports	Exports	Net Exports
Overall manufacturing:			
1960–84	−2,621.3	1,107.1	−1,514.2
1980–84	−1,248.0	−168.4	1,416.5
1970–80	−941.5	946.7	5.2
1960–70	−431.7	328.9	−102.9
Lowest quartile:			
1960–84	−1,021.7	71.8	−950.0
1980–84	−576.2	−60.7	−636.9
1970–80	−307.6	113.3	−194.3
1960–70	−138.0	19.2	−118.8
Second quartile:			
1960–84	−457.2	323.0	−134.1
1980–84	−217.7	10.1	−207.6
1970–80	−177.5	242.8	65.3
1960–70	−61.9	70.1	8.2
Third quartile:			
1960–84	−547.8	271.5	−276.2
1980–84	−220.5	−70.1	−290.6
1970–80	−229.9	251.5	21.6
1960–70	97.4	90.1	−7.2
Highest quartile:			
1960–84	−594.7	440.8	−153.9
1980–84	−233.7	−47.6	−281.3
1970–80	−226.6	339.1	112.5
1960–70	−134.4	149.4	15.0

[a]Industries were ranked by the industry wage premium variable defined in n. b of table 3.4 and placed into quartiles on the basis of 1983 employment.

[b]The loss in employment from imports for industry i from period t to t' is defined as $[(M_{it}' - M_{it}) \cdot (L/Q_i)]$, where M is imports and $(L/Q)_i$ is the ratio of employment to output in industry i in 1984. Imports and output are measured in quantities with their nominal values deflated by the four-digit SIC industry shipments deflator from the Annual Survey of Manufactures. The gain in employment from exports is analogously defined with exports replacing imports. The trade flow, employment, and output data are from the NBER trade–immigration–labor market data set.

industries. Between 1960 and 1980, the number of jobs displaced by imports was approximately equal to the number of jobs created by exports. Particularly during the 1970s, increased imports led to a reallocation of labor out of the lowest-wage jobs in the manufacturing sector. Increased U.S. exports led to increased employment in high-wage sectors of the economy. During the 1980s, the fraction of workers employed in producing tradable goods declined as the trade deficit increased. Between 1980 and 1984, the last year for which we have data available, the increase in the trade deficit was associated with a reduction of 1.4 million workers producing traded manufacturing goods. Over

600,000, or 43 percent, of these workers worked in the quartile of industries that paid the lowest wages. This reflects the substantial increase in import penetration in industries such as apparel during the early 1980s.

These results conflict dramatically with popular stereotypes suggesting that the United States is being forced away from cutting-edge industries. We suspect that the popular misconception results from the fact that traded goods industries as a whole pay higher wages than the rest of the economy. In a period when the trade deficit rises, good jobs are lost. But these jobs are likely to come back when the trade deficit returns to balance.[23] There appears to be little evidence through 1984 of relative deterioration in the high-wage portion of the American traded goods sector.

These patterns should not be surprising. Postulate that "cutting-edge industries" pay wage premia. Following the discussion of Krugman and Baldwin (1987), assume that other nations are catching up with the United States. They then make incursions into the least progressive sectors of our economy, causing U.S. workers to move toward high-wage industries.

3.4 Conclusions

The analysis in the preceding sections suggests that imperfections in the labor market may have at least as much significance as imperfections in product markets for trade policies. Labor market rents earned by workers in high-wage industries are very large relative to plausible estimates of monopoly profits. Unlike the case of product market imperfections, where optimal policies are not robust to small changes in assumptions about corporate strategies, the theoretical case for policies that promote high-wage premium industries is reasonably robust. Given that export industries in the United States have considerably higher wages than import-competing industries even after controlling for observed worker skill measures, our theoretical arguments suggest that export-promoting policies are much more likely to promote economic welfare than import-competing policies.

There are of course a number of other considerations that must be weighed before any policy judgments are made. First, following much of the literature, we have abstracted from the possibility that some industries generate technological externalities. If such externalities are generated and are limited by national borders, there is a strong case for encouraging the growth of externality-generating industries. Second, if wages are very sensitive to the rents earned by firms, it is possible that product market effects are more important than we have suggested but show up as labor market rents.[24] Third, we have ignored input-output considerations in our discussion, implicitly assuming that all output is produced in the industry making a given shipment.[25] Fourth, we have ignored political considerations that might lead activist policymakers to take steps that reduce rather than increase efficiency once the decision to undertake industrial policy was made.

Despite these limitations, we believe that our results strengthen the economic case against import-protecting policies and for export-promoting policies. In future research, it would be useful to employ a general equilibrium model such as those developed by Shoven and his collaborators to explore more precisely the effect of various policies in the presence of noncompetitive wage differentials. Of particular interest would be a reevaluation of the 1986 Tax Reform Act, which appears to have heavily burdened the high-wage durable goods manufacturing sector of the economy.

Notes

1. An analysis of labor rents and trade policies paralleling ours in many respects is presented in Dickens and Lang (1988). Our analysis differs in contrasting the relative importance of labor market and product market imperfections, focusing on the manufacturing sector, and making international comparisons of wages and trade flows. A more extensive treatment of the topics covered in this paper is available in Katz and Summers (1989).

2. A prominent exception to this criticism is Krugman (1984), who emphasizes the potential importance of wage differentials caused by unions.

3. The presumption that labor rents are much greater than rents received by firms does not necessarily mean that product market imperfections are a minor source of rents. A large fraction of the rents earned by workers may arise from the ability of both union and nonunion labor to share in product market rents. For example, Salinger (1984) presents evidence indicating that union labor captures most of the monopoly rents in heavily unionized industries.

4. This conclusion is hardly new. It was noted by Adam Smith and highlighted by Sumner Slichter (1950), and it has been emphasized by institutionally oriented labor economists for many years.

5. Although the CPS is partially a panel data set, only individuals in outgoing rotation groups are asked about earnings. Further, people exit the sample only once a year. Thus, all observations reflect unique individuals.

6. We eliminated employees who reported earning less than $1.00 an hour or greater than $250 an hour.

7. The industry labor cost and wage data are reported in the National Income and Product Accounts (NIPAs) and were previously utilized in Krueger and Summers (1988).

8. Since the NIPA and CPS industry classification schemes do not match exactly, caution should be taken in comparing the results in col. 3.

9. The nonunion sample consists of workers not covered by collective bargaining agreements. The results are almost identical when the union membership is used as the criterion for excluding a worker from the nonunion sample.

10. The estimates are taken from table 2 of Krueger and Summers (1988).

11. In contrast, Murphy and Welch (1988) document that the earnings of "skilled" (college-educated) workers rose dramatically relative to those of less-educated workers from 1979 to 1985. They provide some suggestive evidence that increased net imports in manufacturing may have played an important role in the widening of skill differentials.

12. For contrasting findings using matched March CPS data, see Murphy and Topel (1987). Gibbons and Katz (1987) discuss in detail potential reasons for differences in findings in alternative longitudinal data sets.

13. At the cost of some complexity, the special assumption that capital is not used in producing secondary-sector output could be relaxed. It does capture the stylized fact noted in the previous section that high-wage sectors tend to be capital intensive.

14. For an explicit derivation of a $d(L^P)$ schedule from an efficiency wage model, see Bulow and Summers (1986).

15. The optimal subsidy will be set at $d(L^{P'})$, where $L^{P'}$ is the level of primary-sectory employment at which $p(Y^P)F(K^P,L^P) = w_0$.

16. We focus on the "small open-economy case" to highlight the implications of wage differentials for trade policy. In the case of open economies large enough to affect the prices at which they buy and sell, there are traditional optimal tariff considerations as well. These suggest the desirability of taxing rather than subsidizing exports when expanding exports can lead to at least a moderate terms-of-trade deterioration. In this case, our analysis of employment subsidies is correct if it is assumed that optimal tariffs (taxes) based on these traditional considerations are already in place.

17. This point has also been made by Dickens and Lang (1988).

18. This point is well known from the development literature on project evaluation (e.g., Sah and Stiglitz 1985).

19. Since each new job created in the primary sector removes $1/(1 - u)$ workers from secondary employment, and since $w^0/(1 - u)$ w^P, the social opportunity cost of labor for an additional job in the primary sector equals the marginal product of labor in the primary sector.

20. For a more detailed discussion of wait unemployment and the measurement of the social opportunity cost of labor, see Sah and Stiglitz (1985) and the references cited therein.

21. The issue is a complex because policies that tax high-wage workers for the benefit of low-wage workers will, at least in some efficiency wage models, have perverse effects on the composition of output by reducing the relative utility of primary-sector workers. Thus, income redistribution policies may undo the allocative effects of subsidies to sectors that pay wage premia.

22. For consideration of the relation between U.S. trade and wages outside the manufacturing sector, see Dickens and Lang (1988).

23. On the other hand, for an argument that transitory exchange rate shocks may permanently affect an economy's ability to compete in some industries, see Baldwin and Krugman (1986).

24. Rent-sharing considerations are examined in detail in Katz and Summers (1989).

25. Dickens and Lang (1988) find that taking into account input-output relations does not greatly affect one's conclusions concerning the cross-sectional relations among wage premiums and trade flows in the United States.

References

Akerlof, George A. 1984. Gift exchange and efficiency wages: Four views. *American Economic Review* 74(May):79–83.

Baldwin, Richard, and Paul Krugman. 1986. Persistent trade effects of large exchange rate shocks. NBER Working Paper no. 2017. Cambridge, Mass.: National Bureau of Economic Research, September.

————. 1987a. Industrial policy and international competition in wide-bodied jet aircraft. Cambridge, Mass.: National Bureau of Economic Research, June. Mimeo.

————. 1987b. Modelling international competition in high technology industries: Lessons from aircrafts and semiconductors. NBER Conference Paper. Cambridge, Mass.: National Bureau of Economic Research, September.

Bhagwati, Jagdish N., and V. K. Ramaswami. 1963. Domestic distortions, tariffs and the theory of the optimum subsidy. *Journal of Political Economy* 71(February):44–50.

Bhagwati, Jagdish N., and T. N. Srinivasan. 1983. *Lectures on international trade.* Cambridge, Mass.: MIT Press.

Brander, James A., and Barbara J. Spencer. 1983. International R&D rivalry and industrial strategy. *Review of Economic Studies* 50:707–22.

————. 1984. Tariff protection and imperfect competition. In *Monopolistic competition and international trade,* ed. H. Kierzkowski. Oxford: Oxford University Press.

Bulow, Jeremy, and Lawrence H. Summers. 1986. A theory of dual labor markets with application to industrial policy, discrimination, and Keynesian unemployment. *Journal of Labor Economics* 4(July):376–414.

Dickens, William T., and Lawrence F. Katz. 1987a. Inter-industry wage differences and industry characteristics. In *Unemployment and the structure of labor markets,* ed. K. Lang and J. Leonard. Oxford: Basil Blackwell.

————. 1987b. Inter-industry wage differences and theories of wage determination. NBER Working Paper no. 2271. Cambridge, Mass.: National Bureau of Economic Research, June.

————. 1988. Further notes on the inter-industry wage structure. Harvard University, August. Mimeo.

Dickens, William T., and Kevin Lang. 1988. Why it matters what we trade. In *The dynamics of trade and employment,* ed. L. Tyson, W. Dickens, and J. Zysman. Cambridge, Mass.: Ballinger.

Dixit, Avinash. 1987. Strategic aspects of trade policy. In *Advances in economic theory—fifth world congress,* ed. Truman Bewley. Cambridge: Cambridge University Press.

————. 1988. Optimal trade and industrial policy for the U.S. automobile industry. In *Empirical research in international trade,* ed. R. Feenstra. Cambridge, Mass.: MIT Press.

Doeringer, Peter, and Michael J. Piore. 1971. *Internal labor markets and manpower analysis.* Lexington, Mass.: D. C. Heath.

Freeman, Richard B., and Lawrence F. Katz. 1987. Industrial wage and employment determination in an open economy. Paper presented at the NBER Conference on Immigration, Trade, and the Labor Market, Cambridge, Mass., September.

Gibbons, Robert S., and Lawrence F. Katz. 1987. Learning, mobility, and inter-industry wage differences. Massachusetts Institute of Technology, December. Mimeo.

Hagen, E. 1958. An economic justification for protectionism. *Quarterly Journal of Economics* 62(November):496–514.

Harberger, Arnold C. 1971. On measuring the social opportunity cost of labour. *International Labour Review* 103:559–79.

Harris, J., and M. Todaro. 1970. Migration, unemployment and development: A two-sector analysis. *American Economic Review* 60(March):126–43.

Holzer, Harry, Lawrence F. Katz, and Alan B. Krueger. 1988. Job queues and wages: Some new evidence on the minimum wage and inter-industry wage structure. NBER Working Paper no. 2561. Cambridge, Mass.: National Bureau of Economic Research.

Katz, Lawrence F. 1986. Efficiency wage theories: A partial evaluation. In *NBER Macroeconomics Annual 1986*, vol. 1, ed. Stanley Fisher, 235–76. Cambridge, Mass.: MIT Press.

Katz, Lawrence F., and Lawrence H. Summers. 1989. Industry rents: Evidence and implications. *Brookings Papers on Economic Activity, Microeconomics 1989* (in press).

Krueger, Alan B. 1987. Ownership, agency, and wages: An empirical analysis. Princeton University. Mimeo.

Krueger, Alan B., and Lawrence H. Summers. 1987. Reflections on the inter-industry wage structure. In *Unemployment and the structure of labor markets*, ed. K. Lang and J. Leonard. Oxford: Basil Blackwell.

————. 1988. Efficiency wages and the inter-industry wage structure. *Econometrica* 56(March):259–94.

Krugman, Paul. 1984. The U.S. reponse to foreign industrial targeting. *Brookings Papers on Economic Activity*, no. 1:77–121.

————. 1986. *Strategic trade policy and the new international economics.* Cambridge, Mass.: MIT Press.

Krugman, Paul, and Richard E. Baldwin. 1987. The persistence of the U.S. trade deficit. *Brookings Papers on Economic Activity*, no. 1:1–44.

Magee, S. P. 1976. *International trade and distortions in factor markets.* New York: Marcel Dekker.

Mars, Gerald. 1982. *Cheats at work.* London: Unwin.

Mathewson, Stanley B. 1969. *Restriction of output among unorganized workers.* Carbondale: Southern Illinois University Press.

Murphy, Kevin M., and Robert H. Topel. 1987. Unemployment, risk, and earnings. In *Unemployment and the structure of labor markets*, ed. K. Lang and J. Leonard. Oxford: Basil Blackwell.

Murphy, Kevin M., and Finis Welch. 1988. The structure of wages. Los Angeles: Unicon Research Corp. Mimeo.

Pencavel, John. 1970. *An analysis of the quit rate in American manufacturing.* Princeton, N.J.: Industrial Relations Section, Princeton University.

Sah, Raaj, and Joseph E. Stiglitz. 1985. The social cost of labor and project evaluation: A general approach. *Journal of Public Economics* 28:135–61.

Salinger, Michael A. 1984. Tobin's q, unionization, and the concentration-profits relationship. *Rand Journal of Economics* 15(Summer):159–70.

Shapiro, Carl, and Joseph E. Stiglitz. 1984. Equilibrium unemployment as a worker discipline device. *American Economic Review* 74(June):433–44.

Slichter, Sumner. 1950. Notes on the structure of wages. *Review of Economics and Statistics* 32:80–91.

Stiglitz, Joseph E. 1985. Equilibrium wage distributions. *Economic Journal* 95(September):595–618.

————. 1987. The causes and consequences of the dependence of quality on price. *Journal of Economic Literature* 25(March):1–48.

Weiss, Andrew. 1980. Job queues and layoffs in labor markets with flexible wages. *Journal of Political Economy* 88(June):526–38

Comment   Kenneth A. Froot

Lawrence F. Katz and Lawrence H. Summers have written a very nice paper. Its principle point is to remind "new wave" trade economists that factor market distortions are likely to be an important consideration in designing commercial policy. Of course, factor market distortions already occupy a prominent place in the traditional trade literature. Stephen Magee's (1969) famous survey cites over one hundred papers and books going back to Cairnes (1874), Ohlin (1933), and Viner (1964). It is probably fair to say that our current understanding about the first- to the nth best treatment of wage distortions in the absence of product market distortions has not changed much since Bhagwati (1971).

Katz and Summers in a sense rejuvenate this older literature. They argue that, in fact, product market distortions, which are the focus of much new wave trade theory, are likely to be small in comparison with labor market distortions. They provide an impressive array of evidence from the United States and a number of other countries that (1) intersectoral wage differentials are large, with a standard deviation of 13–18 percent; (2) the differentials are highly persistent over time and very similar across countries; and (3) export industries tend to have higher wages than import industries. The paper then argues that these differentials do in fact constitute distortions or rents. In other words, intersectoral wage differentials cannot be explained by unobserved differences in the quality of workers or of jobs. Katz and Summers also review briefly the efficiency wage explanation for why such differentials persist.

Whether these differentials are noncompetitive in nature is the subject of debate in labor economics and could not possibly be resolved here. I want to focus instead on the paper's arguments for intervention, taking for granted that the differentials do in fact represent distortions and assuming, as Katz and Summers do, that there are no product market distortions. In short, under these circumstances the paper suggests that intersectoral wage differentials may justify export-promoting policies to improve U.S. welfare.

To study the effects of export promotion, Katz and Summers build a two-sector economy in which labor in the "primary" sector earns a wage higher than the wage in the numeraire sector. The wage premium is a rent. In equilibrium, when the wage is set to the marginal product of labor, the output of the primary good is too low. The first-best allocation of labor can be achieved by a subsidy to employment in the primary sector. In a closed economy, the price of the primary good falls as output expands, yielding a gain in consumer surplus.

Kenneth A. Froot is Ford International Assistant Professor of Management at the Sloan School, Massachusetts Institute of Technology, and a faculty research fellow at the National Bureau of Economic Research.

Katz and Summers turn to consider this small economy once it is opened internationally. The effect of trade in their model is to fix the price of the primary good. I wonder whether the fixed-price assumption is appropriate. First, most of the discussion in the paper centers on wage differentials and trade policy in the United States, where the small-country assumption clearly does not hold. Second, manufactured goods, which form the bulk of traded goods in the United States, are often highly differentiated. Even the small country that produces these goods in a perfectly competitive export sector will face declining international demand.

It is easy to show that the case for export promotion relies heavily on the fixed-price assumption. As I show below, a relatively mild terms-of-trade deterioration due to an export expansion program is likely to be enough to reverse the paper's policy conclusions. Ignoring these effects may lead to an overly optimistic view of the scope for intervention. At one point, Katz and Summers suggest that home subsidies that are matched by foreign subsidies are likely to raise welfare in both countries. This result is in contrast to the negative effects on home-country welfare of foreign retaliation in the presence of imperfect competition. Katz and Summers's assertion will depend critically on the terms-of-trade effects of the subsidies and on whether the home country is a net importer or exporter of the primary good.

To demonstrate how sensitive the results are to the terms-of-trade effects, consider a version of the Katz and Summers model. To make the point as starkly and simply as possible, I will assume that the country exports all its primary-good output. The social planner faces a noncompetitive wage distortion and must decide whether to subsidize or tax output in the primary sector. Using Katz and Summers's notation, the planner maximizes the value of total output less wage costs:

$$\max_{s} Y^n + PY^p - w_0 L - PY^{p,}$$

where $L = L^p + L^n$ is the country's total labor force, P is the price of primary output paid by foreigners, the price of numeraire output is one, and s is the subsidy rate. Note that the assumption that primary output is entirely exported makes a production subsidy equal to an export subsidy. Note also that the social planner evaluates the cost of labor at its opportunity cost—the cost of labor in the numeraire sector, w_0. To keep things simple, assume that labor is the only input into production of the primary good, $Y^p = f(L^p)$. (This implies that a production subsidy is also equivalent to a subsidy to employment.) Using the rest of the model as specified in Katz and Summers, we have the standard first-order condition:

(1) $Pf_L(1/\epsilon^p + 1) - w = 0,$

where ϵ^p is the price elasticity of foreign primary product demand.[1] Primary-product producers are on their labor demand curve, given the level of the subsidy, s, and size of the wage differential, d:

(2)
$$Pf_L = \left(\frac{1 + d}{1 + s}\right)w_0.$$

Combining equations (1) and (2) yields the optimal export subsidy:

(3)
$$s^* = d^* - \frac{1 + d^*}{\epsilon^{p^*}},$$

where the asterisk indicates the variable is evaluated at s, the optimal subsidy. Katz and Summers find that a reasonable estimate for d is about 0.25. This implies that, if the price elasticity of exports is five, the optimal subsidy is exactly zero. Most reasonable estimates of export-price elasticities are much less than five. In this case, the optimal policy is an export *tax*. Katz and Summers suggest that, by eliminating the $150 billion U.S. trade deficit entirely through export expansion, U.S. welfare would increase by $12 billion.[2] If this enormous 60 percent expansion of U.S. exports resulted in an 8 percent decline in export prices—an elasticity of roughly eight—the welfare gain would be completely negated. If the price elasticity is lower, as it no doubt is in industries such as aircraft, this method of reducing the trade deficit would reduce welfare, even in the presence of wage distortions.

Notice that this standard result ignores imperfect competition in the primary-product market, which is what justifies export promotion in newer trade models. I do not think that export sectors are perfectly competitive and that the right policy for the United States would be a tax on exports. Rather, my point is that, even in the presence of wage distortions, most arguments for export promotion will ultimately rely on some product market distortion. Indeed, it is quite likely that these factor and product market distortions interact in practice. For example, unions might bid wages up in order to absorb profits generated by imperfect competition in the product market. A more sophisticated theory might even have organized labor in an oligopolistic industry bid up wages not only to absorb current profits but also to restrict output. By forcing firms to up their labor demand curves, unions could reproduce the monopolistic outcome while absorbing all the profits. In such cases, the right policies will be those that undo the underlying product market imperfections. Causality could also run in the opposite direction. Competing firms might find product market collusion more credible if they face similar factor market distortions. Then the right policies will target the labor market distortions. The Katz and Summers paper provides an important stepping stone to this kind of topic.

Notes

1. I assume that the cross-price elasticity is zero.
2. This is $150 \times 0.8 = 12$, where 0.8 is the difference in wages between the average export worker and the average import worker.

References

Bhagwati, J. 1971. The generalized theory of distortions and welfare. In *Trade, balance of payments, and growth: Papers in international economics in honor of Charles P. Kindleberger.*

Cairnes, J. E. 1874. *Some leading principles of political economy.* London: Macmillan.

Magee, Stephen P. 1969. Factor market distortions and the pure theory of international trade. Ph.D. diss., Massachusetts Institute of Technology.

Ohlin, Bertil. 1933. *Interregional and international trade.* Cambridge, Mass.: Harvard University Press.

Viner, Jacob. 1964. *Studies in the theory of international trade.* London: George Allen & Unwin

Comment   Raquel Fernandez

The main contribution of this paper is to bring to the attention of trade theorists a great deal of what is known about interindustry wage differentials and a discussion of some of the possible reasons for its causes. The authors quite convincingly show that the wage differential is still large when observed characteristics are controlled for and that job attributes on their own are unlikely to explain the wage differential. Their arguments against unmeasured labor quality are somewhat weaker, but their most convincing counterargument is the fact that wages are correlated across occupations in an industry and that there is no good reason to expect an industry that needs especially good engineers also to need especially good secretaries. Most of the alternative efficiency wage (EW) hypotheses, however, are also unable to account for the correlation of wages across occupations in an industry. As Katz and Summers (K&S) admit, in order to explain this fact it is necessary to marry some sort of Akerlof/egalitarianism type of story to an EW story. But it is also possible to combine an equity story to either unobserved job attributes or labor quality, which would then allow either alternative hypothesis to command more explanatory power than before.

Efficiency Implications of Wage Subsidies

Acknowledging the diversity of reasons that may underlie interindustry wage differentials, K&S nonetheless state that the implications of noncompetitive wage differentials among nonunion workers for trade policies do not depend on their precise cause. Is this really true? Consider the following scenario. Suppose that there are two industries and two occupations: managers

Raquel Fernandez is assistant professor of economics at Boston University and a faculty research fellow at the National Bureau of Economic Research.

The author wishes to thank Jacob Glazer, Michael Manove, Andy Weiss, and especially Hector Fernandez and Kevin Lang for helpful suggestions.

and engineers. For simplicity, assume that the marginal product of labor in each occupation is independent of the number of workers employed in the other occupation. Furthermore, suppose that engineers in industry 1 earn higher wages than engineers in industry 2 (i.e., $w_2 = w_1 + \alpha$) because work conditions for engineers in industry 1 are more unattractive. Let us argue, moreover, that managers in industry 1 also earn higher wages than managers in industry 2 for sociological/social equity types of reasons. Concretely, let us assume that each percentage increase in the wage of engineers must be met by an equal percentage increase in the wage of managers. What would be the effect if, following K&S's prescription, we were to subsidize all employment in industry 1? The effect of a wage subsidy s is shown in figure 3C.1. The employment of engineers in industry 1, previously socially efficient, would increase, creating an allocative distortion in the market for engineers. The wage of engineers also increases (but by less than the full amount of the subsidy). More surprisingly, however, while the subsidy would tend to increase the employment of managers in industry 1, thus increasing efficiency (since the value of the marginal product of managers is greater in industry 1), the increased wage of engineers sets up a countervailing force since the wage of managers must increase by at least the same percentage. If managers' wages had originally been greater than those of engineers, then it is possible, as shown in figure 3C.1, that the economy could end up with less managers employed in industry 1 than there were prior to the subsidy, thus increasing inefficiency in both labor markets. Note that this effect is not due to the assumption of the way that the market for engineers functions. Suppose that the higher wages for engineers in industry 1 were really a result of some EW story. A subsidy would now create an improvement in the allocation of engineers, but it is still possible that the employment of managers in industry 1 could fall and that overall efficiency would worsen by a sufficient degree.

There are other reasons why a labor subsidy might be counterproductive. Schumpeterian considerations, such as the hypothesis that the existence of rents causes firms to be less innovative since there is less competitive pressure, imply that subsidizing high-wage firms may also have unfavorable effects on the effort that firms expend on research and development activities. Indeed, the positive empirical correlation between rents and high wages may simply imply that the distortion is occurring in the product market and then being passed on to the labor market through some bargaining mechanism. In this case, a first-best policy would probably imply some intervention on the product rather than on the labor market side. On the whole, while many scenarios do have a high wage being indicative of a higher value of the marginal product of labor and result in a labor subsidy improving allocative efficiency, the fact that the implications of bargaining in the workplace and of the strategic interactions of the product market with the labor market have only recently received attention leads me to be rather more wary than the authors about the efficiency implications of a labor subsidy.

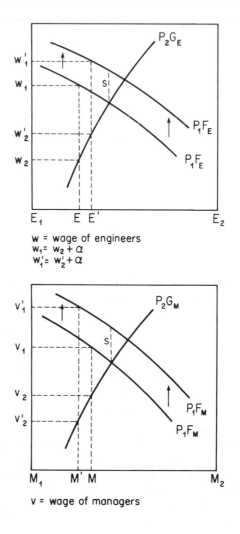

w = wage of engineers
$w_1 = w_2 + \alpha$
$w_1' = w_2' + \alpha$

v = wage of managers

Fig. 3C.1

Welfare Consequences

The welfare consequences of labor subsidies, on the other hand, have the property in almost every plausible scenario of not being Pareto improving and, moreover, worsening the distribution of income. In the example discussed by K&S, it is necessary to assume that workers are homogeneous and that the movement of workers between sectors is characterized by a Markovian process in order that a labor subsidy be Pareto improving. The second assumption is especially objectionable, and any relaxation of it results in a labor subsidy not being Pareto improving. Nor can one wave the usual magic wand and appeal to some income distributional mechanism to take care of this redistributive aspect. Indeed, one of the main benefits of a model in which labor market distortions are endogenous is that it allows one to examine the feasibility of different redistributive measures. Whereas the study of labor market interactions with trade often assumes that the labor market distortion is exogenous (e.g., rigid exogenous wage differentials) and thus is able to claim that a system of lump-sum taxes and subsidies will take care of compensation problems, the taxation of workers in sector 1 in an EW model reduces those workers' after-tax income (presumably what they care about) and must be counteracted by the firm by an increase in the wage in order to leave the after-tax income at its optimal level. Consequently, unless firms are generating a sufficient amount of rent that may be taxed without creating a distortion, the tax to pay for the wage subsidy must fall on sector 2 workers, thus serving to worsen the distribution of income. This seems a strong reason to recommend against the subsidization of employment in high-wage industries.

Strategic Trade Policy Implications

Katz and Summers observe that the wage differential between the typical worker in import- and export-intensive industries is about 8 percent (in favor of the export-sector worker). This suggests to them that, for the United States, policies that succeed in promoting trade and increases in the volume of export and imports will tend to raise welfare by moving workers from the lower- to the higher-wage industries. Once again, the aforementioned caveats regarding welfare apply. Moreover, Dickens and Lang (1988), who include the agricultural and service sector in their study, conclude that the average wage surplus in the export sector relative to the import sector is approximately equal. Furthermore, arguing in favor of export subsidies is potentially dangerous. Retaliation in the form of a tariff that, say, leaves the total quantity of the good imported by the foreign country at the same level it was at prior to the subsidy simply allows the foreign country to capture the revenue associated with the tariff without producing any compensatory allocational effects at home. Labor subsidies, while not only being first best, also have less of a chance of being retaliated against since GATT rules may allow subsidies whose primary purpose is not seen as expanding exports.

The Deindustrialization Debate

Katz and Summers attempt to debunk the idea that the United States is losing its cutting-edge, high-wage industries. Although they note that, during the period 1980–84, the increase in the trade deficit was associated with a reduction of 1.4 million workers producing traded manufacturing goods, they do not find this to be a cause for concern since these jobs will come back when the trade deficit returns to balance. Their faith on this eventuality rests on the transversality condition: the United States cannot run a trade deficit forever. Accepting this, nonetheless, there is no a priori reason to believe that, by the time the United States eventually does run a trade surplus, the composition of exports will still have a preponderance of high-wage occupations. That is, in order to be able to discuss the legitimacy of the deindustrialization arguments sensibly, one must be able to say something about what our comparative advantage will be in the future. Standard neoclassical economic theory, however, has very little to tell us about the dynamic determinants of a country's comparative advantage. It may very well be that the latter depends very heavily on the policies that our and foreign governments follow today. Hence, we may interpret the deindustrialization debate as telling us that we must worry about the dynamic consequences of the trade deficit.

General Considerations

The factors that result in efficiency wages may also produce other important distortions. The hiring of other productive factors will also be distorted. More important, it may be that if, as in some EW stories, firms fear the power of workers to disrupt the workplace (say, by destroying costly capital equipment) those firms are led to expend less resources than what is socially optimal in technological innovation or perhaps to place too great an emphasis on labor-saving technology. Hence, another avenue that the authors may find interesting to explore is whether wage differentials are more significant in some countries than in others and thus whether social institutions, worker-management schemes, profit-sharing mechanisms, and so on are capable of playing a role that firms in the United States may also profitably use to deal with the reasons that efficiency wages arise.

To conclude, I found K&S's reminder to trade theorists of the significance of labor market rents both timely and important, as demonstrated by the ability of labor rents to overturn the welfare implications of the Airbus subsidy and as they enable us to make some economic sense of the significance of the deindustrialization debate.

Reference

Dickens, William T., and Kevin Lang. 1988. Why it matters what we trade. In *The dynamics of trade and employment,* ed. L. Tyson, W. Dickens, and J. Zysman. Cambridge, Mass.: Ballinger.

4

Dynamic Duopoly with Output Adjustment Costs in International Markets: Taking the Conjecture out of Conjectural Variations

Robert Driskill and Stephen McCafferty

Microeconomics in general and trade economists in particular have made wide use of the conjectural variations approach to modeling oligopolistic behavior. Most users of this approach acknowledge its well-known shortcomings but defend its use as a "poor man's" dynamics, capable of capturing dynamic considerations in a static framework. As one example, Eaton and Grossman (1986) organize discussion about optimal trade policy in international oligopolistic markets around the question of whether conjectural variations are Nash-Cournot, Bertrand, or consistent in the sense of Bresnahan (1981). Their primary finding is that the optimal policy might be a tax, a subsidy, or free trade, depending on whether the exogenous conjectural variation is Nash-Cournot, Bertrand, or consistent.

In this paper, we construct a dynamic differential game of duopolistic trade in an international market. We show that the steady state of the closed-loop, subgame perfect equilibrium of our game can be replicated by a conjectural variations equilibrium of an analogous static game. The difference, though, is that the term in our steady-state equilibrium that corresponds to the conjectural variations term in the static game is itself a function of structural parameters in the model. The endogeneity of the conjectural variation allows us to pin down the optimal policy in terms of tax, subsidy, or laissez faire, depending on the structural aspects of our model. The optimal policy no longer depends on an assumed, exogenous value of a conjectural variation. In our particular model, we find that the optimal policy is an export subsidy that credibly shifts profits to the domestic firm.

Our work also has implications for the empirical study on optimal trade and industrial policies of Dixit (1988). Dixit employs a conjectural variations

Robert Driskill and Stephen McCafferty are professor of economics and associate professor of economics, respectively, at Ohio State University.

model to analyze the U.S. automobile industry. In his analysis, Dixit treats these conjectural variations as "parameters that measure the degree of competition or collusion in market conduct" (p. 142). He is most interested in the equilibrium values of the conjectural variation terms as implied by the historical data. However, he does express some concern that such equilibrium conjectural variations might be functions of tariffs and other policy variables. The term in our dynamic model corresponding to the conjectural variations term in the analogous static model is a function of such taste, technology, and policy parameters. Hence, Dixit's concerns about the validity of using a constant conjectural variation term in the face of policy changes seems well founded.

While our analysis is amenable to easy comparison with works that adopt the conjectural variations framework, we do not claim to rebut those critics who find conjectural variations a flawed behavioral concept. Rather, we view current users of conjectural variations as believing that the concept captures in a static framework the long-run behavior of some unspecified dynamic game.

For our analysis, we develop a duopoly model in which firms incur costs associated with how fast they change their level of output. By positing these adjustment costs, we create what James Friedman (1974) has called a "time-dependent" or "structurally linked" dynamic game and cast the duopoly problem as a differential game. In this game, firms take levels of output as state variables and choose how fast they adjust output.

We think our approach is a natural extension of traditional duopoly theory and especially of the conjectural variations approach. Even though not explicit, dynamics lurks just offstage in these static theories. Both Cournot's discussion of move and countermove and the naming of static first-order conditions as "reaction curves" reflect a concern with dynamics not captured in the formal models. By explicitly introducing a time-dependent structure into a model, we can naturally address these dynamic considerations. An interesting characteristic of such a game is that, in the steady state, the closed-loop, subgame perfect equilibrium differs from the equilibrium of a static, one-shot Nash game. This makes the steady state of our game amenable to comparison with conjectural variations equilibria. We also believe that our approach provides a justification for the reasonableness of the conjectural variations approach.

Our main result is that output in the steady state of our game is greater than it would be in an analogous static Nash-Cournot equilibrium. This holds true even in the limiting case where the adjustment cost term that gives rise to the intrinsic dynamics of the model shrinks to zero. Our steady-state equilibrium can also be replicated by a static game whose players have negative conjectural variations of a particular magnitude. While we do not obtain analytic results concerning optimal taxes or subsidies, we do compute the optimal policy for a number of numerical examples. We find in all cases that the optimal policy is a subsidy on exports. Intuition that suggests this finding is robust is gleaned from comparing our steady state with the consistent conjectures equilibrium of the analogous static game. We find that output in our steady state is always less than that in the consistent conjectures equilibrium. Results from Eaton and Grossman (1986) tells us that, in a static conjectural variations framework, when output is below the consistent conjectures level, the optimal policy is a subsidy.

We should note that in a companion paper (Driskill and McCafferty 1988) we model a dynamic game where the intrinsic dynamics arise from dynamic demand. In that model, steady-state output is above that of the associated consistent conjectures equilibrium, and the optimal policy is a tax on exports. The general lesson seems to be that, while the outcome of a dynamic game can be replicated by a conjectural variations equilibrium, this outcome is dependent on the specific features of the dynamic game, including values of policy parameters.

4.1 The Model

Following Eaton and Grossman (1986), among others, we consider the case of two duopolists, each from a different country, competing in a third country. The government of each duopolist's respective country is assumed to commit, prior to the start of the game, to an ad valorem tax or subsidy on the exports of the domestic firm. Throughout the game, each firm and government takes as given the tax or subsidy imposed by each government. Each firm's objective is the maximization of the present discounted value of profits.

Both firms face a common linear demand curve, given by

$$(1) \qquad\qquad p = a - u_1 - u_2,$$

where a is a positive constant and u_i is the output of the ith firm.

We assume that costs depend both on the level of output and on the time derivative of output, reflecting costs associated with changing output quickly rather than slowly. Furthermore, we assume that the cost of changing output infinitely quickly is infinite: the force of this assumption is to make output levels state variables that do not jump discontinuously but rather evolve smoothly through time. What firms control, then, are rates of change of output. We assume that both firms have identical cost functions given by

$$(2) \qquad\qquad C_i = cu_i + (A/2)(x_i)^2,$$

where c and A are positive constants and $x_i \equiv \dot{u}_i$, where ($\dot{\ }$) denotes a time derivative. We could add a cost term quadratic in the level of output, but we believe that it would add nothing to the analysis except increased algebraic complexity.

The key assumption about strategic behavior is that each firm's strategy is restricted to be a function only of the current state, that is, a function only of the output levels of both firms. This assumption restricts our equilibria to be "closed loop." We briefly point out the properties of the model when strategies are path strategies, that is, not conditional on the state of the system. Equilibria predicated on path strategies have the undesirable property of not being perfect. The reasonableness and usefulness of the state-space restriction is discussed by Fudenberg and Tirole (1983). Basically, it rules out other perfect equilibria in which strategies depend on "irrelevant" history; in particular, it rules out trigger-strategy equilibria.

Each firm is thus assumed to solve the following problem:

$$\max_{x_i} \int_0^\infty [(a - u_1 - u_2)u_i(1 - t_i) - cu_i - (A/2)x_i^2]e^{-\delta t}dt$$

subject to

$$\dot{u}_i = x_i, \quad \dot{u}_j = x_j(u_i, u_j), \quad i, j = 1, 2, i \neq j,$$

where t_i is the tax or subsidy rate and δ is the common discount rate.

The above maximization problems constitute a differential game. We now state and prove the following theorem.

THEOREM 1: Let

(3) $$x_i^* = K_i + k_{ii}u_i + k_{ij}u_j, \quad i, j = 1, 2, i \neq j,$$

where k_{ii} and k_{ij} solve the following equations:

(4) $$k_{ii} = \{[2(1 - t_i) - Ak_{ij}k_{ji}](k_{jj} - \delta) - Ak_{ii}^2(k_{ii} - \delta) \\ + 2k_{ii}(1 - t_i) - Ak_{ii}k_{ij}k_{ji} + A(k_{ii} - \delta)k_{ji}k_{ij} \\ - Ak_{ij}k_{ji}k_{jj}\}/A(k_{ii} - \delta)(k_{jj} - \delta),$$

(5) $$k_{ij} = \{[(1 - t_i) - Ak_{ij}k_{jj}](k_{jj} - \delta) - Ak_{ii}k_{jj}(k_{ii} - \delta) \\ + 2k_{ij}(1 - t_i) - Ak_{ij}^2k_{ji} - Ak_{ij}k_{jj}(k_{ii} - \delta) \\ + k_{jj}(1 - t_i) - Ak_{ij}k_{jj}^2\}/A(k_{ii} - \delta)(k_{jj} - \delta),$$

(6) $$k_{ii} + k_{jj} < 0,$$

(7) $$k_{ii}k_{jj} - k_{ij}k_{ji} > 0,$$
$$i, j, = 1, 2, i \neq j.$$

If such k_{ij} exist, then the pair x_1^*, x_2^* constitute a stable, closed-loop Nash equilibrium for the dynamic game under consideration.

Proof: We need to show that the stipulated strategies satisfy the Pontryagin necessary conditions for the two players. The first-order conditions for player i are

(8) $$H_{x_i}^i = -Ax_i + \lambda_{ii} = 0,$$

(9) $$-H_{u_i}^i + \lambda_{ii}\delta = \dot{\lambda}_{ii} = -[a(1 - t_i) - c] \\ + 2(1 - t_i)u_i + u_j(1 - t_i) - \lambda_{ij}k_{ji} + \lambda_{ii}\delta,$$

(10) $$-H_{u_j}^i + \lambda_{ij}\delta = \dot{\lambda}_{ij} = u_i(1 - t_i) - \lambda_{ij}k_{jj} + \lambda_{ij}\delta,$$

where H^i is the discounted Hamiltonian, $H^i_{(\cdot)}$ is the partial derivative of H^i with respect to $(\cdot)$, and λ_{ii}, λ_{ij} are the costate variables. Substituting (8) into (9), time-differentiating (8) and substituting into (9), time-differentiating that relation and combining it with (10), and rearranging, we get the following relation between x_i and u_1, u_2:

$$
\begin{aligned}
(11) \quad u_i = {}& K_i + (\{[2(1 - t_i) - Ak_{ij}k_{ji}](k_{jj} - \delta) - Ak_{ii}^2(k_{ii} - \delta) \\
& + 2k_{ii}(1 - t_i) - Ak_{ii}k_{ij}k_{ji} + A(k_{ii} - \delta)k_{ji}k_{ij} \\
& - Ak_{ij}k_{ji}k_{jj}\}/A(k_{ii} - \delta)(k_{jj} - \delta))u_i + (\{[(1 - t_i) \\
& - Ak_{ij}k_{jj}](k_{jj} - \delta) - Ak_{ii}k_{jj}(k_{ii} - \delta) + 2k_{ij}(1 - t_i) - Ak_{ij}^2k_{ji} \\
& - Ak_{ij}k_{ji}(k_{ii} - \delta) + k_{jj}(1 - t_i) - Ak_{ij}k_{jj}^2\}/A(k_{ii} - \delta)(k_{jj} - \delta))u_j,
\end{aligned}
$$

where K_i is a constant. Hence, if k_{ii}, k_{ij} equal the coefficients on u_i, u_j, respectively, then the stipulated pair of strategies satisfies the Pontryagin first-order conditions. If they also satisfy the auxiliary conditions that $k_{ii} + k_{jj} < 0$ and $k_{ii}k_{jj} - k_{ij}k_{ji} > 0$ (i.e., if they satisfy the Routh-Hurwicz conditions), then the strategies are also stable; that is, for any arbitrary initial values $u_i(0)$, $u_j(0)$, u_i and u_j converge to finite steady-state values. Q.E.D.

In general, we do not know under what parameter values such strategies exist or, if they do, whether they are unique. In Driskill and McCafferty (in press), we prove existence and uniqueness of a symmetric linear set of strategies for the special case $t_i = t_j = 0$. In this paper, we compute equilibria numerically for a wide variety of parameter values.

4.2 The Steady State

We wish to emphasize two aspects of the steady state of our dynamic game: first, that our equilibrium can be replicated by a conjectural variations equilibrium and, second, that output in our equilibrium steady state is higher than it would be in a static Nash-Cournot game played under the same demand and cost conditions except with no adjustment costs.

Setting all time derivatives to zero, we can derive the following relation from each player's maximization problem:

$$
(12) \qquad u_i = \{[a - c(1 - t_i)]/[2 + r_j]\} - u_j/(2 + r_j),
$$

where

$$
(13) \qquad r_j = -k_{ji}/(k_{jj} - \delta).
$$

We will refer to (12) as a *steady-state reaction curve*.

Now consider the static conjectural variations analogue to our dynamic problem, that is, the same demand and cost conditions except for the lack of adjustment costs. The reaction curve for each player is readily derived as

$$
(14) \qquad u_i = \{[a - c(1 - t_i)]/[2 + \theta_j]\} - u_j/(2 + \theta_j),
$$

where θ_j is firm i's conjecture about firm j's response to a change in u_i.

Note that the steady state of our game and the outcome of the conjectural variations game are identical if $\theta_j = r_j$. This means that there is a conjectural variation that replicates the steady state of our game. In the conjectural variations approach, though, the value of the conjectural variation is taken as exogenous, except in the consistent conjectures approach. The r_j in our dynamic game is, in contrast, a function of demand, cost, and policy parameters.

To compare output between the static Nash-Cournot analogue of our game and the steady state of our game, we need to know the sign of r_j. In Driskill and McCafferty (in press), we prove that, for the special case of $t_i = t_j = 0$, there exist symmetric negative k_{ij}'s that uniquely solve the Pontryagin first-order conditions for each firm's maximization problem and that give rise to r_j's strictly between zero and minus one. For this case, it is straightforward that output in the steady state is greater than output in the static Nash-Cournot game, which corresponds to the static case in which $\theta_1 = \theta_2 = 0$. For the asymmetric case we study in this paper, we are forced to compute solutions to equations (4) and (5) numerically. For a wide variety of parameter values, we always find $r_j \epsilon (-1, 0)$. For $r_j \epsilon (-1, 0)$, a straightforward inequality comparison exercise on equations (12) shows that output for the industry is unambiguously higher than in the static Nash-Cournot case.

What pushes output beyond the static Nash-Cournot level is a purely strategic force associated with the closed-loop aspect of our game. In the closed-loop game, each firm takes account of the effect that the value of the state variable has on its rival's optimal response. Consequently, each firm knows that, if it expands output, its rival's response is to reduce its rate of change of output, leading to a lower level of its output through time. This occurs since the k_{ij}'s are negative. Thus, each firm has an incentive to increase output even more since this shifts out its future residual demand curve.

4.3 Welfare

Following Eaton and Grossman (1986), we measure welfare contributions to each country by national product generated in the steady state by the home firm:

$$(15) \qquad\qquad w_i = pu_i - cu_i .$$

We look only at the steady state in considering welfare effects. Our purpose is to compare conjectural variations results with those derived from the steady state of a completely specified dynamic game; our interpretation of the conjectural variations justification as "poor man's dynamics" is that conjectural variations equilibria can be thought of as just such a steady state. A truly dynamic welfare analysis, while perhaps desirable, is also beyond our computational abilities at this time.

While we have no analytic results to report, we did solve our model numerically for a wide variety of parameter values and compute associated welfare levels. A representative display of our findings is presented in table 4.1, where welfare levels for each country are shown as functions of both countries' tax rates. The table shows that, for a zero foreign-country tax rate, the optimal home-country response is a subsidy of about 34 percent. For all the different parameter values we tried, the optimal response was qualitatively the same: a subsidy.

In the spirit of Eaton and Grossman, we can also use table 4.1 to analyze optimal foreign policy response. That is, we can think of both governments setting tax rates before the start of the dynamic game between the two competing firms so as to maximize their own steady-state welfare. More precise numerical calculations than those presented in the table demonstrate that the resulting Nash equilibrium would be a 25 percent subsidy granted by

Table 4.1   **Welfare Levels for Various Tax/Subsidy Rates**

T2	T1							
	− .40	− .34	− .28	− .22	− .16	− .10	.0	.10
− .60:								
W1	.0446	.0462	.0475	.0482	.0483	.0474	.0430	.0325
W2	.0546	.0612	.0686	.0770	.0867	.0980	.1211	.1519
− .50:								
W1	.0519	.0534	.0545	.0551	.0550	.0538	.0490	.0380
W2	.0579	.0643	.0715	.0798	.0893	.1004	.1231	.1533
− .40:								
W1	.0607	.0620	.0630	.0633	.0630	.0617	.0563	.0447
W2	.0607	.0669	.0740	.0821	.0914	.1021	.1244	.1541
− .30:								
W1	.0715	.0727	.0734	.0735	.0729	.0713	.0654	.0531
W2	.0627	.0687	.0756	.0834	.0924	.1029	.1246	.1537
− .20:								
W1	.0850	.0859	.0864	.0862	.0853	.0834	.0768	.0638
W1	.0633	.0691	.0757	.0833	.0920	.1022	.1232	.1514
− .10:								
W1	.1021	.1028	.1029	.1025	.1012	.0989	.0915	.0775
W1	.0617	.0672	.0735	.0807	.0891	.0989	.1192	.1465
.0:								
W1	.1244	.1247	.1245	.1237	.1220	.1192	.1109	.0958
W2	.0563	.0615	.0674	.0743	.0822	.0915	.1109	.1371
.10:								
W1	.1541	.1540	.1534	.1521	.1499	.1465	.1375	.1206
W2	.0447	.0495	.0550	.0614	.0689	.0775	.0958	.1206

Note: W1 = country 1 welfare, W2 = country 2 welfare, T1 = tax rate for country 1, T2 = tax rate for country 2, $A = 1.0$, $a = 2.0$, $c = 1.0$, and $\delta = .05$.

both governments. Much as in the Eaton and Grossman analysis, allowing for foreign response leaves the basic results unchanged.

In Driskill and McCafferty (1988), we modeled competing international duopolists facing slow price adjustment along the lines developed by Fershtman and Kamien (1987). In that paper, we found that the optimal policy was about a 5 percent tax imposed by the government. We argued that this finding could be understood with the help of Eaton and Grossman's results about optimal policy under different conjectural variations. Basically, what they found was that, for consistent conjectures, the optimal policy was no tax or subsidy; for conjectures smaller in absolute value than the consistent conjecture, the optimal response was a subsidy; and for conjectures greater in absolute value than the consistent conjecture, the optimal policy was a tax (at least for the case of linear demand and quadratic marginal cost). In our model with sticky price adjustment, we showed that the conjectural variations equilibrium that replicated our steady-state equilibrium had a conjecture greater in absolute value than the consistent conjecture. Hence, Eaton and Grossman's analysis suggests that the optimal policy would be a tax. Of course, the Eaton and Grossman results did not apply exactly since in our model the terms corresponding to the conjectural variations term in the static game were themselves not exogenous but functions of the tax rates.

In this paper, with output adjustment costs instead of sticky price adjustment, analogous reasoning can be used to gain some insight. We find it useful to recast the Eaton and Grossman results in our special case of linear demand and linear costs. Consider the welfare function (15), $w_i = w_i(u_i, u_j)$. Graphically, we depict w_1 in figure 4.1 as a family of isowelfare curves in the (u_1, u_2) plane. The salient characteristics of this graph are that each isowelfare curve is concave, with a maximum at

(16)
$$u_1 = \frac{a - c - u_2}{2}$$

and with partial derivatives

(17)
$$\partial w/\partial u_2 < 0, \quad \partial u_2/\partial u_1 > -2,$$

for $\partial u_2/\partial u_1 < 0$. Note that the Nash-Cournot one-shot game reaction curve for the country 1 firm is that line along which $\theta_2 = \partial u_2/\partial u_1 = 0$.

Maximization of country 1's welfare calls for picking the pair (u_1, u_2) along country 2's reaction curve that is tangent to an isowelfare locus. This point is illustrated in figure 4.1 as point A. Since the isowelfare curve is concave with a slope that decreases from zero along the Nash-Cournot reaction curve for the country 1 firm, this constrained optimum is necessarily to the right of the Nash-Cournot reaction curve. The question answered by Brander and Spencer is how a country can obtain point A when its firm's reaction curve is the Nash-Cournot one. The answer is that a subsidy will twist out the home firm's

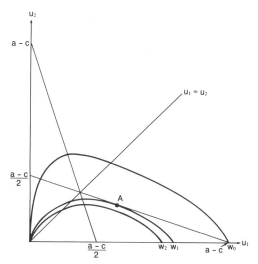

Fig. 4.1 The welfare maximizing output level for country 1

reaction curve so as to intersect the foreign reaction curve at point A. To make the point more clear, we write the home firm's reaction curve when the firm is subsidized at rate t_1 as

(18) $u_1 = [a(1 - t_1) - c]/[2(1 - t_1)] - (u_2)(1 - t_1)/[2(1 - t_1)]$.

As t_1 decreases from zero, the intercept moves up, and the slope grows flatter. An appropriate subsidy can twist the curve through point A.

Now consider the same problem but assume no taxes. Instead, consider how different conjectural variations twist the Nash-Cournot reaction curve. The conjectural variation reaction curve for country 1 is

(19) $u_1 = (a - c)/(2 + \theta_2) - (u_2)/(2 + \theta_2)$.

As θ_2 varies from zero (Cournot) to minus one, the reaction curve twists out. Clearly, there is some θ_2 that will make the home-country firm's reaction curve go through point A, the welfare optimum. Eaton and Grossman have proved what this conjectural variation is: the "consistent" one in the sense of Bresnahan (1981) and Perry (1982). With the consistent conjecture, Eaton and Grossman prove that the optimal subsidy is zero. Hence, the consistent conjecture reaction curve must pass through point A. For conjectural variations greater in absolute value than the consistent one, the optimal policy would be a tax; this, for example, is the case in our linear example with Bertrand conjectures. That is, the Bertrand conjecture in terms of quantities is greater in absolute value than the consistent conjecture. For conjectures smaller in absolute value than the consistent one, the optimal policy is a subsidy.

Since for a wide variety of parameter values we compute that welfare is optimized with the imposition of a subsidy, one might guess that r_2, the term in our steady-state reaction curve that occupies the same spot that the conjectural variations term occupies in the one-shot reaction curve, is in fact less in absolute value than the consistent conjecture of the one-shot game. If this is true, it is of interest not only because it helps us understand the welfare simulations but also because it means that the steady-state output of this dynamic game is always less than the output of the one-shot game with consistent conjectures. To show that this may in fact be the case, at least in the neighborhood where $t_i = t_j = 0$, we first calculate r_j (which also equals r_i in this symmetric case) in the limiting case when $A \to 0$.

The solution to our game obtained when $A \to 0$ is called the limit game solution. Recall that A is the cost-of-adjustment parameter. If we were to simply set $A = 0$ at the start of the problem and solve the game, we would find that the steady-state output of that game is identical to static Nash-Cournot. In contrast, as we take the limit as $A \to 0$ of our closed-loop Nash equilibrium, steady-state output tends not to static Nash-Cournot but rather to some level strictly between perfect competition and static Nash-Cournot. This is a standard feature of closed-loop equilibria of differential games (see Fershtman and Kamien 1987; Reynolds 1987; and Driskill and McCafferty 1988, in press).

We now state and prove the following theorem.

THEOREM 2: For $t_i = t_j = 0$, the steady-state output level for each firm in the limit game of $A \to 0$ is strictly greater than static Nash-Cournot but strictly less than the output level in the static consistent conjectures equilibrium.

Proof: First, we set t_i and t_j to zero in equations (4) and (5) and restrict ourselves to symmetric solutions where $k_{ii} = k_1$ and $k_{ij} = k_{ji} = k_2$. Equations (4) and (5) then become

(20) $$k_1 = \{-Ak_2^2[3k_1 - 2\delta] + 2(k_1 - \delta)\}/ \\ [A(k_1 - \delta)(2k_1 - \delta) + Ak_2^2 - 2],$$

(21) $$k_2 = \{-Ak_1k_2[3k_1 - 2\delta] + 2k_1 - \delta\}/ \\ [A(k_1 - \delta)(2k_1 - \delta) + Ak_2^2 - 2].$$

Rearranging (20), we can write

(22) $$k_2 = \phi(k_1) = [(Ak_1^2 - A\delta k_1 - 2)/(-2A)]^{1/2}.$$

Consider the value of k_1 where $\phi(k)_1 = k_1$. This value, call it $\bar{k}_1$, is always greater than any equilibrium value k_1^* because of stability condition (6). Now $\bar{k}_1$ is given by

(23) $$\bar{k}_1 = \{(\delta/3) \pm (1/2)[(\delta/3)^2 + (8/3A)]^{1/2}\}.$$

Hence, as $A \to 0$, both $\bar{k}_1$ and k_1^* go to $-\infty$. Now, rearranging (22), we get

(24) $$A = 2/[2k_2^2 + k_1(k_1 - \delta)].$$

Dividing (21) by (20), and substituting (24) for A in the resulting expression, we get:

(25) $(k_2/k_1) = \{-2[3 - (2\delta/k_1)](k_2/k_1) + [2 - (\delta/k_1)][1 - (\delta/k_1)]$
$\qquad + [2(k_2/k_1)^2]\} + \{-2[(k_2/k_1)^2 - 1 + (2\delta/k_1) - (\delta/k_1)^2]\}.$

Define $\lim\limits_{A \to 0} (k_2/k_1) \equiv -r$. Using the well-known properties of limits, and remembering that, as $A \to 0$, $k_1 \to -\infty$, we then have

(26) $$-r = (6r + 2 + 4r^2)/[-2(r^2 - 1)].$$

Rearranging (26), we get

(27) $$2r(r^2 - 4) - 2(1 + 2r^2) \equiv \Omega(r) = 0.$$

Over the interval $(-1, 0)$, $\Omega(r)$ is a strictly concave function, with $\Omega(-1) = 0$, $\Omega(0) = -2$, and $\Omega'(-1) > 0$. Thus, $\Omega(r) = 0$ once and only once over the interval $(-1, 0)$. Now, $r = -1$, which satisfies (27), is inconsistent with stability, as it implies that $k_1 = k_2$, which in turn violates the Routh-Hurwicz condition. Hence, r is strictly greater than -1, and steady-state output is greater than it would be under static Nash-Cournot, which corresponds to $r = 0$. The consistent conjecture for the analogous static problem is given by

(28) $$\theta_{cc} = -1.$$

Hence, in this symmetric case with $t_1 = t_2 = 0$, our steady-state reaction curve is always steeper than the consistent conjecture equilibrium reaction curve, and steady-state output is less than under consistent conjecture equilibrium. Q.E.D.

At least for the limiting case $A \to 0$, theorem 2 tells us that our steady-state reaction curve with $t_1 = t_2 = 0$ intersects the other firm's reaction curve to the left of point A in figure 4.1. We illustrate this in figure 4.2. Now, for the given values of r_2, we know that a tax will shift our reaction curve out toward point A. What complicates our analysis relative to the static one of Eaton and Grossman, though, is that changing t_i, the tax rate, changes r_1 and r_2. We are unable to determine analytically how these changes in t_i change r_1 and r_2. Such changes in r_1 and r_2 twist and shift both reaction curves, and we have been unable to prove whether these twists and shifts can overwhelm the welfare-improving shift occurring directly from the increase in the tax rate. Our numerical calculations suggest that this in fact does not happen.

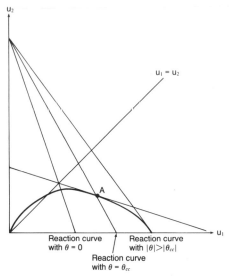

Fig. 4.2   The limit game of $A \to 0$

4.4   Conclusions

By explicitly solving a dynamic game, we find that steady-state output for two duopolists competing in a third-country market is greater than the output that would be produced under identical cost conditions at a Nash-Cournot equilibrium for a one-shot, static game. We also find that our steady state can be replicated by a static conjectural variations equilibrium. The gain from the explicit solution of the dynamic game is that the conjectural variation that replicates the dynamic outcome is specified as a function of underlying taste and technology parameters and is not simply an assumed, exogenous value. Given Eaton and Grossman's (1986) findings concerning the relation between optimal taxes and conjectural variations, this result has important implications for welfare analysis of the optimal tax. Furthermore, our dynamic analysis points out that welfare analysis is perhaps more complex than the static conjectural variations approach would suggest: for the dynamic analysis, the conjectural variation that replicates the dynamic outcome is itself a function of tax parameters and cannot be assumed to be constant across policy experiments.

For the explicit game we study, we find that the optimal policy under a wide variety of parameter values is a subsidy on exports. This finding seems related to the fact that our steady-state level of output is less than would arise at a consistent conjectures equilibrium. For the linear example we study, an implication of Eaton and Grossman's analysis is that, for conjectural variations equilibria with output less than would arise under consistent conjectures, the optimal policy would be a subsidy. Eaton and Grossman's result thus suggests that the optimal policy in our model should be a subsidy, not a tax. Their result is suggestive, but not definitive, for our model because their analysis takes conjectural variations as exogenous and unchanging in the face of policy changes.

Our results are of course derived from a very specific model. On the basis of other work on dynamic games, we think that some of our results generalize. Work by Driskill and McCafferty (1988) on models with slow price adjustment instead of costs of output adjustment also finds that steady-state output is greater than would occur at a static Nash-Cournot equilibrium. These models can also be thought of as being replicable by a static conjectural variations equilibrium. The optimal policy in such models, though, seems to be a tax instead of a subsidy.

References

Brander, J. A. 1981, Intra-industry trade in identical commodities. *Journal of International Economics* (11(1):1–14.

Brander, J. A., and B. J. Spencer, 1984. Tariff protection and imperfect competition. In *Monopolistic competition in international trade*, ed. H. Kierzkowski, 194–206. Oxford: Oxford University Press.

———. 1985. Export subsidies and international market share rivalry. *Journal of International Economics* 18(1/2):83–100.

Bresnahan, T. F. 1981. Duopoly models with consistent conjectures. *American Economic Review* 71(5):934–45.

Dixit, A. 1988. Optimal trade and industrial policies for the U.S. automobile industry. In *Empirical methods for international trade*, ed. R. Feenstra, 141–65. Cambridge, Mass.: MIT Press.

Driskill, R., and S. McCafferty. 1988. Trade industrial policy, and dynamic duopoly: Taking the conjecture out of conjectural variations. Mimeo.

———. In press. Dynamic duopoly with adjustment costs: A differential game approach. *Journal of Economic Theory*.

Eaton, J., and G. Grossman. 1986. Optimal trade and industrial policy under oligopoly. *Quarterly Journal of Economics* 101(2):383–406.

Fershtman, C., and M. Kamien. 1987. Dynamic duopolistic competition with sticky prices. *Econometrica* 55(5):1151–64.

Friedman, J. 1974. Non-cooperative equilibria in time-dependent supergames. *Econometrica* 42(2):221–37.

Fudenberg, D., and J. Tirole. 1983. Dynamic models of oligopoly. Stanford University. Mimeo.

Perry, M. K. 1982. Oligopoly and consistent conjectural variations. *Bell Journal of Economics* 13(2):197–205.

Reynolds, S. S. 1987. Capacity investment, preemption and commitment in an infinite horizon model. *International Economic Review* 28(1):69–88.

Spencer, B. J., and J. A. Brander. 1983. International R&D rivalry and industrial strategy. *Review of Economic Studies* 50(4):702–22.

Comment   Elias Dinopoulos

The paper by Driskill and McCafferty develops a dynamic differential game with two firms competing in a third market and facing output adjustment costs. The main finding is that the steady-state equilibrium of the dynamic game can be replicated by a static game with conjectural variations. Comparing the steady-state equilibrium to that of the one-shot static game, the authors find several differences: the term that corresponds to conjectural variations of the static game is a function of the parameters of the dynamic game; when output adjustment costs approach zero, the steady-state output of each firm is higher than that of the static Cournot game and lower than that of the static consistent conjectures game; and, when firms face output adjustment costs, an export subsidy maximizes steady-state welfare, whereas, in the case of price adjustment costs, steady-state welfare maximization requires a tax. In the following discussion, I would like to interpret the results of the paper in the context of the existing literature on conjectural variations and trade policy and offer some remarks on comparative dynamics, steady-state welfare, and adjustment processes.

Bresnahan (1981) introduced the concept of consistent conjectures in an attempt to provide the "right" alternative to Cournot and Bertrand equilibria in a static framework. Eaton and Grossman (1986) used Cournot, Bertrand, and consistent conjectures to show that the optimal trade policy depends crucially on the nature of conjectural variations. They found that Cournot conjectures require an export subsidy, that Bertrand conjectures are associated with an export tax, and that under consistent conjectures free trade is the optimal policy.[1] Conjectural variations were criticized by Stanford (1986). He showed that, in an infinitely repeated game with discounting and discrete time, the only reaction function equilibria that are subgame perfect are those with static Cournot or Bertrand conjectures.

The present paper models the dynamic game using continuous time and obtains results that are similar to those of Stanford with respect to consistent conjectures. It shows that the steady-state output of each duopolist is *different* than the output of the analogous one-shot static game with consistent conjectures. In this sense, it implies some form of trade intervention that is discussed in the welfare section. One of the virtues of the paper is that the authors do an excellent job of indicating the formal connections and the economic intuition that relate the results to particular assumptions. The discussion of why the steady-state output is higher than the static Cournot output is extremely useful. The use of numerical simulations to investigate the nature of the steady-state solution is common practice in problems involving differential games.

Elias Dinopoulos is associate professor of economics at the University of Florida, Gainesville.

Most of the analysis of the paper focuses on comparing a steady-state equilibrium to the analogous static game. One of the weaknesses of the paper is that it does not deal with issues of existence and uniqueness of the steady-state equilibrium. The lack of a formal proof of the existence of steady-state equilibrium does not allow the reader to compare the results of the present paper to those of Stanford (1986). Moreover, Fisher and Wilson (1988) show that a static Bertrand duopoly game with a homogeneous product and differential tariffs does not possess pure strategy equilibria. Consequently, it is possible that the class of steady-state solutions for the differential game with nonzero tariffs might not exist. The issue of uniqueness is equally important because the existence of multiple steady-state equilibria would question the relevance of comparative dynamics exercises. These exercises are used implicitly in the maximization of steady-state welfare.

Personally, I found the discussion of optimal policies and welfare somewhat unsatisfactory. The paper concentrates on policies (in the form of export taxes or subsidies) that maximize the value of steady-state welfare (sec. 4.3). Given the explicit dynamic framework of the game, optimum policies should be intertemporally efficient in the sense that they maximize the present discounted profits. Starting at a steady-state equilibrium, any change of a tax rate is associated with a time path that drives the system from the old to the new steady state. The transition from one steady state to another involves welfare changes that should be taken into account when comparing the two original steady-state equilibria. Samuelson (1975) and Srinivasan and Bhagwati (1983) show that, in general, a path that maximizes steady-state welfare is not necessarily intertemporally efficient in the sense that it maximizes the present discounted value of welfare. The proper way of calculating optimal taxes or subsidies in the present context is to have each government maximizing the present discounted profits of its firm taking the tax rate of the other government as given and acting as a Stackelberg leader vis-à-vis the game of the two firms. The optimal tax path of each government will be intertemporally efficient, and it could converge into a steady-state value. This value could then be examined in terms of its positive or negative sign. Indeed, it is peculiar to have firms engaged in intertemporal optimization and governments in steady-state optimization. If firms maximize steady-state instead of present discounted profits, I suspect that there will be no difference between the steady-state and the analogous static Cournot game output. However, if the proper methodology is followed, I have no reason to expect that the steady-state values and signs of intertemporally efficient taxes or subsidies are the same as those that maximize steady-state welfare. I realize that the computation of intertemporally efficient policy instruments is analytically difficult, if not impossible. Perhaps an appropriate variant of Diamond's (1980) methodology[2] or even an additional numerical simulation exercise will illuminate the nature of the proper optimal policy instruments.

My final remark concerns the symmetric structure of output adjustment costs. In the present model, each firm faces costs that are quadratic in the rate of output change. I feel slightly uncomfortable with this specification because it implies that a reduction in the rate of output increases costs by the same amount as a raise in the rate of output. Models that focus on capacity constraints assume that increasing output beyond a certain range is not possible in the short-run but that output reduction does not affect variable costs. I would expect more economic intuition on the choice and the role of the output adjustment structure.

To conclude, I think that the paper makes an important contribution to the literature of conjectural variations and trade policy. It suggests that consistent conjectures cannot be rationalized by a dynamic differential game with adjustment costs. However, its normative conclusion, which advocates some form of trade intervention, is based on steady-state welfare maximization and not intertemporally efficient policy paths. I hope that future work in this area will clarify the normative issues that were raised by the present paper.

Notes

1. Cheng (1988) has provided a similar analysis in the context of a home market that is supplied by a domestic and a foreign firm.
2. Diamond has proposed a simple expression for the present discounted value of a change in welfare from one steady state to another along a convergent path.

References

Bresnahan, T. F. 1981. Duopoly models with consistent conjectures. *American Economic Review* 71(5):934–45.

Cheng, L. K. 1988. Assisting domestic industries under international oligopoly: The relevance of the nature of competition to optimal policies. *American Economic Review* 78(4):746–58.

Diamond P. A. 1980. An alternative to steady-state comparisons. *Economic Letters* 5:7–9.

Eaton, J., and G. M. Grossman. 1986. Optimal trade and industrial policy under oligopoly. *Quarterly Journal of Economics* 51(May):383–406.

Fisher, E., and C. Wilson. 1988. International duopoly with tariffs. Cornell University. Mimeo.

Samuelson, P. A. 1975. Trade pattern reversals in time-phased Ricardian systems and intertemporal efficiency. *Journal of International Economics* 5(November):309–64.

Srinivasan, T. N., and J. Bhagwati. 1983. Trade and welfare in a steady state. In *Essays in international economic theory,* ed. R. Feenstra, 1:136–48. Cambridge, Mass.: MIT Press.

Stanford, W. G. 1986. Subgame perfect reaction function equilibria in discounted duopoly supergames are trivial. *Journal of Economic Theory* 39(1):226–32.

Comment   Ronald D. Fischer

In my view, this paper has two main objectives: (i) to provide a foundation for conjectural variations equilibrium and a model of how the conjectures are generated and (ii) to apply the model to international trade in order to determine the optimal tariff or subsidy and compare it to the corresponding results of the static model of Eaton and Grossman (1986), henceforth EG.

Driskill and McCafferty use a dynamic Cournot game with adjustment costs to generate conjectural variations. They show that, in their model, the reaction functions corresponding to linear output changes (the instruments) do not correspond to those of the static Cournot model. These reaction functions can be written in a form reminiscent of the reaction functions of static conjectural variations models. As the term corresponding to the conjectures is written in terms of the fundamentals of their model, they conclude that their model can be seen as endogenizing the conjectures. This provides support for conjectural variations models against the static Cournot model. But is this really true? Since they restrict themselves to linear instruments,

$$x_i = \dot{u} = K_i + k_{ii}u_i + k_{ij}u_j \,,$$

and consider the steady state $x_i = 0$, the relation (reaction function) between u_i and u_j must be linear. As they have included adjustment costs, it is clear that the reaction functions will normally be different from the ones derived from a static Cournot model. Consider a better analogue of their model: a two-period model with quadratic adjustment costs (the discount factor is assumed to be zero),

$$\Pi^i = \Pi^i_1 + \Pi^i_2, \quad i = 1, 2,$$

where subscripts denote periods and superscripts denote firms. Writing the profit functions explicitly,

$$\Pi^i_1 = (1 - q^1_1 - q^2_1)q^i_1,$$
$$\Pi^i_2 = (1 - q^1_2 - q^2_2)q^i_2 - A(q^i_2 - q^i_1)^2, \quad i = 1, 2.$$

Here q^i_j represents output of firm i in period j and A is a constant, common to both firms. Solving this two-period model recursively, one obtains higher first-period outputs than in the Cournot equilibrium. The reason is that the adjustment cost allows the firms to try to precommit to higher output (as in the Spencer and Brander [1985] models of investment in research and development). Since the firms are symmetric, higher output results in the equilibrium. This replicates the results of the dynamic model, which suggests that it is the

Ronald D. Fischer is assistant professor of economics at the University of Virginia.

The author wishes to thank Gerhard Glomm for his many helpful comments on the subject of these comments.

different specification (i.e., the inclusion of adjustment costs) that leads to the results and not that the Cournot model is inappropriate.

This raises the question, Does this represent support for conjectural variations? I think it does not. What it shows is that conjectural variations can be used as static shorthand to encompass different models that have their own logical foundations. The dynamic game studied by Driskill and McCafferty is interesting in its own right, not because it has a relation to conjectural variations.

There are two big differences between the two-period model and dynamic models. The first is that the solution of the two-period model is nonstationary. Second, in the two-period model, as the adjustment cost A tends to zero, the solution converges to that of a two-period Cournot model. In the dynamic model, output remains larger even in the limit. It would be interesting to know the source of this difference.

Is such a project of supporting conjectural variations desirable? The notion of conjectural variations, though superficially attractive, suffers from internal inconsistencies. Unless conjectures are restricted in some way, any equilibrium is possible. Certain seemingly plausible restrictions have been proposed but have been shown to be irrational. Daugherty (1985) proved that the only "consistent" conjectural variations equilibrium is the Nash equilibrium. Makowski (1987) has shown that so-called rational and reasonable conjectures are neither.

Consider now the second objective, that is, the applications to trade. In EG (see their n. 2, p. 386), the conjectural variations model is used as a convenient framework that includes conjectures ranging from Cournot to Bertrand. It is also used because it highlights the source of the potential benefits from policy intervention: the difference between conjectural and actual responses.

Driskill and McCafferty confirm the results in EG for quantity competition, showing that, for a range of parameter values, a subsidy on exports will be optimal. The authors relate this result to the fact that the conjectures (in the conjectural variations analogue of their model) are smaller than the consistent conjectures. Eaton and Grossman have shown that in their model the choice between a subsidy and a tax on exports depends on the conjectures being smaller or larger than the consistent conjectures.

Finding another model that supports the results of EG is nice, but is it interesting? In my interpretation, the models of international trade that analyze profit shifting without home consumption are examples designed to show that the classical propositions of trade theory may no longer be valid in a world of imperfect competition. But, as Dixit argues, "It is my belief that research will reveal the profit-shifting argument to be of significance in only a small number of selected industries" (Dixit 1986, p. 291). In EG, the real welfare analysis begins when home consumption is included in the model. This type of analysis is difficult to do in the present model. It is in this sense that I find that the real interest of the model lies in industrial organization rather than in its application to international trade.

The authors have characterized the linear closed-loop solutions to their dynamic model (when they exist). Another interesting question is the possibility of cooperation. Since the model is the continuous version of a repeated Cournot game with adjustment costs, can collusive solutions be supported? Suppose that the firms decide on the following trigger strategy: play collusively, and, if the other firm defects, use the above closed-loop solution. If detection is immediate, the gains from deviating are zero, but the use of the closed-loop strategy in the future represents a loss with respect to cooperation. Thus, the collusive outcome may be supported. In fact, given a low enough discount rate, this is probably true even if detection of defection is delayed (for related work, see Benhabib and Radner 1988). It does not seem to me that such equilibria depend on "irrelevant" history as the authors claim.

References

Benhabib, J., and R. Radner, 1988. Joint exploitation of a productive asset: A game-theoretic approach. Working paper. New York University, 17 March.

Daugherty, A. 1985. Reconsidering Cournot: The Cournot equilibrium is consistent. *Rand Journal of Economics* 16(1):368–79.

Dixit, A. K. 1986. Trade policy: An agenda for research. In *Strategic trade policy and the new international economics*, ed. P. Krugman. Cambridge, Mass.: MIT Press.

Eaton, J., and G. Grossman. 1986. Optimal trade and industrial policy under oligopoly. *Quarterly Journal of Economics* 101(May):383–406.

Makowski, L. 1987. Are "rational conjectures" rational? *Journal of Industrial Economics* 36(1):35–47.

Spencer, B., and J. Brander. 1985. Industrial R&D rivalry and industrial strategy. *Review of Economic Studies* 50:702–22.

5 Differentiated Products, Economies of Scale, and Access to the Japanese Market

Gary R. Saxonhouse

5.1 The Low Share of Manufactures in Japanese Consumption

By comparison with other advanced industrialized economies (see table 5.1), Japan imports a remarkably small share of the manufactured goods it consumes. Unlike the experience of other advanced industrialized economies, this small share has been virtually constant for decades. This distinctive trade structure is regularly cited by policymakers as evidence that foreign manufacturers are systematically denied access to the Japanese market (McDonald 1982). Foreign manufacturers who have tried unsuccessfully to sell in the Japanese market always concede that formal barriers to imports of manufactured goods are low by any reasonable standard. They argue, however, that the regulatory environment within which most Japanese firms operate allows wide scope for arrangements keeping out those foreign manufactures that are

Table 5.1   **Imports of Manufactures as Percentages of Nominal GNP of Selected Countries, 1962–85**

	1962	1973	1985
Japan	2.8	2.8	2.7
U.S.	1.3	3.4	6.5
Federal Republic of Germany	6.0	9.1	15.0
France	4.8	9.5	13.1
United Kingdom	4.7	12.0	16.3

Source: Bank of Japan, *Kokusai hikaku tōkei* (International comparative statistics), various issues.

Gary R. Saxonhouse is professor of economics at the University of Michigan.

directly competitive with domestic Japanese production (Schlosstein 1984). These disappointed competitors suggest that it is a mistake to look at lists of vanishing Japanese tariffs and quotas. It is said that a protectionist record can be clearly seen in Japan's distinctive trade structure, which otherwise seems to defy conventional economic explanation.

5.2   What the Theory of Comparative Advantage Tells Us

While a large literature has collected the complaints of foreign manufac-turers trying unsuccessfully to sell in Japan, there have also been a number of studies that have attempted to provide an alternative explanation of Japan's distinctive trade structure (Saxonhouse and Stern 1989). This work has investigated how well traditional models of comparative advantage can explain Japanese trade structure. In particular, both Leamer (1984, 1987) and Saxonhouse (1983, 1986) have estimated sectoral trade equations directly derived from Heckscher-Ohlin factor endowment theories of trade structure. Within the Heckscher-Ohlin framework, much of Japan's distinctive trade structure can be explained by Japan's distinctive pattern of factor endow-ments. If Japanese formal barriers are low and Japan's trade structure can be explained by conventional economic reasoning, it is difficult to take seriously the avalanche of complaints about Japan's supposedly distinctive protectionist trade and industrial policies.

Are such results believable? Their great virtue is that they are nonarbitrary. The specification used in these empirical analyses is dictated by the most widely known and widely taught theory of international trade. This is also their great problem. The assumptions behind the Heckscher-Ohlin frame-work, which Leamer and Saxonhouse estimate, are severe. This empirical work assumes that national economies differ not in their technologies and preferences but only in their factor endowments. Scale economies and market power are assumed to be absent, and consumption preferences are assumed to be unaffected by income. Factors must be perfectly mobile within countries and totally immobile across national boundaries. Even factor endowments cannot be so dissimilar across countries that each good is not produced in each country.[1]

5.3   What Traditional Theory Leaves Out

Lawrence (1987) has argued persuasively that empirical work on trade barriers using Heckscher-Ohlin equations misses out on at least one critical issue in current policy discussions. Heckscher-Ohlin equations are defined for net trade, yet it is frequently suggested that what is distinctive about Japan's trade pattern is its very meager participation in conventionally defined intraindustry trade in manufacturing (Sazanami 1981). The structure of Japan's net trade flows might appear normal even while, as seen in table 5.2, its gross trade pattern might be highly distinctive.

Table 5.2   **Intraindustry Manufacturing Trade Indices, 1980**

Country	21 Sectors	94 Sectors
Australia	.41	.22
Belgium	.87	.79
Canada	.67	.68
Finland	.58	.49
France	.88	.82
Germany	.69	.66
Italy	.71	.61
Japan	.30	.25
Netherlands	.77	.78
Norway	.62	.51
Sweden	.66	.68
United Kingdom	.82	.78
United States	.67	.60
Korea	. . .	.48
Switzerland	. . .	.61

Source: Lawrence (1987), using

$$\text{Index } j = \frac{\sum_{i=1}^{n} [(X_{ij} + M_{ij}) - |X_{ij} - M_{ij}|]}{\sum_{i=1}^{n} (X_{ij} + M_{ij})},$$

where i denotes manufacturing category, j denotes country, and X and M are exports and imports, respectively.

It has been argued that this lack of participation in intraindustry trade is at the heart of Japan's diplomatic difficulties during the last ten or fifteen years. The Federal Republic of Germany, which has comparably large net exports of manufactures, is rarely the object of protectionist complaints. Germany is an active participant in intraindustry trade in manufactures. Throughout the postwar period, Germany has imported lots of manufactured products. Perhaps, foreign manufacturers hurt by German competition have difficulty developing a unified position against German trade because, within any foreign manufacturing industry, Germany, by virtue of its manufacturing imports, will have allies to balance against its enemies (Lawrence 1987).

It is difficult to know whether such analyses are good political economy. Trade research that uses net trade as a dependent variable does ignore the possibility that Japanese policy may have worked to keep down both imports *and* exports. From the point of view of the trade policy debate in the United States, however, this may not be a serious omission. This research says that it is unlikely that, compared to other countries, Japanese policy has unfairly kept down imports in dozens of manufacturing sectors unless it is simultaneously keeping down exports in precisely the same sectors. From the American side, U.S.-Japanese economic conflict is surely not about Japan exporting too little, and, from an economic point of view, it is, unhappily, often about quite narrowly defined sectoral trade balances. Economists have learned from American congressmen about the auto deficit, the steel deficit, the textile deficit, and the semiconductor deficit, among others. It would seem that this politically salient part of the trade debate is well handled by investigations that use the Heckscher-Ohlin specification and look at sectoral net trade.

5.4 New Research Findings

Notwithstanding the virtues of looking at sectoral net trade, the determinants of gross imports and gross exports and therefore intraindustry trade also deserve close scrutiny. The very development of the concept of intraindustry trade went hand in hand with the recognition that this type of trade does not reflect comparative advantage. Its existence reflects the importance of product differentiation and scale economies, among other influences. Two economies with very similar factor endowments may still engage in substantial two-way trade if consumers in each have similar tastes for a wide variety of imperfectly substitutable products, most of which are produced under conditions of increasing returns to scale (Helpman and Krugman 1985).

Assume that all manufactured goods are differentiated by country of origin. Given the same identical homothetic preferences usually assumed in the Heckscher-Ohlin research, each economy will consume identical proportions of each variety of each good. This means that country j's consumption of all the different varieties of good i can be described by

(1) $$C_{ij} = M_{ij}^+ + C_{ij}^i,$$

(2) $$M_{ij}^+ = S_j\left(\overline{Q}_i - Q_{ij}\right),$$

(3) $$C_{ij}^i = S_j Q_{ij},$$

where[2]

$C_{ij} \equiv$ consumption of good i by country j;

$C_{ij}^i \equiv$ consumption of variety j of good i by country j;

$M_{ij}^+ \equiv$ imports of good i by country j;

$Q_{ij} \equiv$ production of good i in country j;

$\overline{Q}_i \equiv \sum_j Q_{ij} \equiv$ global production of good i;

$\Pi_j \equiv \sum_i \equiv$ GNP of country j;

$$\Pi \equiv \sum_j \Pi_j \equiv \text{global GNP; and}$$

$$S_j \equiv \frac{\Pi_j}{\Pi} \equiv \text{share of country } j \text{ in global GNP.}$$

Equations (2) and (3) can be combined to obtain:

(4)
$$\frac{M_{ij}^+}{M_{ij}^+ + S_j Q_{ij}} = \frac{S_j(\overline{Q}_i - Q_{ij})}{M_{ij}^+ + S_j Q_{ij}} = \frac{S_j(\overline{Q}_i - Q_{ij})}{S_j(\overline{Q}_i - Q_{ij}) + S_j Q_{ij}}$$

$$= \frac{S_j(\overline{Q}_i - Q_{ij})}{S_j \overline{Q}_i} = 1 - \frac{Q_{ij}}{\overline{Q}_i}.$$

Equation (4) states that imports of good i by economy j as a proportion of total use of i by j will be equal to the proportion of good i that is produced outside j. The less competitive a country is in the production of good i, the more it will import.

Alternatively,

(4')
$$\frac{M_{ij}^+}{M_{ij}^+ + S_j Q_{ij}} = 1 - \frac{Q_{ij}}{\overline{Q}_i} = 1 - \frac{(1 - S_j)Q_{ij}}{(1 - S_j)\overline{Q}_i} = 1 - \frac{X_{ij}^+}{(1 - S_j)\overline{Q}_i},$$

where $X_{ij}^+ \equiv$ exports of good i by economy j.

Imports of good i by economy j as a proportion of total consumption of i by j will be equal to the proportion of foreign consumption of i that is foreign produced. By global homotheticity, foreign and domestic consumption of any variety of any good will be proportionally the same.

Equations (4) and (4') provide the basic framework for Lawrence's empirical work on cross-national trade structure. Lawrence, however, does not use cross-national data on trade structure and production to test the restrictions implied by (4) and (4'). Rather, he argues that (4) and (4') apply only to a world where distance imposes no cost on trade. In a world where transport costs are nonzero and a determinant of trade structure, Lawrence prefers to estimate the logarithmic version of (4) and (4'):

(4a)
$$\log \frac{M_{ij}^+}{M_{ij}^+ + Q_{ij}} = u_i + v_i \log \frac{Q_{ij}}{\overline{Q}_i} + y_i \log T_j$$

and/or

(4a')
$$\log \frac{M_{ij}^+}{M_{ij}^+ + Q_{ij}} = u_i^* + v_i^* \log \frac{X_{ij}^+}{(1 - s_j)\overline{Q}_i} + y_i^* \log T_j,$$

where $T_j \equiv$ transport costs or distance and $u_i, u_i^*, v_i, v_i^*, y_i,$ and y_i^* are all parameters.

When estimating (4a) and (4a'), Lawrence finds that he can confirm the impression given by table 5.2. For many manufacturing sectors, Japanese shares of global production and/or of global export markets are too small to explain the small share that imports play in total Japanese consumption. Japan does not appear to be competitive enough abroad to explain why it has such a large market share at home.

Lawrence's work is most attractive in that it allows for important phenomena that cannot be considered by approaches based on the Heckscher-Ohlin framework. His use of production shares and export shares as explanatory variables, however, makes homotheticity the driving force of his interpretation of differences in trade structure. Indeed, his empirical findings can be viewed primarily as a test of this assumption. The quality of this test may be qualified by a number of specification errors.

Quite apart from unresolved issues such as what functional form is appropriate when transport costs are introduced into the Helpman-Krugman model and whether it is appropriate to introduce transport costs at all into an export share version of this model, Lawrence's import share, export share, and production share variables are all jointly determined. The issue of simultaneity here is a very real one. In addition to nontrivial estimation bias, there are some important identification issues. While Lawrence is careful in interpreting his results to suggest that there is something distinctive about Japanese trade structure, he does not make clear why this distinctiveness should be associated with possible Japanese import barriers. For example, in his export share model, out of twenty manufacturing sectors only three appear to have unduly low imports in 1970, but no less than nine do in 1983. Is it really plausible to infer that Japanese protection for manufacturing increased substantially between 1970 and 1983? This is precisely the period when virtually all formal Japanese barriers to the import of manufactured goods were eliminated. If Japanese trade structure did become more distinctive between 1970 and 1983, this can be more properly attributed to increasing foreign barriers to Japanese exports. Japan's import shares of manufactures may be a better index of Japanese competitiveness than its export shares.

5.5   Factor Endowments and Intraindustry Trade

In fact, neither export shares nor production shares need be used as explanatory variables in estimating the Helpman-Krugman model. From (2) and (4'),

$$M_{ij}^+ = S_j(Q_i - Q_{ij}),$$

$$X_{ij}^+ = (1 - S_j)Q_{ij},$$

but

(5)
$$S_j = \frac{\Pi_j}{\Pi} = \frac{\sum_s W_{sj} L_{sj}}{\sum_i \overline{Q}_i},$$

where $L_{sj} \equiv$ endowment of factor of production s in economy j and $W_{sj} \equiv$ rental for factor of production s.

Following the approach taken in Heckscher-Ohlin analyses, if factor price equalization is assumed, then, by Hotelling's lemma, if Π_j is differentiated,[3]

(6)
$$Q_{ij} = \sum_{s=1}^{K} R_{is} L_{sj},$$

where R_{is} is a function of the parameters of Π_j and output prices, which are assumed to be constant.

Substituting (5) and (6) into the expressions for gross imports and gross exports we get

(7) $$M_{ij}^+ = \sum_{s=1}^{K} B_{is}^+ L_{sj} - \sum_{s=1}^{K} \sum_{r=1}^{K} D_{isr}^+ L_{sj} L_{rj}, \quad i = 1, \ldots, N,$$

(8) $$X_{ij}^+ = \sum_{s=1}^{K} R_{is} L_{sj} - \sum_{s=1}^{K} \sum_{r=1}^{K} D_{isr}^+ L_{sj} L_{rj}, \quad i = 1, \ldots, N,$$

where B_{is}^+ and D_{isr}^+ are functions of parameters of Π_j and where output prices will be constant under the assumptions already made. The linear factor endowments terms in (7) represent economy j's demand for good i, while the linear terms in (8) represent economy j's supply of good i. The interaction terms in equations (7) and (8) represent economy j's supply of good i. The interaction terms in equations (7) and (8) represent economy j's demand for its domestically produced variety j of good i. The term M_{ij}^+ in (7) can be interpreted as that part of economy j's demand for good i that cannot be satisfied by the domestically produced variety j. The term X_{ij}^+ in (7) is the supply of variety j of good i available after domestic demand has been met. Neither M_{ij}^+ nor X_{ij}^+ can be negative. If (7) is subtracted from (8), net exports will be given by[4]

(9) $$\left(X_{ij}^+ - M_{ij}^+ \right) = \sum_{s=1}^{K} \left(R_{is} - B_{is}^+ \right) L_{sj}, \quad i = 1, \ldots, N.$$

Net exports reflect the balance between domestic demand for and supply of good i by economy j. Since domestic demand for the domestic variety of good i appears in both equations (7) and (8), these terms cancel out in equation (9).

By contrast with (7) and (8), (9) is the traditional Heckscher-Ohlin equation with net exports as a linear function of factor endowments (Saxonhouse 1983; and Leamer 1984). Within the Heckscher-Ohlin framework, the nonlinear terms in (7) and (8) cancel out. Since (9) can be derived from the Helpman-Krugman equations (7) and (8), this should demonstrate the compatibility of these two approaches. Contrary to what is often alleged (e.g., Zysman and Tyson 1983, p. 30), the incorporation of scale economies and product differentiation into conventional methods of international trade in order to account for intraindustry trade need not invalidate the Heckscher-Ohlin interpretation of interindustry trade (Helpman and Krugman 1985, p. 131).

Equations (7) and (8) can be estimated in an effort to reconcile the contrasting approaches of Leamer/Saxonhouse and Lawrence. As in the Lawrence approach, equations (7) and (8), by using gross imports or gross exports as a dependent variable, do not net out intraindustry trade. As in the Leamer and Saxonhouse approaches, however, simultaneity problems are avoided by using factor endowments as the central explanatory variables.

The structure embodied in equations (7), (8), and (9) results from relaxing many of the strictest assumptions of the Heckscher-Ohlin model in order to incorporate hitherto neglected phenomena. Still further relaxation of assumptions is possible. For example, suppose that the assumption that strict factor price equalization across countries is dropped. Suppose rather that international trade equalizes factor prices only when factor units are normalized for differences in quality. For example, observed international differences in the compensation of ostensibly unskilled labor may be accounted for by differences in labor quality.[5] Instead of (7), (8), and (9), we have

$$(7') \quad M_{ij}^+ = \sum_{s=1}^{K} B_{is}^+ a_s L_{sj} - \sum_{s=1}^{K} \sum_{r=1}^{K} D_{isr}^+ a_s L_{sj} a_r L_{rj}, \quad i = 1, \ldots, N,$$

$$(8') \quad X_{ij}^+ = \sum_{s=1}^{K} R_{is} a_s L_{sj} - \sum_{s=1}^{K} \sum_{r=1}^{K} D_{is}^+ a_s L_{sj} a_r L_{rj}, \quad i = 1, \ldots, N,$$

$$(9') \quad (X_{ij}^+ - M_{ij}^+) = \sum_{s=1}^{K} (R_{is} - B_{is}^+) a_s L_{sj}, \quad i = 1, \ldots, N,$$

where $a_s \equiv$ quality of factor s.

5.6   Estimation Procedures

Equation (9') can be estimated for N commodity groups from cross-national data. The term a_s is not directly observable but can be estimated from (9'). Formally, the estimation of (9') with a_s differing across countries and unknown is a multivariate, multiplicative errors in variable problem. Instrumental variable methods will allow consistent estimates of the $R_{is} - B_{is}^+$. For any given net trade cross section, a_s will not be identified. In the particular specification adopted in (8'), however, at any given time there are N cross sections that contain the identical independent variables. This circumstance can be exploited to permit consistent estimation of the a_s.[6] Since the same error will recur in equation after equation owing to the unobservable quality terms, it is possible to use this recurring error to obtain consistent estimates of the quality terms. These estimates of a_s can then be used to adjust the factor endowment data in (7') and (8') to obtain more efficient estimates of R_{is}, B_{is}^+, and D_{isr}^+.[7] In estimating (7') and (8'), the D_{isr}^+ can be constrained to be the same in both equations.

5.7   Estimating an Interindustry Trade Model

Equation (9') is estimated with data taken from the forty-one countries listed in table 5.3.[8] Equation (9') is estimated for each of the sixty-one trade sectors listed in table 5.4 for 1979. The six factor endowments used in this estimation include directly productive capital stock, educational attainment, labor, petroleum reserves, coal, and arable land. Unlike Lawrence's work and earlier work by Saxonhouse (1983, 1986), distance is not treated as an independent variable, and the Heckscher-Ohlin equations are assumed to hold up to an additive stochastic term.

Table 5.3   **Country Sample for Empirical Work**

Argentina	Japan
Australia	South Korea
Austria	Malaysia
Belgium & Luxembourg	Malta
Brazil	Mexico
Canada	Netherlands
Sri Lanka	Nigeria
Cyprus	Norway
Denmark	Philippines
Finland	Portugal
France	Singapore
West Germany	Spain
Greece	Sweden
Honduras	Switzerland
Hong Kong	Thailand
Iceland	Turkey
India	United Arab Republic
Indonesia	United Kingdom
Ireland	United States
Israel	Yugoslavia
Italy	

Table 5.4   Trade Sectors in Sample

Petroleum, petroleum products (PETRO33)	Travel goods, handbags (LAB83)
Crude materials, crude fertilizer (MAT27)	Clothing (LAB84)
Metalliferous ores, metal scrap (MAT28)	Footwear (LAB85)
Coal, coke briquettes (MAT32)	Miscellaneous manufactured articles not
Gas, natural & manufactured (MAT34)	elsewhere specified (LAB89)
Electrical energy (MAT35)	Postal pack not classified according to kind
Nonferrous metals (MAT68)	(LAB91)
Wood, lumber, cork (FOR24)	Special transactions not classified according
Pulp, waste paper (FOR25)	to kind (LAB93)
Wood, cork manufactures (FOR63)	Coins, nongold, noncurrent (LAB96)
Paper, paperboard (FOR64)	Leather, dressed furskins (CAP61)
Fruit, vegetables (TROP5)	Rubber manufactures, not elsewhere
Sugar, sugar preparations, honey (TROP6)	specified (CAP62)
Coffee, tea, cocoa, spices (TROP7)	Textile, yarn, fabrics (CAP65)
Beverages (TROP11)	Iron and steel (CAP67)
Crude rubber (TROP23)	Manufactures of metal (CAP69)
Live animals (ANL0)	Sanitary fixtures, fittings (CAP81)
Meat, meat preparations (ANL1)	Machinery, other than electrical (MACH71)
Dairy products, eggs (ANL2)	Electrical machinery (MACH72)
Fish, fish preparations (ANL3)	Transport equipment (MACH73)
Hides, skins, furskins, undressed (ANL21)	Professional goods, watches, instruments
Crude animal, vegetable minerals (ANL29)	(MACH86)
Animal, vegetable oils, fats, processed	Firearms, ammunition (MACH95)
(ANL45)	Chemical elements, compounds (CHEM51)
Animals, not elsewhere specified (ANL94)	Mineral tar & crude chemicals from coal,
Cereals, cereal preparations (CER4)	petroleum & natural gas (CHEM52)
Feeding stuff for animals (CER8)	Dyeing, tanning, coloring matter (CHEM53)
Miscellanous food preparations (CER9)	Medicinal, pharmaceutical products
Tobacco, tobacco manufactures (CER12)	(CHEM54)
Oil seeds, oil nuts, oil kernels (CER22)	Essential oils, perfume matter (CHEM55)
Textile fibers (CER26)	Fertilizers, manufactured (CHEM56)
Animal oils, fats (CER41)	Explosives, pyrotechnic products (CHEM57)
Fixed vegetable oils (CER42)	Plastic materials, cellulose (CHEM58)
Nonmetallic mineral manufactures (LAB66)	Chemical materials, not elsewhere specified
Furniture (LAB82)	(CHEM59)

The results of estimating equation (9') are given in tables 5.5 and 5.6. Note that fifty-four of the sixty-one sectoral net trade regressions are significant. For individual factor endowments, out of sixty-one estimated equations, capital has significant coefficients in twenty-eight, labor has fourteen, education has nineteen, oil has sixteen, coal has twenty-two, and land has twenty-two. Generally speaking, physical capital and human capital are sources of comparative disadvantage in the interindustry trade in natural resource and labor-intensive products and sources of comparative advantage for trade in capital-intensive and machinery products. Labor is a source of comparative disadvantage in interindustry trade in natural resource products. Surprisingly, it has little influence on the trade of what are normally thought to be labor-intensive products. As expected, oil and arable land are sources of comparative

Table 5.5   **Estimation of Equation (9′)**

$$(X_{ij}^+ - M_{ij}^+) = N_0 + N_1\text{CAPITAL} + N_2\text{LABOR} + N_3\text{EDUC} + N_4\text{OIL} + N_5\text{COAL} + N_6\text{LAND ARA}$$

	R^2	$F(6/34)$		R^2	$F(6/34)$
PETRO33	.952	112.**	CER42	.096	.60
MAT27	.747	16.8**	LAB66	.574	7.63**
MAT28	.798	22.4**	LAB82	.202	1.44
MAT32	.835	28.6**	LAB83	.535	26.52**
MAT34	.461	4.78**	LAB84	.413	3.99**
MAT35	.295	2.37**	LAB85	.515	6.02**
MAT68	.687	12.4**	LAB89	.754	17.4**
FOR24	.652	10.6**	LAB91	.540	6.64**
FOR25	.424	4.18**	LAB93	.5701	7.51**
FOR63	.476	5.15**	LAB96	.137	.90
FOR64	.305	2.48**	CAP61	.591	8.19**
TROP5	.428	4.24**	CAP62	.850	32.2**
TROP6	.699	13.2**	CAP65	.590	8.16**
TROP7	.683	12.2**	CAP67	.848	31.6**
TROP11	.697	13.0**	CAP69	.891	46.4**
TROP23	.177	1.22	CAP81	.309	2.54**
ANL0	.045	.27	MACH71	.843	30.3**
ANL1	.454	4.71**	MACH72	.928	72.5**
ANL2	.115	.74	MACH73	.930	75.3**
ANL3	.953	116.**	MACH86	.700	13.2**
ANL21	.587	8.05**	MACH95	.953	114.**
ANL29	.334	2.84**	CHEM51	.693	12.8**
ANL43	.323	2.71**	CHEM52	.382	3.51**
ANL94	.436	4.38**	CHEM53	.510	5.89**
CER4	.942	92.7**	CHEM54	.599	8.47**
CER8	.653	10.7**	CHEM55	.650	10.6**
CER9	.403	3.82**	CHEM56	.240	1.78
CER12	.823	26.3**	CHEM57	.573	7.60**
CER22	.894	47.6**	CHEM58	.689	12.6**
CER26	.739	16.1**	CHEM59	.793	21.7**
CER41	.865	36.5**			

$**F(6, 34)_{.05} = 2.34.$

advantage for trade in natural resources and sources of comparative disadvantage for trade in virtually all manufactured products. By contrast, coal is a source of comparative disadvantage for most natural resource products, save coal itself, and a source of comparative advantage for trade in machinery and chemicals.

Apart from their statistical significance, how important are each of these variables in explaining trade structure? Table 5.7 presents beta coefficients for each of the six explanatory variables for each of the sixty-one net trade equations (Kmenta 1986, pp. 422–23). These beta coefficients are directly proportional to the contribution that each variable makes to a prediction of net trade (Leamer 1978). Since equations such as (9′) are used to predict Japanese trade structure, these results are of particular interest.

Table 5.6 Numbers of Significant (.05) Coefficients in Equation (9′) by Sectoral Grouping, Factor Endowment, and Sign

	Capital		Labor		Education		Petroleum		Coal		Land	
	+	−	+	−	+	−	+	−	+	−	+	−
(7) Petroleum and raw materials (PETRO33, MAT27–68)	...	3	...	1	...	1	2	...	1	...	2	...
(4) Forest products (FOR24–63)	...	1	1	...	...	...	...	...	...	1	1	...
(5) Tropical products (TROP5–23)	...	3	1	...	...	3	...	2	...	3	2	...
(8) Animal products (ANL0–94)	...	3	1	...	...	1	1	...	...	...	2	...
(8) Cereals (CER4–42)	1	1	1	...	...	3	3	...	1	...	4	...
(9) Labor-intensive manufactures (LAB66–96)	1	1	1	...	1	1	...	2	1	2	...	1
(6) Capital-intensive manufacturing (CAP61–81)	4	...	2	1	3	...	...	2	2	1	...	3
(5) Machinery (MACH71–95)	4	...	3	...	4	...	1	...	4	...	...	4
(9) Chemical products (CHEM51–59)	4	2	3	2	2	1	...	3	6	...	...	4

Note: Numbers in parentheses at the left of sectoral grouping rows indicate the number of equations in each sectoral grouping.

Table 5.7   **Beta Values from Equation (9′)**

	N_1	N_2	N_3	N_4	N_5	N_6
PETRO33	−1.16	−.20	.22	.68	−.15	−.15
MAT27	−.63	−.75	−.20	1.09	−.13	.85
MAT28	−1.62	1.42	−1.79	−.45	−.48	1.93
MAT32	−.83	−.68	−.26	−.21	1.85	.48
MAT34	−.94	.97	−.91	.10	−.96	.86
MAT35	.48	−1.15	.21	1.06	−1.12	.71
MAT68	.41	−2.36	.71	.32	.01	.62
FOR24	−1.59	.88	−.88	.58	−.24	.75
FOR25	.48	−1.19	−.02	.97	−1.33	1.12
FOR63	−.11	−1.31	.16	.36	−.17	.74
FOR64	1.16	−1.76	−.48	.88	−1.26	.71
TROP5	−.29	−.28	−.22	.96	−1.20	.94
TROP6	−.86	1.19	−1.59	−1.70	−.22	1.91
TROP7	−1.02	1.48	−.62	−.20	−1.08	.42
TROP11	−1.47	4.57	−2.60	−1.77	−1.54	1.01
TROP23	−.13	.83	1.04	1.13	−.07	−1.00
ANL0	−.38	.71	−.62	−.42	.18	.38
ANL1	−.28	−.52	−.58	−.10	−.43	1.37
ANL2	.06	.52	−.98	−.42	−.85	1.21
ANL3	−1.15	.21	.20	.64	−.13	−.12
ANL21	−.91	.32	−.80	.14	.44	.90
ANL29	−.88	.82	−.54	.54	−1.05	.65
ANL43	−1.69	1.58	−.96	−.16	.29	.22
ANL94	−2.06	2.22	−1.50	−.61	.52	.58
CER4	−.33	.69	−1.22	.18	−.20	1.24
CER8	−.77	.98	−.66	.62	−.48	.73
CER9	.15	−.07	−.09	.32	.21	.09
CER12	−.75	.47	−.47	.78	−.04	.57
CER22	.00	.02	.01	.00	.29	.01
CER26	−.68	−.15	−1.18	−.66	.78	1.79
CER41	.41	−.99	−.14	.68	.00	.91
CER42	−.33	−.37	.38	.80	−.04	−.31
LAB66	.01	.62	.25	−1.11	.63	−.81
LAB82	.51	−1.52	1.18	−.15	1.12	−.95
LAB83	−.09	.01	.24	−.02	−.57	−.20
LAB84	−.50	.47	−.13	.11	−.75	.13
LAB85	−.28	.87	−.42	−.31	−1.03	.31
LAB89	1.23	−1.28	1.56	−.22	.44	−1.50
LAB91	−2.18	3.91	−1.48	−1.34	1.06	−.82
LAB93	−.18	1.66	−.95	−.57	−1.61	.63
LAB96	.57	−1.74	1.05	.62	.82	−.57
CAP61	−.90	1.84	−.47	−.75	−.56	.70
CAP62	.75	1.27	−.12	−1.00	−.67	−.55
CAP65	1.67	−1.72	1.85	.38	.08	−1.20
CAP67	2.69	−2.88	1.91	.08	−.13	−.80
CAP69	1.62	−1.00	1.04	−.88	.88	−1.04
CAP81	.45	−.55	.69	−.36	1.25	−.95

(*continued*)

Table 5.7   (continued)

	N_1	N_2	N_3	N_4	N_5	N_6
MACH71	1.07	−1.27	1.08	−.17	1.60	−1.19
MACH72	2.22	−2.15	1.79	−.02	.67	−1.36
MACH73	2.12	−1.41	1.22	−.31	.16	−.88
MACH86	2.08	−2.86	2.26	.62	.97	−1.63
MACH95	.18	.35	−.17	.54	.46	−.12
CHEM51	1.58	−2.71	1.61	.13	1.76	−1.04
CHEM52	−.70	.07	−.63	.92	−1.00	.71
CHEM53	.63	−1.09	.87	−.89	2.05	−1.06
CHEM54	−1.22	2.22	−1.04	−.96	1.33	−.43
CHEM55	−1.57	4.35	−2.27	−1.72	.29	.27
CHEM56	1.45	−3.15	1.35	1.16	.20	−.29
CHEM57	−1.46	2.98	−1.21	−1.04	1.05	−.56
CHEM58	1.38	−1.82	1.45	.16	1.30	−1.24
CHEM59	.21	−.53	.54	−.37	1.99	−.99

The beta values in table 5.7 indicate the amount of change in standard deviation units of the net trade variable induced by a change of one standard deviation in the factor endowment. Following Leamer, if 0.5 is defined as a significant beta value, then education or human capital is significant in fifty-one out of sixty-one net trade equations. Arable land is significant forty-seven times, labor forty-three times, capital forty-one times, coal thirty-four times, and oil thirty-three times.

5.8   Cross-national Differences in Factor Quality and Measurement Error

In table 5.8, Hausman's (1978) Test is used to check for unmeasured differences in factor quality and other errors in factor measurement across countries. In no less than forty-two out of a total of sixty-one sectoral trade equations, the hypothesis that there are no cross-national unmeasured differences in factor quality cannot be accepted. This result is hardly surprising in view both of the quality of the data being used and of the widely observed differences across countries in the compensation of ostensibly similar factors of production. In consequence, using the multiplicative errors in variables methods previously outlined, these differences have been estimated.

Cross-national estimate of factor quality and measurement error for forty-one countries are presented in table 5.9. These estimates are very difficult to interpret. They do not conform to any a priori beliefs about the relative quality of the various factors of production across countries. Cypriot, Honduran, Icelandic, and Maltese workers are not credibly three or four times more efficient than their American counterparts. Rather, these estimates may be dominated by errors of measurement that simply reflect poor data collection. For some countries, the estimated a_s may also reflect government policies aimed not so much as protecting particular sectors as at protecting

Table 5.8   **Hausman's Test on Factor Endowments, *F*-Test on Errors in Capital, Labor, and Education Variables**

PETRO33	31.82*	CER42	1.44
MAT27	12.38*	LAB66	1.69
MAT28	21.97*	LAB82	3.94*
MAT32	2.00	LAB83	3.10*
MAT34	4.81*	LAB84	1.64
MAT35	3.54*	LAB85	6.85*
MAT68	1.68	LAB89	2.77*
FOR24	2.71*	LAB91	44.37*
FOR25	3.05*	LAB93	3.71*
FOR63	2.90*	LAB96	.81
FOR64	1.10	CAP61	2.36*
TROP5	7.74*	CAP62	8.62*
TROP 6	.32	CAP65	3.43*
TROP7	3.51*	CAP67	4.31*
TROP11	1.05	CAP69	6.32*
TROP23	1.59	CAP81	5.07*
ANL0	27.30*	MACH71	3.28*
ANL1	5.64*	MACH72	12.89*
ANL2	1.17	MACH73	27.75*
ANL3	1.17	MACH86	8.68*
ANL21	.23	MACH95	1.99
ANL29	1.54	CHEM51	7.52*
ANL43	8.48*	CHEM52	5.62*
ANL94	14.13*	CHEM53	11.41*
CER4	1.11	CHEM54	4.28*
CER8	7.01*	CHEM55	.81
CER9	6.15*	CHEM56	6.11*
CER12	10.70*	CHEM57	3.53*
CER22	13.89*	CHEM58	3.46*
CER26	10.35*	CHEM59	1.78
CER41	2.95*		

*Significant at .05 level.

particular factors of production. For example, Indonesian capital may greatly benefit by government policy at the expense of skilled and unskilled labor, while Turkish, Norwegian, and Danish labor may benefit at the expense of capital. It is also possible that some of the unusual findings in table 5.9 are purely artifacts of the estimation procedures used. Cyprus, Honduras, Iceland, and Malta, with by far the highest measured factor efficiency, also have the smallest factor endowments of capital and skilled and unskilled labor in the forty-one-country sample. While using rank order by size of factor endowments generates instruments that, in general, are closely correlated with the factor endowments, some countries obviously remain outliers.[9]

5.9   Estimating an Intraindustry Model of Trade

Unlike the net trade equation (9′), the dependent variables in the gross trade equations (7′) and (8′) will never be negative, but they will occasionally be

Table 5.9   Cross-national Estimates of Factor Quality and Measurement
                 Error a_s

	Capital	Labor	Education
Argentina	.96	1.17	1.18
Australia	1.08	1.09	1.26
Austria	.87	1.28	1.23
Belgium & Luxembourg	.98	1.36	1.18
Brazil	.71	.70	.83
Sri Lanka	2.48	1.07	1.36
Cyprus	4.13	3.76	5.04
Denmark	.85	1.51	.89
Finland	.95	1.33	.93
France	.76	1.00	.82
West Germany	1.15	1.03	1.06
Greece	.78	1.13	1.39
Honduras	4.07	2.35	3.01
Hong Kong	1.78	1.22	1.30
Iceland	3.13	4.16	3.62
India	1.37	.91	1.00
Indonesia	2.62	.83	.79
Ireland	2.61	1.57	1.44
Israel	1.40	1.38	1.17
Italy	.93	.94	.87
Japan	.93	.89	.94
Korea	1.22	.83	1.09
Malaysia	1.69	.99	1.04
Malta	5.01	3.97	4.16
Mexico	1.16	.98	1.02
Netherlands	.87	1.13	.82
Nigeria	1.93	1.02	1.10
Norway	.78	1.54	1.09
Philippines	1.40	.67	.85
Portugal	1.53	1.41	1.43
Singapore	1.67	1.70	1.48
Spain	.77	1.06	1.11
Sweden	1.00	1.32	.89
Switzerland	.95	1.38	1.03
Thailand	1.13	.85	1.31
Turkey	.82	1.43	1.36
United Arab Republic	1.56	1.33	.86
United Kingdom	10.99	.76	.85
United States	1.00	1.01	1.01
Yugoslavia	1.14	.84	.91

zero. As seen in table 5.10, some of the import equations and most of the export equations will contain some zero observations. This suggests that equations (7′) and (8′) should be specified as a Tobit model.[10]

The presence of factor endowment interaction terms in equations (7′) and (8′) presents additional estimation problems. Given the available sample size and the large number of interaction terms, multicollinearity among the

Table 5.10   **Proportion of Zero Observations in Gross Trade Equations**

	Imports	Exports		Imports	Exports
PETRO33	0	.073	CER9	0	0
MAT27	0	.024	CER12	.049	.049
MAT28	0	.195	CER22	.024	.073
MAT32	0	.195	CER26	0	0
MAT34	.049	.268	CER41	0	.146
MAT35	.634	.683	CER42	0	.049
MAT68	0	0	CAP61	0	0
FOR24	0	.098	CAP62	0	.024
FOR25	.049	.098	CAP65	0	0
FOR63	0	0	CAP67	0	.049
FOR64	0	0	CAP69	0	0
TROP5	0	.024	CAP81	0	.049
TROP6	0	.049	MACH71	0	.024
TROP7	0	.024	MACH72	0	.049
TROP11	0	.049	MACH73	0	.024
TROP23	0	.122	MACH86	0	.049
ANL0	.268	NA	MACH95	.171	.366
ANL1	.024	.024	CHEM51	0	.024
ANL2	0	.073	CHEM52	0	.220
ANL3	0	0	CHEM53	0	0
ANL21	.073	0	CHEM54	0	.024
ANL29	0	0	CHEM55	0	.024
ANL43	0	.122	CHEM56	.024	.146
ANL94	0	.122	CHEM57	0	.146
CER4	0	.024	CHEM58	0	.049
CER8	0	0	CHEM59	0	0

independent variables is likely to make precise estimation difficult.[11] In order to avoid this problem, recall that from (5) and (7') that

$$M_{ij}^+ = \sum_{s=1}^{K} B_{is}^+ a_s L_{sj} - \sum_{s=1}^{K} \sum_{r=1}^{K} D_{irs}^+ a_s L_{sj} L_{rj}$$

$$= \frac{\Pi_j}{\Pi} \overline{Q}_i - \frac{\Pi_j}{\Pi} \sum_{s=1}^{K} R_{is} a_s L_{sj} .$$

Dividing through by Π_j we get

$$(10') \qquad \frac{M_{ij}^+}{\Pi_j} = \frac{\overline{Q}_i}{\Pi} - \frac{1}{\Pi} \sum_{s=1}^{K} R_{is} a_s L_{sj} = F_i - \sum_{s=1}^{K} R_{is}^* a_s L_{sj} ,$$

where $F_i \equiv \overline{Q}_i/\Pi \equiv$ global sector i as a proportion of global GNP and $R^*_{is} \equiv R_{is}/\Pi$.

Equation (10') makes it very easy to demonstrate that, in a world with intraindustry trade, trade volume as a proportion of GNP can vary. By contrast, in the Heckscher-Ohlin world of equation (9'), trade volume as a proportion of GNP cannot vary. From (10') it is clear that, if two economies are alike in all respects except size, the larger economy will have the relatively smaller foreign trade sector.

The results of estimating (10'), using the quality adjusted factor endowment data but excluding Japan from the sample, are presented in tables 5.11 and 5.12. In general, the results are interesting, occasionally surprising, but mostly plausible. For example, forty-nine out of sixty-one gross import regressions are statistically significant. These results mean that it is possible to get a good explanation of the commodity structure of intraindustry trade even without any treatment of distance between trading partners.

Table 5.11   The Estimation of
$$P_0 + P_1\text{CAPITAL} + P_2\text{LABOR} + P_3\text{EDUC}$$
$$+ P_4\text{OIL} + P_5\text{COAL} + P_6\text{LAND ARA}$$

	R^2	$F(6/33)$		R^2	$F(6/33)$
PETRO33	.999	6610.00**	CER42	.746	18.3**
MAT27	.378	3.34**	LAB66	.646	10.0**
MAT28	.149	.97	LAB82	.280	2.14
MAT32	.120	.75	LAB83	.796	21.4**
MAT34	.059	.34	LAB84	.483	5.14**
MAT35	.085	.51	LAB85	.430	4.14**
MAT68	.502	5.55***	LAB89	.805	22.7**
FOR24	.475	4.99**	LAB91	.033	.18
FOR25	.205	1.42	LAB93	.362	3.12**
FOR63	.589	7.89**	LAB96	.370	3.23**
FOR64	.523	6.10**	CAP61	.545	6.58**
TROP5	.820	25.1**	CAP62	.454	4.57**
TROP6	.420	3.98**	CAP65	.818	24.7**
TROP7	.716	13.9**	CAP67	.815	24.2**
TROP11	.607	8.49**	CAP69	.780	19.5**
TROP23	.920	62.8**	CAP81	.705	13.2**
ANL0	.688	12.1**	MACH71	.864	34.9**
ANL1	.570	7.28**	MACH72	.903	51.3**
ANL2	.582	7.65**	MACH73	.914	58.6**
ANL3	.999	1870.0**	MACH86	.792	20.9**
ANL21	.076	.46	MACH95	.132	.84
ANL29	.654	10.4**	CHEM51	.374	3.28**
ANL43	.899	48.7	CHEM52	.064	.38
ANL94	.691	12.3**	CHEM53	.834	27.6**
CER4	.397	3.62**	CHEM54	.466	4.80**
CER8	.435	4.23**	CHEM55	.711	13.5**
CER9	.536	6.34**	CHEM56	.108	.66
CER12	.395	3.59**	CHEM57	.738	15.5**
CER22	.243	1.77	CHEM58	.255	16.9**
CER26	.559	6.97**	CHEM59	.416	3.92**
CER41	.067	.39			

**Significant at the .05 level, $F(6,33)_{.05} = 2.33$.

Table 5.12 Number of Significant (.05) Coefficients in Equation (10′) by Sectoral Grouping and Factor Endowment and Sign

	F_i	Capital		Labor		Education		Oil		Coal		Arable Land	
		+	−	+	−	+	−	+	−	+	−	+	−
(7) Petroleum and raw materials (PETRO33, MAT27–68)	3	2	1	1	1	1	1	...	2	...	1	...	2
(4) Forest products (FOR24–63)	2	1	...	2	1	...	2	...	2	...	...	2	...
(5) Tropical products (TROP5–23)	5	3	1	1	3	2	2	3	1	1	3	...	...
(8) Animal products (ANL0–94)	7	4	2	2	3	4	1	4	2	4	2	1	5
(8) Cereals (CER4–42)	6	3	2	...	4	3	2	1	2	1	3	0	5
(9) Labor-intensive manufactures (LAB66–96)	7	3	2	...	6	3	2	3	2	3	3	2	3
(6) Capital-intensive manufactures (CAP61–81)	6	2	4	2	2	2	3	3	2	1	3	3	1
(5) Machinery (MACH71–95)	4	1	3	1	2	1	3	1	1	...	4	3	2
(9) Chemical products (CHEM51–59)	7	2	5	1	4	1	3	3	1	...	5	3	1

Note: Numbers in parentheses at the left of sectoral grouping rows indicate the number of equations in each sectoral grouping.

The results here also appear to be generally in accord with the theory motivating equation (10'). Since it is impossible to have imports of a product that is nowhere produced, from (10') it is clear that F_i, the constant term in this equation, should be positive. In fifty out of the sixty-one estimated gross import share equations, the F_i are statistically significantly greater than zero. From (6), it is also clear that the signs of the coefficients on the factor endowments in (10') will be opposite to those of the corresponding second derivatives of the GNP function. This means that at least some of the sixty-one coefficients on each factor endowment in (10') are negative and that in the absence of widespread specialization by sector at least some of the coefficients on factor endowments in each of the sixty-one import equations will also be negative (Diewert 1974, p. 143). As estimated, equation (10') meets both these conditions.

For individual factor endowments, by marked contrast with the estimated interindustry trade model, the intraindustry trade model has a great many more significant coefficients. What are the determinants of gross imports? Capital once again has the most significant coefficients with forty-three, education has thirty-three, oil has thirty-four, and coal, land, labor all have thirty-five. The determinants of gross imports do appear quite similar to the determinants of net trade. Endowments of capital and human capital do encourage imports of natural resource products and labor-intensive products while discouraging imports of capital-intensive, machinery, and chemical products. As expected, arable land has just the opposite effect. Perversely, endowments in labor do appear to discourage imports of what are thought to be labor-intensive products along with the imports of most natural resource products. Factor endowments of oil, while encouraging net exports of many natural resource products, with the obvious exception of energy products, do encourage the gross imports of natural resource products. Coal's effect is just the opposite. With the exception of energy products, endowments of coal appear to encourage net imports of natural resource products. At the same time, however, they appear to discourage gross imports of these products.

5.10   Is Japanese Trade Behavior Distinctive?

Equation (10') has been estimated without using Japanese observations.[12] Following earlier work by Saxonhouse (1983, 1986), forecasts are made successively on Japanese, Canadian, U.S., and Korean sectoral import shares using equation (10'). These forecasts are then compared with actual import shares. To the extent that equation (10'), estimated with non-Japanese evidence, can replicate Japan's trade structure, it is difficult to argue that Japanese sectoral policies are yielding distinctive outcomes. This does not necessarily mean that Japan has a liberal trade regime. If all countries with relatively small amounts of arable land protect their wheat growers, Japan's behavior will not be seen as distinctive. At the same time under these circumstances, a change in Japanese trade policy will yield an increase in Japanese wheat imports. It should also be understood that, even if equation (10′) cannot replicate Japan's trade structure, such a failure cannot necessarily be attributed to Japanese trade barriers. There may be other important variables, besides trade barriers, that have been excluded from the model underlying equation (10′).

The results of estimating (10′) are presented in tables 5.13 and 5.14. Of the sixty-one actual observations on Japanese import shares, only eight do not appear to come from the same population used to estimate (10′). These findings for gross import shares appear broadly consistent with earlier findings by Leamer and Saxonhouse for net trade. Japanese sectoral policies do not appear to be yielding distinctive outcomes.

Tables 5.13 and 5.14 contain findings for individual sectors. In order to test the null hypothesis that the ex post forecasts on all the extra sample values of

Table 5.13   **Extreme Observations on Imports, 1979**

Japan:	United States:
Wood, lumber, cork	Metalliferous ores
Wood, cork, manufactures	Petroleum products
Meat, meat preparation	Plastic materials
Dairy products & eggs	Rubber manufactures, not elsewhere specified
Feedstuff for animals	Textile yarn, fabrics
Tobacco, tobacco products	Clothing
Clothing	Footwear
Footwear	

Canada:	Korea:
Dairy products, eggs	Coal, coke briquettes
Fish, fish prepartion	Fruit, vegetables
Oil seeds, oil nuts, oil kernels	Cereals, ceral preparation
Wood, lumber, cork	Tobacco, tobacco manufactures
Wood, cork manufactures	Oil seeds, oil nuts, oil kernels
Leather, dressed	Textile fibers
Rubber manufactures	Hides, skins, furskins, undressed
Paper, paperboard, & manufactures	Crude animals, vegetables, minerals
Textile yarn, fabrics	Wood, lumber, cork
Manufactures of metal machinery	Wood, cork manufactures
	Footwear
	Rubber manufactures, not elsewhere specified
	Metal manufactures
	Machinery, other than electrical
	Electrical machinery
	Transport equipment
	Plastic materials, cellulose
	Chemical materials, not elsewhere specified

Table 5.14   Does Forecasted $\dfrac{M_{ij}}{\Pi_j}$ Come from the Same Population as Actual $\dfrac{M_{ij}}{\Pi_{j'}}$?

	Japan	United States	Canada	Korea
PETRO33	.33	2.38*	.67	.67
MAT27	.84	.84	.91	1.41
MAT28	1.56	2.53*	.89	1.25
MAT32	1.07	1.85	1.36	3.16*
MAT34	1.50	.61	1.28	1.48
MAT35	.74	1.21	1.03	1.19
MAT68	1.37	1.02	1.84	1.02
FOR24	2.14*	1.56	2.61*	2.68*
FOR25	.85	1.36	1.50	1.61
FOR63	2.68*	.28	2.50*	4.51*
FOR64	1.08	.74	3.02*	1.03
TROP5	.19	.04	1.08	2.87*
TROP6	1.08	1.02	.84	1.02
TROP7	.06	1.71	1.36	1.50
TROP11	.61	.28	1.48	.42
TROP23	.17	.34	1.33	.28
ANL0	.63	.02	.79	.68
ANL1	2.85*	1.03	.81	.41
ANL2	2.31*	1.63	2.21*	.54
ANL3	1.43	.35	.02	.42
ANL21	1.02	.51	1.46	.07
ANL29	.67	.55	1.27	3.11*
ANL45	.41	.94	1.02	.82
ANL94	.77	1.48	.81	1.19
CER4	.48	.41	.59	.50
CER8	2.96*	.81	1.27	.92
CER9	.27	.83	.80	.94
CER12	2.51*	.81	1.01	.02
CER22	.31	.25	3.41*	4.32*
CER26	.34	.47	.27	2.90*
CER41	.36	.47	1.26	.43
CER42	.51	.77	.21	.89
LAB66	.61	.87	.97	.85
LAB82	.85	.33	.69	.69
LAB83	.85	.41	.87	.96
LAB84	2.38*	2.64*	.68	1.89
LAB85	3.09*	3.16*	.43	1.15
LAB89	1.17	.48	.71	.66
LAB91	.69	.24	.57	.52
LAB93	.65	.37	.60	1.04
LAB96	.09	.09	.11	.06
CAP61	.11	.75	2.80*	1.64
CAP62	.08	2.67*	3.24*	2.98*
CAP65	.35	3.50*	.67	1.18
CAP67	1.23	1.44	1.84	.28
CAP69	.69	.61	2.73*	2.27*

Table 5.14   (continued)

	Japan	United States	Canada	Korea
CAP81	.01	.93	.85	1.28
MACH71	.97	1.02	.28	6.18*
MACH72	.69	.61	.91	3.76*
MACH73	.38	.87	.01	6.59*
MACH86	.67	.63	1.21	1.50
MACH95	.88	.39	.96	1.11
CHEM51	.77	1.23	.60	1.16
CHEM52	.21	.54	.56	1.06
CHEM53	.01	.46	.37	.77
CHEM54	.22	.44	.05	1.49
CHEM55	.55	.93	.57	.95
CHEM56	1.36	1.07	1.04	1.07
CHEM57	.62	1.00	.82	.86
CHEM58	.54	2.51*	.66	4.73*
CHEM59	1.42	1.48	1.39	3.20*

*Hypothesis that forecast and historical values come from same population not accepted (critical region = .05) using t-tests.

Japanese, Canadian, Korean, and U.S. trade structure, respectively, do not differ significantly from their historical values, the chi-square test statistic

(11) $$ P = \sum_{i=1}^{61} [(\hat{\phi}_{ij} - \phi_{ij})/\hat{\sigma}_{\phi ij}]^2 , $$

where $\hat{\phi}_{ij}$ ≡ forecast of gross imports/GNP in the ith sector in the jth country, where ϕ_{ij} ≡ actual value of gross imports/GNP in the ith sector in the jth country, ≡ and where $\hat{\sigma}_{\phi ij}$ ≡ estimated standard error can be utilized. Since the calculated values of P for Japan, Canada, Korea, and the United States are 89.3, 114.3, 227.6, and 95.4 respectively, for 1979 and the 5 percent critical value is 109.4, it is apparent that for Japan and the United States the null hypothesis cannot be rejected. As before, this suggests whatever Japanese (and American) trade policies (and/or informal barriers) may have been, more than likely they have not been a major determinant of trade patterns. Further investigation of the Canadian and Korean results are clearly in order.

5.11 Conclusions

On the basis of the preceding research, it appears that the removal of the remaining distinctive formal and informal Japanese sectoral barriers to the import of manufactures, while highly desirable from a diplomatic standpoint, may have little effect on Japanese trade structure. Japan's intraindustry trade pattern, like Japan's interindustry trade pattern, looks globally distinctive. When full allowance is made for economies of scale, differentiated products, and Japan's distinctive national endowments, however, Japan's intraindustry trade, like Japan's interindustry trade and like American trade, does conform to international patterns. If Japan is protectionist, it is protectionist in the same ways that other advanced, industrialized countries with scarce natural resources are protectionist. Whatever Japanese trade and industrial policies may have been in the 1950s, 1960s, and 1970s, by the late 1970s it is difficult to find evidence of their distinctive, lasting effect on Japanese trade structure.

Appendix A
Data Sources and Methods

Directly Productive Capital Stock

Benchmarks for 1960 for each of the countries in the sample are estimated by cumulating gross domestic capital formation excluding residential housing investment and inventories from 1948. Estimates of real gross domestic capital formation in common currency terms are available in Robert Summers, Irving Kravis, and Alan Heston, "International Comparison of Real Product and Its Components," *Review of Income and Wealth* ser. 26, no. 1 (March 1980). Residential housing investment and inventories are subtracted from these estimates. These data are available from the World Bank national accounts data sheets for 1950, 1955, and 1960. They are converted to common currency basis using the Summers, Kravis, and Heston purchasing power parity estimates for investment goods. For both the aggregate series and its components, missing years are interpolated. It is assumed that the average annual rate of growth of gross domestic capital formation is the same for 1948–50 as for 1950–55. Gross domestic capital formation is converted to net domestic capital formation by assuming an average asset life of twelve years and applying the appropriate depreciation factor. A capital stock series for 1959–79 is created by using World Bank data following these same procedures.

Labor Force

Benchmarks for 1979 for each of the countries in the sample are taken from the economically active population data given in International Labor Organization, *Yearbook of Labor Statistics* (Geneva: International Labor Organization).

Educational Attainment

Benchmarks for 1979 for each of the countries in the sample (1968 for France, 1971 for the Netherlands, and 1971 for the United Kingdom) are constructed using country-specific survey of labor force data. Occupational groups in each country are aggregated using weights taken from Laurits Christensen, Diane Cummings, and Dale W. Jorgenson, "Economic Growth, 1947–1973: An International Companson," in *New Development in Productivity Measurement and Analysis,* ed. John W. Kendrick and Beatrice Vaccara (Chicago: University of Chicago Press, 1980), 595–698.

Petroleum Resources and Coal Resources

Benchmarks for 1968 for each of the countries in the sample are obtained from the United Nations.

Petroleum resources series and coal resources series for 1959–79 are created by adding or subtracting where appropriate crude petroleum production to the benchmarks. These production data are taken from United Nations, *Yearbook of World Energy Statistics* (New York: United Nations).

Arable Land

Arable land data are available in Food and Agricultural Organization, *Production Yearbook* (Rome: Food and Agriculture Organization).

Trade Data

Trade data are available in United Nations, *Commodity Trade Statistics* (New York: United Nations), and *Yearbook of International Trade Statistics* (New York: United Nations). Some reclassification because of a change in the SITC (Standard Industrial Trade Classification) system in 1960. Trade flows are converted to U.S. dollars using prevailing exchange rates. Trade flows in current U.S. dollars are deflated using U.S. export and import price indices. The price indices used are more aggregated than the commodity breakdown employed in the analysis here.

Appendix B
Estimating Equations (7') and (8')

The results of estimating (7') and (8') jointly, using the quality adjusted factor endowment data, but excluding Japan from the sample, are presented in table 5B.1. Tables 5B.2 and 5B.3 present the results of tests on the explanatory power of equations (7') and (8'). As reported in table 5B.2, fifty- nine out of a total of sixty-one sectoral trade relationships are significant. In table 5B.3 we test whether the nonlinear terms in equations (7') and (8'), taken together, contribute significantly to the explanation of gross trade flows. Does the

Table 5B.1   Numbers of Significant (.05) Coefficients in Equations (7') and (8') by Sectoral Grouping and Factor Endowment

		Linear Terms						Interaction Terms					
		Capital	Labor	Education	Petroleum	Coal	Land	Capital	Labor	Education	Petroleum	Coal	Land
Petroleum and Raw Materials (PETRO33 MAT27–68)	M	3	1	2	3	3	3	6	3	2	8	3	3
Forest Products (FOR24–63)	X	4	2	1	1	4	2	9	5	7	8	7	5
	M	1	2	2	2	0	3						
Tropical Products (TROP5–23)	X	3	3	1	0	0	3	7	3	4	2	2	1
	M	2	0	1	1	2	2						
Animal Products (ANL0–94)	X	1	0	0	2	1	3	12	9	7	3	3	2
	M	1	2	4	0	3	4						
Cereals (CER4–42)	X	2	1	4	4	1	1	6	5	4	1	5	2
	M	0	0	0	1	4	6						
Labor-Intensive Manufactures (LAB66–96)	X	1	1	1	3	6	4	12	5	8	3	8	2
	M	3	0	1	0	5	6						
Capital-Intensive Manufactures (CAP61–81)	X	3	2	4	0	3	5	9	5	6	0	7	3
	M	2	1	3	1	5	3						
Machinery (MACH71–95)	X	2	1	3	1	5	6	9	4	5	0	2	1
	M	1	4	5	1	3	2						
Chemical Products (CHEM51–59)	X	5	2	2	0	2	2	12	11	17	6	12	6
	M	4	3	7	1	7	6						
	X	3	1	0	0	3	4						

Table 5B.2 **Test on the Significance of Each Sectoral Regression,** $F_{.05(33,47)} = 1.70$

PETRO33	30.9*	CER42	12.5*
MAT27	4.8*	LAB66	6.3*
MAT28	21.0*	LAB82	4.8*
MAT32	8.4*	LAB83	37.8*
MAT34	33.0*	LAB84	27.0*
MAT35	9.7*	LAB85	58.8*
MAT68	5.2*	LAB89	19.1*
FOR24	18.1*	LAB91	1.6*
FOR25	71.8*	LAB93	111.0*
FOR63	17.8*	LAB96	1.2
FOR64	4.1*	CAP61	35.4*
TROP5	26.9*	CAP62	30.4*
TROP6	69.0*	CAP65	7.5*
TROP7	31.3*	CAP67	26.4*
TROP17	30.3*	CAP69	9.4*
TROP23	2.0*	CAP81	5.3*
ANL0	14.6*	MACH71	18.4*
ANL1	132.1*	MACH72	12.5*
ANL2	15.9*	MACH73	19.3*
ANL3	33.1*	MACH86	12.8*
ANL21	67.0*	MACH95	3.1*
ANL29	22.9*	CHEM51	9.1*
ANL43	7.0*	CHEM52	176.5*
ANL94	40.5*	CHEM53	6.9*
CER4	3.6*	CHEM54	6.2*
CER8	1.9*	CHEM55	6.7*
CER9	5.2*	CHEM56	21.4*
CER12	7.9*	CHEM57	5.8*
CER22	4.3*	CHEM58	12.1*
CER26	13.3*	CHEM59	8.0*
CER41	2.2*		

*Test statistic significant at .05 level.

Helpman-Krugman specification contribute to the explanation of gross trade flows? The results presented in table 5B.3 indicate that in forty-nine of the sixty-one sectoral regressions, the nonlinear terms do contribute significantly to the explanation.

Notes

1. More detailed discussions of the assumptions behind the Heckscher-Ohlin results can be found in Caves and Jones (1981) and Leamer (1984).

2. The properties of Π, the GNP function, are discussed in more detail in Saxonhouse and Stern (1989).

3. The GNP function, Π_j, has been defined to allow for differentiated products and economies of scale. Following Helpman and Krugman, this can be done by including

Table 5B.3   **Test on the Significance of Each Sectoral Regression's Interaction**
Terms, $F_{.05} = 1.77$
$H_0: D_{11} = D_{12} = D_{13} = \ldots = D_{56} = D_{66} = 0$

PETRO33	3.8*	CER42	1.5
MAT27	1.8	LAB66	2.3*
MAT28	4.1*	LAB82	2.7*
MAT32	1.9*	LAB83	3.3*
MAT34	0.8	LAB84	1.3
MAT35	3.4*	LAB85	3.1*
MAT68	4.7*	LAB89	8.2*
FOR24	8.0*	LAB91	0.3
FOR25	15.2*	LAB93	14.0*
FOR63	6.5*	LAB96	0.8
FOR64	2.2*	CAP61	26.1*
TROP5	1.8	CAP62	3.6*
TROP6	26.5*	CAP65	4.9*
TROP7	4.0*	CAP67	9.1*
TROP11	5.0*	CAP69	3.5*
TROP23	0.5	CAP81	2.4*
ANL0	4.1*	MACH71	4.6*
ANL1	0.5	MACH72	1.9*
ANL2	0.7	MACH73	2.3*
ANL3	3.2*	MACH86	3.4*
ANL21	12.6*	MACH95	2.7*
ANL29	0.2	CHEM51	8.4*
ANL43	1.6	CHEM52	2.2*
ANL94	11.6*	CHEM53	5.1*
CER4	1.9*	CHEM54	5.2*
CER8	2.1*	CHEM55	5.1*
CER9	1.5	CHEM56	4.0*
CER12	2.8*	CHEM57	2.3*
CER22	2.4*	CHEM58	6.0*
CER26	1.9*	CHEM59	4.9*
CER41	0.9		

*Test statistic significant at the .05 level.

optimal firm scale in Π_j. Provided optimal firm scale is small relative to market size, change in industry output can be achieved by changes in the number of firms in the industry. Firms are assumed to be identical. This means that at an industry level there will be constant returns to scale.

4. In the likely case that the number of goods exceeds the number of factors ($N > K$), trade will be indeterminant. In estimating models of this kind, Leamer (1984, p. 18) suggests that this indeterminancy can be resolved by assuming international transportation costs that deter and determine trade but are otherwise negligible. Alternatively, Saxonhouse (1983, 1986) assumes that the $N = K$ but that included and excluded dependent variables have properties such that the exclusion of relevant variables does not bias the parameters that are estimated.

It should be noted that derivation of eq. (9) does not necessarily require that the trade balance be zero or exogenously fixed at all. If securities are incorporated into a Woodland (1982) indirect trade utility function, then, with trade taking place in securities as well as goods, it is possible to use the same model to examine the influence of sectoral trade policy on both trade structure and the overall current account on international transactions. See Helpman and Razin (1978).

5. This line of reasoning was first advanced by Leontief (1956) more than thirty years ago as a possible explanation for the empirical failure of the simple Heckscher-Ohlin model.

6. The approach taken here is analogous to the two-step "jackknife" procedure proposed in Guilkey and Schmidt (1973) and Zellner (1962). As an example of the approach taken here, let $a_s = 1 + a_s'$, assuming $E(a_s') = 0$. Using instrumental variable techniques in the presence of multiplicative errors allows consistent estimates of the $R_{is} - B_{is}^+$. Using these estimates, for each economy an $NX1$ vector $[v_i]$ of the net trade residuals can be formed. Consistent estimates of the quality terms can be obtained from

$$[(R_{is} - B_{is}^+)L_s]'[(R_{is} - B_{is}^+)L_s]^{-1}[(R_{is} - B_{is}^+)L_s]'[v_i].$$

7. Following Durbin (1954), and in common with two stage least squares, the approach taken here uses synthetic instrumental variables. Factor endowments are ordered according to size and rank is used as an instrument.

8. Since the factor endowment variables in (9') explain national development, there is no need to limit the sample used here to just the most advanced economies. In general, less advanced economies impose more protection than the most advanced economies. This development-related protection is explained by changes in the levels of the factor endowments. Typically, the higher the level of factor endowments, the less the protection.

9. These same estimation techniques have been used by Saxonhouse (1983, 1986) in earlier work with multiplicative errors in variables models. Because this work used smaller and more homogeneous samples, the problems associated with using rank-order instrumental variables did not arise.

10. The proportion of zero observations for nine labor-intensive sectors was mistakenly left out of table 5.10 and is available from the author on request. The Tobit estimation methods used here for eqs. 7' and 8' are described in Greene (1981, 1983) and Chung and Goldberger (1984).

11. See, however, the discussion in Saxonhouse and Stern (1989).

12. Equation (10') has also been reestimated including Japan but successively excluding Canada, the United States, and Korea from the sample.

References

Caves, Richard E., and Ronald W. Jones. 1981. *World trade and payments.* 3d ed. Boston: Little, Brown & Co.

Chung, Ching-Fan, and Arthur S. Goldberger. 1984. Proportional projections in limited dependent variable models. *Econometrica* 54 (March): 531–34.

Deardorff, Alan V. 1984. Testing trade theories and predicting trade flows. In *Handbook of international economics,* vol. 1, ed. Ronald W. Jones and Peter B. Kenen. Amsterdam: North Holland.

Diewert, W. E. 1974. Applications of duality theory. In *Frontiers of quantitative economics,* ed. Michael D. Intriligator and David A. Kendrick. Amsterdam: North Holland.

Durbin, James. 1954. Errors in variables. *Review of the International Statistical Institute* 22: 23–32.

Greene, William H. 1981. On the asymptotic bias of the ordinary least squares estimator of the Tobit model. *Econometrica* 49 (March): 505–14.

————. 1983. Estimation of limited dependent variable models by ordinary least squares and the method of moments. *Journal of Econometrics* 21 (February): 195–212.

Guilkey, D. K., and P. Schmidt. 1973. Estimation of seemingly unrelated regressions with vector-autoregressive errors. *Journal of the American Statistical Association* 68 (September): 642–47.

Hausman, Jerry A. 1978. Specification tests in econometrics. *Econometrica* 46: 1251–72.

Havrylyshyn, Oli, and E. Cigan. 1984. Intra-industry trade and the state of development. In *The economics of intra-industry trade*, ed. P. K. M. Tharaken. Amsterdam: North Holland.

Helpman, Elhanan, and Paul R. Krugman. 1985. *Market structure and foreign trade: Increasing returns, imperfect competition and the international economy* Cambridge, Mass.: MIT Press.

Helpman, Elhanan, and Assaf Razin. 1978. Uncertainty and international trade in the presence of stock markets. *Review of Economic Studies* 45 (June): 239–50.

Kmenta, Jan. 1986. *Elements of econometrics*. 2d ed. New York: Macmillan.

Lawrence, Robert Z. 1987. Does Japan import too little: Closed minds or markets. *Brookings Papers in Economic Activity*, no. 2: 517–54.

Leamer, Edward E. 1978. *Specification searches*. New York: Wiley.

————. 1984. *Sources of international comparative advantage*. Cambridge, Mass.: MIT Press.

————. 1987. Measures of openness. Paper presented at the National Bureau of Economic Research Conference on Trade Policy Issues and Empirical Analysis, Cambridge, Mass., February 13–14.

Leontief, W. W. 1956. Factor properties and the structure of American trade: Further theoretical and empirical analysis. *Review of Economic Studies* 38 (November): 386–407.

McDonald, David R. 1982. Statement. In *United States–Japan relations.* Hearings before the Subcommittees on International Economic Policy and Trade and Asian and Pacific Affairs, House Foreign Affairs Committee, U.S. Congress. Washington, D.C.: U.S. GPO.

Saxonhouse, Gary R. 1983. The micro- and macroeconomics of foreign sales to Japan. In *Trade policy for the 1980s,* ed. William R. Cline. Cambridge, Mass.: MIT Press.

————. 1986. What's wrong with Japanese trade structure? *Pacific Economic Papers,* No. 137 (July): 1–36.

Saxonhouse, Gary R., and Robert M. Stern. 1989. An analytical survey of formal and informal barriers to international trade and investment in the United States, Canada and Japan. In *Trade and investment relations among the United States, Canada, and Japan,* ed. Robert M. Stern, ch. 9. Chicago: University of Chicago Press.

Sazanami, Yoko. 1981. Possibilities of expanding intra-industry trade in Japan. *Keio Economic Studies* 18(2): 27–44.

Schlosstein, Steven. 1984. *Trade war.* New York: Congdon & Weed.

Woodland, A. D. 1982. *International trade and resource allocation.* Amsterdam: North Holland.

Zellner, Arnold. 1962. An efficient method of estimating seemingly unrelated regressions and tests for aggregative bias. *Journal of American Statistical Association.* 57 (June): 348–68.

Zysman, John, and Laura Tyson. 1983. American industry in international competition. In *American industry in international competition,* ed. John Zysman and Laura Tyson. Ithaca, N.Y.: Cornell University Press.

Comment   Laura D'Andrea Tyson

There is a wealth of anecdotal evidence not just from U.S. producers but from producers in other countries in both the developed and the developing world that there are significant barriers to market access in Japan. Whether as a result of official policies or the unofficial practices of Japanese firms—which often exhibit a definite preference for Japanese products over foreign ones, even when the latter are cheaper—foreign firms seeking to sell in Japan frequently encounter serious obstacles. These obstacles have led many in business communities both at home and abroad to conclude that the Japanese market is relatively closed compared to markets in the other advanced industrial countries.

A pattern of market closure has also been suggested by aggregate trade statistics. As Saxonhouse himself reports, by comparison with other advanced industrial countries, Japan imports a remarkably small share of the manufacturing goods it consumes. And this share has been virtually constant for decades while comparable shares have risen in most other developed market economies. It is important to note that relative market closure does not imply that the structure of Japan's trade should diverge from the structure predicted by standard comparative advantage considerations. Closure might result in less or chronically unbalanced trade but a structure of trade that reflects Japan's relatively poor resource and land endowments and its relative richness in skilled labor, capital, and technological know-how. Thus, a finding of closure is perfectly consistent with earlier empirical research by Saxonhouse indicating that Japan's pattern of trade conforms to Heckscher-Ohlin principles.

Saxonhouse's new research attempts to look at the market closure argument in an empirical framework that extends these principles to allow for intraindustry trade flows. He builds on earlier work by Lawrence, who uses a simple model of intraindustry trade in manufactured goods based on scale economies and product differentiation to examine the issue of market closure in Japan.

Lawrence's results suggest that there is something distinctive about Japan—that, in many manufactured goods, import penetration ratios are lower than levels predicted by the behavior of a sample of other industrial countries and that the gap between Japanese behavior and comparable behavior elsewhere has actually increased over time.

Saxonhouse questions these results because they are based on a methodology that explains the share of imports in total domestic use of a particular product in a particular country by that country's share of world production or

Laura D'Andrea Tyson is professor of economics at the University of California, Berkeley, and director of research at the Berkeley Roundtable on the International Economy.

world exports of that product. As Saxonhouse correctly notes, there is a serious simultaneity problem inherent in this methodology: export shares, import shares, and production shares are jointly determined. This poses both an estimation problem and an even more serious interpretation problem.

Even if import shares are reasonable given a country's share in global production, market-closing policies may still be a significant determinant of that country's trade behavior if such policies have affected its production share over time. And that is precisely the objective of market-closing policies based on infant-industry considerations. The question of closure is not whether imports are a relatively low share of domestic use in products, such as automobiles, in which Japan has a substantial share of global production but rather whether closure played or plays a role in the global production base in automobiles and other industries that the Japanese have built. Neither the Lawrence methodology nor the Saxonhouse methodology is equipped to answer this question.

To understand why this is so, it is necessary to clarify how market closure has influenced the evolution of Japan's competitive strength in a variety of industries. Industry studies by scholars at the Berkeley Roundtable on the International Economy (BRIE) and elsewhere indicate that temporary market closure, achieved by both formal and informal means and cooperatively supported by government and industry, has been and continues to be an important component of Japan's development strategy.[1] Protectionist measures, along with other critical elements of this strategy, such as low-cost capital, research and development and other subsidies, and preferential tax policies, have been used to promote the domestic development of industries targeted by the Japanese as critical to long-run growth and technological change. These policies have had permanent or dynamic effects so that, even after they are removed, the Japanese market remains difficult to penetrate in the targeted industries.

At different times in industries such as steel, automobiles, consumer electronics, semiconductors, computers, and sophisticated telecommunications equipment, a constellation of protectionist and promotional policies has encouraged the buildup of domestic capacity by Japanese producers seeking to compete with one another for market share in the large protected domestic Japanese market. Foreign producers who might have gained a foothold in this market on the basis of their real competitive advantage in price, quality, or some other factor have confronted a variety of barriers that have either strictly controlled or effectively precluded their access to this market.

Fostered by their infant-industry environment and responding to the availability of cheap capital and other policy incentives, Japanese firms in targeted industries have built domestic capacity and expanded production in response to the rapidly growing Japanese market. As production levels have increased, Japanese firms have realized significant scale and learning economies in their production costs, and these economies in turn have been one of the factors behind their growing competitive strength. The strong competition among Japanese firms to exploit the cost and learning advantages that accompany growing production volumes has led to the development of excess capacity for the domestic market and has fostered a competitive search for growing markets abroad. By the time this search has begun, however, the Japanese firms are in a strong enough position on the basis of the scale and learning economies they have enjoyed in the protected Japanese market to be fierce competitors on world markets against foreign firms with whom they would not have been able to compete earlier. At this point, active measures to close the Japanese market to such firms are no longer necessary—the effects of past protection are long lived and not readily reversible.

If this argument is correct, the fact that formal or informal barriers to the Japanese market in a particular industry do not exist at the moment in time does not mean that such barriers have not played an important role in the evolution of Japan's competitive strength in that industry. The history of past protection matters to current market outcomes in industries that are characterized by large economies of scale and learning economies. And such economies have been nothing short of spectacular in the industries that the Japanese have chosen to target over time.

What would Japan's trade in automobiles look like today if the Japanese domestic market had not been closed to foreign auto imports in the 1960s, when at the very least Fiat, if not General Motors, had a competitive product to offer Japanese consumers? Would the Japanese semiconductor industry have its technological and competitive edge today if not for the closure of the Japanese market to low-cost, high-quality 16k DRAMs produced by U.S. firms in the 1970s? And would Japan be at the cutting edge in fiber optics today if NTT had not orchestrated closure of the Japanese market to Corning Glass to encourage the development of a domestic production and research and development capability? These are the types of questions that must be addressed if the role of market closure in Japan is to be properly assessed.

Unfortunately, such questions cannot be answered with the model employed by Saxonhouse. This model rests on a number of assumptions that are at odds with reality in significant ways. Particularly debilitating is the fact that these assumptions are inherently static and overlook the dynamic effects of temporary closure on trade outcomes.

Saxonhouse's model assumes that consumer tastes are identical and homothetic across countries. Most of the industries that have been targeted by the Japanese have income elasticities in excess of one—as income rises, consumers both at home and abroad permanently spend a larger fraction of their incomes on such goods. The products involved are not divisible in consumption, as the model assumes—you cannot consume a little of your automobile from a Japanese source, a little from an American source, and a little from an Italian source. Most consumers must be content with at most one or two choices from the many national varieties of automobiles available. Tastes themselves are not given but are affected by what is available. If Japanese consumers had been allowed to buy Italian cars in the 1960s, they might have learned to love them. It is often alleged that Japanese consumers show a definite preference for Japanese goods, but perhaps that is because market closure has encouraged or necessitated such a preference.

Saxonhouse's model assumes that production technologies are identical across nations. But there is ample evidence that the investment and research and development spending encouraged by protectionist and promotional policies generated production innovations by Japanese firms. Aggressive competition among Japanese producers for the protected but rapidly growing domestic market resulted in real technological breakthroughs in production that are today the envy of producers around the world (Cohen and Zysman 1988). We do not know whether these breakthroughs would have occurred in the absence of closure and promotion, but we do know that a model that overlooks such breakthroughs cannot address an important factor behind Japan's competitive strength and trade performance in a variety of industries.

Finally, most of the industries that have been the targets of promotion and protection in Japan have enjoyed ''large'' economies of scale rather than the ''small'' economies of scale assumed in the Saxonhouse model. When economies of scale are large, and when distances between trading partners are great, as in the Japanese case, it is easy to imagine how a ''temporary'' market closure policy can have permanent effects on a country's share of world production and the share of imports in its total use of particular products.

Using the questionable assumptions of identical and homothetic tastes, identical production technologies, factor price equalization, and ''small'' economies of scale, Saxonhouse expands on Lawrence's model to explain each country's share of world production of particular products by the factor intensities involved in these products and the country's factor endowments. In this way, he blends a Heckscher-Ohlin explanation of production shares with the Helpman-Krugman-type model used by Lawrence, in which product differentiation and small economies of scale are important determinants of trade flows. As Saxonhouse correctly observes, under his limiting assumptions, the incorporation of scale economies—provided they are small—and product differentiation into conventional models of international trade in order to account for intraindustry trade does not invalidate the Heckscher-Ohlin interpretation of interindustry trade. But both approaches are equally ill suited to deal with the dynamic effects of market closure on national production structures and trade patterns over time.

Ultimately, Saxonhouse presents empirical estimates of a standard Heckscher-Ohlin net trade equation for interindustry trade and a derived intraindustry trade equation for gross import shares expressed as a percentage of GNP. Both equations are estimated using data for forty-one countries and sixty-one commodities.

The interindustry results are predictable and commonsensical. About half the sixty-one products are food and resource products, in which Japan tends to be at a comparative disadvantage given its relatively poor land and resource base. It should hardly be a surprise to find that Japan is a net exporter of manufactured goods and a net importer of resource-intensive products. Indeed, it is the linchpin of Japan's development strategy that Japan had to develop a competitive manufacturing base because, as the Japanese themselves point out, they could not afford to become a "second-rate agrarian power."

The intraindustry results form the core of Saxonhouse's argument. His equation explains the gross import share of each product in the GNP of each country on the basis of that country's factor endowments. As an illustration, the imports of transportation equipment as a share of GNP for each country are explained as a function of that country's factor endowments. He estimates equations of this form for each individual product. He finds that Japan's import behavior is consistent with the behavior of the other countries in his sample. In other words, in most products Japan's import- GNP ratio can be predicted by the estimates of the import-GNP ratio for the other countries in his sample, and the import-GNP ratio for most products in turn can be explained by factor endowments. Saxonhouse's results are questionable given the inappropriate assumptions and model on which they rest. But, even accepting his model for the sake of argument, there remains one serious shortcoming of his empirical results. The closure hypothesis, as usually understood, argues that Japan is relatively closed to imports of manufactured goods compared to the other advanced industrial countries. But Saxonhouse bases his estimation on a sample of countries, more than half of which are developing or newly industrializing countries and most of which have significant barriers to imports of manufactured products. Perhaps Japan's import behavior is consistent with this larger sample but still out of line with the behavior of the other advanced industrial countries. Lawrence used a smaller sample of advanced industrial countries and found that Japan's behavior differed from the behavior of these countries. It would be interesting to discover if Saxonhouse's results would hold up for Lawrence's sample of countries.

What can we conclude about the effects of market closure on Japan's pattern of trade on the basis of Saxonhouse's paper? Saxonhouse concludes that, even if such closure exists, it has had negligible effects on trade patterns for most products. But his conclusions are based on a model that is at odds in fundamental ways with the reality he is trying to explain. His model cannot be taken as an adequate test of the hypothesis that temporary market closure has had long-term effects on the competitiveness of Japanese producers in a variety of industries targeted as part of Japan's development strategy.

Note

1. The relevant case studies by BRIE scholars include Borrus, Tyson, and Zysman (1986), Stowsky (1987), and Borrus (1988). The argument that market closure has played a role in Japan's industrial policy is elaborated in greater detail in Johnson, Tyson, and Zysman (1989). Dosi, Tyson, and Zysman (1989) and Tyson and Zysman (1989) contain many of the arguments on which this review of Saxonhouse's paper rests.

References

Borrus, Michael. 1988. *Competing for control: America's stake in microelectronics.* Cambridge, Mass.: Ballinger.
Borrus, Michael, Laura Tyson, and John Zysman. 1986. How government policies shape high technology trade. In *Strategic trade policy and the new international economics,* ed. Paul Krugman. Cambridge, Mass.: MIT Press.
Cohen, Steve, and John Zysman. 1988. Manufacturing innovation and American industrial competitiveness. *Science* 239(4 March):1110–15.
Dosi, Giovanni, Laura Tyson, and John Zysman. 1989. Trade, technologies, and development: A framework for discussing Japan. In *Politics and productivity: The real story of how Japan works,* ed. Chalmers Johnson, Laura Tyson, and John Zysman. Cambridge, Mass.: Ballinger.
Johnson, Chalmers, Laura Tyson, and John Zysman, eds. 1989. *Politics and productivity: The real story of how Japan works.* Cambridge, Mass.: Ballinger.
Stowsky, Jay. 1987. The weakest link: Semiconductor production equipment, linkages, and the limits to international trade. Working Paper no. 27. Berkeley, Calif.: Berkeley Roundtable on the International Economy, August.
Tyson, Laura, and John Zysman. 1989. Politics and productivity: Developmental strategy and production innovation in Japan. In *Politics and productivity: The real story of how Japan works,* ed. Chalmers Johnson, Laura Tyson, and John Zysman. Cambridge, Mass.: Ballinger.

Comment   Harry P. Bowen

In his paper, Gary Saxonhouse proposes to determine if the distinctiveness of Japan's trade pattern is the result of a distinctive structure of protection or if it instead reflects distinctiveness in Japan's pattern of resource supplies. As evidence of Japan's distinctive trade structure, Saxonhouse reports data indicating that Japan's import share of manufactured goods has remained remarkably low and stable between 1962 and 1985 and that Japan's share of

Harry P. Bowen is associate professor of economics and international business at the Graduate School of Business, New York University, and a National Bureau of Economic Research faculty research fellow.

intraindustry trade in manufactures is low in relation to both developing and advanced countries. As he notes, these features of Japan's trade are often cited as evidence that Japan is restrictive compared to other countries.

To examine whether Japan's trade structure reflects an unusual pattern of protection, Saxonhouse proposes to estimate equations explaining the trade in each of sixty-one "commodities" in terms of countries' resource supplies. The estimated equations are then used to predict Japan's trade pattern given its resource supplies, and those sectors in which actual trade deviates significantly from its predicted trade are identified as "restrictive."

This method of identifying departures of the trade pattern from that predicted on the basis of fundamentals is based on earlier work by Saxonhouse and others. However, a novel feature of the current analysis is that equations are developed to explain not only net trade but also exports and imports separately. Important is that these latter equations are derived from a model that admits differentiated products and economies of scale. While this is an important empirical extension of the standard trade model, an unsatisfying feature of the model is that it assumes homothetic preferences. While this assumption has a long tradition in trade analyses, recent empirical work has questioned the validity of this assumption (e.g., Hunter and Markusen 1988). Thus, it would be useful, and I think not too difficult, to extend the model to include the possibility that consumption patterns depend on income per capita as well as the level of income.

Saxonhouse's data set consists of a 1979 cross section on the trade in each of sixty-one "sectors" and the resource supplies of forty-one countries. Six explanatory variables are employed in the analysis: capital, educational attainment, labor, petroleum reserves, coal, and arable land.

Estimating first the (traditional) equations explaining net trade, Saxonhouse notes that the capital coefficient is generally positive in those sectors thought to be capital intensive but that, surprisingly, the labor coefficient is generally negative in those sectors thought to be labor intensive.

Although Saxonhouse is uncomfortable with the results for labor, I think one should not place much emphasis on this type of inference. As stated in Bowen (1983), the coefficients derived from the net trade model have no direct relation to what are usually defined as factor intensities. In particular, the coefficients are theoretically estimates of parameters that include both Rybczynski production effects and consumption effects. Thus, it appears that raising the supply of labor raises consumption relative to production in labor-intensive sectors.

Aside from concern over the "wrong" signs, Saxonhouse finds that the equations explaining net trade fit the data quite well. However, his interest is to explain not the pattern of Japan's net trade but rather the pattern of Japan's imports. In this regard, he modifies his basic import equation so that the dependent variable is the ratio of a sector's imports to GNP. Moreover, he assumes that there are multiplicative errors associated with the resource variables. These errors are thought to reflect differences in the quality of the resources across countries.

While the specification of quality differences seems appropriate for capital, labor, and land, I am less sure if it should be applied to coal and oil reserves. I have in mind the possibility of adjusting these latter variables to reflect differences in quality prior to estimation. It would require a bit more data collection, but different grades of oil can be identified, as can different grades of coal. I mention this to suggest that one may get a sense of the extent to which pure measurement error can be separated from differences in factor quality. In this regard, Saxonhouse does not present estimates of the error coefficients for coal or oil, and thus one wonders how close to unity they were.

Continuing on the issue of measurement errors, recent work by Bowen, Leamer, and Sveikauskas (1987) suggests that an additional confounding element may be present in Saxonhouse's error specification: technological differences. Thus, his estimates of the multiplicative error coefficients may include all three elements: factor quality differences, technological differences, and pure measurement errors. This confounding may help to explain the peculiar estimates he obtains for differences in labor quality across countries. It should be noted that Bowen, Leamer, and Sveikauskas also obtained peculiar estimates when the coefficients were specified to reflect only technological differences.

Despite the above remarks, Saxonhouse's intent is to predict trade patterns and not to derive estimates of factor quality. Thus, the source of the measurement error does not matter. What does matter is accounting for it, and Saxonhouse's approach is one such method.

Estimating the import model for 1979, Saxonhouse then predicts Japan's pattern of imports given its resource endowments and finds that the prediction errors in only eight of the sixty-one sectors are statistically significant. Saxonhouse concludes from this that Japan's pattern of imports is reasonably well explained by its resource patterns and that removal of barriers would be unlikely to alter Japan's pattern of trade in manufactured goods. This is a "satisfying" conclusion that is consistent with previous studies.

One question that arises from this analysis is whether the residuals for these "rogue" sectors are positive or negative. That is, were Japan's imports in these sectors lower or higher than predicted? This question seems important since his analysis initially pointed to the peculiarly *low* level of Japan's imports. Thus, in addition to testing the significance of the residuals, it would be useful to report the number of sectors for which the model predicted a higher ratio of imports to GNP.

Another issue is that the success of Saxonhouse's approach in identifying trade restrictions requires the assumptions that trade barriers are the only excluded variables and that these trade barriers are uncorrelated with resource supplies. Since trade barriers are often thought to protect certain (e.g., scarce) factors of production, the assumption of orthogonality is suspect. Of course, violating this assumption means that the explanatory variables (and not the residuals) would pick up the effects of any trade barriers. There is not much one can do about this except to note that one may be picking up only trade barriers that are uncorrelated with endowments. However, what this does suggest is that a careful examination of the residuals to detect possibly omitted resource variables is warranted. Only then can one be reasonably confident that peculiar residuals reflect barriers to trade.

Finally, the model is estimated in cross section, and the resulting estimates may have little to do with the evolution of trade patterns over time. This seems important since we would like to know if Japan is getting more or less protective relative to other countries. Thus, it may be appropriate to utilize another cross section and to estimate regressions in change form. This approach would yield the benefit of reducing additive measurement errors that are relatively constant over time and would allow one to determine if Japan's import pattern has deviated from the pattern that would be consistent with the changes in its resource supplies.

The above remarks have pointed to a number of caveats concerning the use of Saxonhouse's methodology for identifying trade barriers. However, these remarks should not overshadow the importance of the empirical specifications developed to incorporate differentiated products and economies of scale within the standard, factor supply, framework. Given this framework, it is perhaps surprising that Saxonhouse's implementation of the model dealt only with Japan's imports from the world and thus did not attempt to differentiate trade by country of origin (i.e., differentiated products). I suspect that this will be the subject of future work. I look forward to that, and other, applications of this empirical framework.

References

Bowen, Harry P. 1983. Changes in the international distribution of resources and their impact on U.S. comparative advantage. *Review of Economics and Statistics* 65(3):402–14.

Bowen, Harry P., Edward E. Leamer, and Leo Sveikauskas. 1987. Multicountry, multifactor tests of the factor abundance theory. *American Economic Review* 77(5):791–809.

Hunter, Linda, and James R. Markusen. 1988. Per-capita income as a determinant of trade. In *Empirical methods for international trade,* ed. Robert C. Feenstra, 89–109. Cambridge, Mass.: MIT Press.

6 Export Prices and Exchange Rates: An Industry Approach

Lawrence Schembri

The ability of domestic firms to compete with foreign firms in domestic and foreign markets is greatly influenced by the relative price of domestic- and foreign-produced goods. This relative price is, in part, determined by the level of the exchange rate. Under purchasing power parity (PPP), relative prices should change in proportion to any exchange rate movement. However, since 1980, the U.S. dollar has appreciated and then depreciated by roughly 50 percent vis-à-vis the Japanese yen and the West German mark, while the prices of many traded goods exported to the United States have moved much less. As a result, U.S. import prices expressed in foreign currency have moved sharply relative to foreign exporters' domestic prices. This failure of foreign-produced traded goods prices to respond to exchange rate changes has had a significant effect on the international competitiveness of U.S. firms.

Recently, several studies (most notably Krugman 1987; Dornbusch 1987; and Giovannini 1988) have tried to explain this "pricing to market" phenomenon by appealing to various theories of imperfect competition.[1] Both Krugman (1987) and Giovannini (1988) note that a complete explanation must include two elements. First, the exporting firm must be able to price discriminate across markets (i.e., it must face different elasticities of demand across markets, and arbitrage across markets must be less than perfect). Second, the firm must incur dynamic costs of adjustment on the supply side

Lawrence Schembri is assistant professor in the Department of Economics at Carleton University, Ottawa.

The author would like to thank John Baldwin, Alberto Giovannini, Robert Feenstra, Catherine Morrison, and Thomas Rymes for helpful advice, Paul Reed, Peter Koumanakos, Jean Leger, Barb Slater, and Danny Triandafillou for encouraging this research, and John McVey and his staff in the Business Microdata Integration and Analysis Section, Statistics Canada, for their cooperation. Generous support from the Social Sciences and Humanities Research Council of Canada and Statistics Canada is gratefully acknowledged. The responsibility for the thoughts expressed in this paper and any errors therein rest solely with the author.

(and also perhaps on the demand side [see Krugman 1987; and Froot and Klemperer 1988]) that affect the exporting firm's reaction to an exchange rate change. In general, the firm's reaction to an exchange rate change that alters foreign demand conditions will depend on the expected magnitude and permanence of the change. That is, a large exchange rate change that is perceived as being permanent may cause the exporting firm to adjust its export price expressed in foreign currency and expand or contract its productive capacity and its foreign sales and distribution networks. However, if the change is perceived as being temporary, the firm's reaction will be much more muted in that it will probably maintain export prices and quantities at relatively constant levels and absorb the exchange rate change in its profit margin.

Most of the empirical work that has been done on this issue consists of either simple comparisons of domestic and imported goods prices in the aggregate or by sectors (see, e.g., Mann 1986; Dornbusch 1987; and Krugman 1987) or the estimation of pass-through equations (see, e.g., Feinberg 1987; and Feenstra 1987). This evidence clearly demonstrates the existence of the pricing to market phenomenon, especially in differentiated goods markets. Hence, while this evidence has limited explanatory power, it does indicate that pricing to market seems to occur in markets where firms are likely to be able to set different prices.

Giovannini (1988) estimates a nonstructural time-series model to explain deviations from PPP for selected categories of Japanese export goods to the United States. While he finds that deviations from PPP are forecastable, he cannot consistently distinguish between the two possible explanations of this occurrence, ex ante price discrimination or exchange rate surprises in conjunction with long-term price setting. Furthermore, although his model has the appearance of being dynamic because firms maximize the expected present discounted value of profits, it is essentially static; dynamic costs of adjustment are not modeled.

Knetter (1989) estimates an export-pricing equation for selected U.S. and German export goods to determine whether firms in the domestic export industry price discriminate across markets in different countries. He uses a panel data set consisting of export prices over time and across markets that allows him to control for shifts in the marginal cost of production that are unobservable but common to all markets and to isolate discriminatory country-specific effects. These effects arise in part because of movements in bilateral exchange rates that affect the elasticity of demand in export markets. These country-specific exchange rate effects are found to be significantly different across markets, indicating that price discrimination is being practiced. The simplicity of the model precludes a structural interpretation of the effect of exchange rate changes on export prices.

The purpose of this paper is to build a structural model of an export industry that can be empirically implemented to estimate the effect of an exchange rate change on domestic prices, export prices, and industrial activity and to test directly for differences in the price elasticities of demand across markets. While the model employed in the paper is static, which implies that any exchange rate change is expected to be permanent, it is still possible to obtain meaningful estimates of the elasticities of demand and to determine how the exchange rate changes that did occur affected markups (the price–marginal cost differential) in the domestic and export markets. Furthermore, this structural model provides a framework that can be extended to include dynamic costs of adjustment.

The model described in this paper is an extension of the closed-economy industry model of Applebaum (1979). Since the theoretical model is of a single export industry, it is necessarily partial equilibrium in nature. However, its usefulness derives from the fact that both the demand and the supply side of the industry are explicitly modeled.

The empirical version of the model is estimated using a carefully collected data set on a major Canadian export industry.[2] This export industry produces almost exclusively for sales in the Canadian and U.S. markets. More than three-quarters of the output of the industry is exported, and its sales to the United States account for more than half of U.S. consumption. The output of this industry is a relatively homogeneous commodity so that high-quality price data are available on domestic and export sales. Therefore, this Canadian industry provides a good case study for the empirical implementation of the theoretical model and the test of different price elasticities of demand.

In figure 6.1, the percentage difference between the U.S. export price and the Canadian domestic price (both prices expressed in Canadian dollars) is

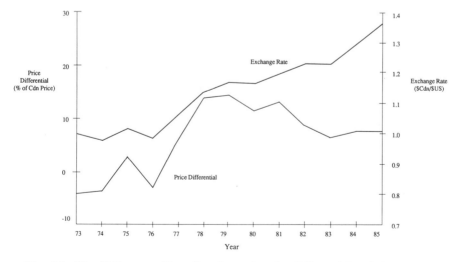

Fig. 6.1   The U.S. export/Canadian domestic price differential and the bilateral exchange rate

plotted along with the Canadian exchange rate ($Canadian/U.S.$) over the years 1973–85. It is important to note that, whenever the Canadian dollar depreciated (e.g., 1976–79 and 1983–85), the export/domestic price differential increased sharply. Indeed, the U.S. export price was significantly above the Canadian price for most of this period. Hence, it appears that Canadian exporters were pricing to market as they tried to maintain the local prices of their goods in the face of sizable exchange rate movements.

6.1 Theoretical Framework

The theoretical model is of an industry in the domestic country that produces an intermediate good that is primarily exported but is also sold domestically. To develop the structure of the model, consider the export industry as a single firm, a monopolist, that sells in two markets, domestic and foreign or export. The monopolist's technology is defined by the production function F, where $y_0 = F(z)$ is the output of the intermediate good produced by an n-dimensional vector of inputs z and F is a continuous-from-above, nondecreasing, and quasi-concave function.[3] In addition, assume that the intermediate good, y_0, is consumed as an input by two sets of firms that operate in a final goods industry in the domestic and foreign countries. Therefore, $y_0 = y_1 + y_2$, where y_1 and y_2 denote domestic and foreign consumption of the intermediate good, respectively.

Each firm in the domestic final goods industry has a production function defined by G_1, where $x_{10} = G_1(y_1, x_1)$ is the output produced and x_1 is an m-dimensional vector of inputs other than y_1 used in the production process. Similarly, each firm in the foreign final goods industry has a production function defined by G_2, where $x_{20} = G_2(y_2, x_2)$ is the output and x_2 is the m-vector of other inputs. If the firm production functions at home and abroad, G_1 and G_2, are subject to constant returns to scale (in addition to being quasi concave and nondecreasing) and all firms in the final goods industry in each country face the same prices and act competitively, then G_1 and G_2 can be interpreted as the industry production functions for the two sets of firms that employ y_0 as a productive input.

Let the prices of y_1, y_2, and z in domestic currency be p_1, p_2, and q, the prices of x_{10} and x_1 in domestic currency be w_{10} and w_1, and the prices of x_{20} and x_2 in foreign currence be w_{20}^* and w_2^* (asterisks denote value in foreign currency).[4]

If domestic and foreign firms in the final goods industry competitively maximize profits, then profit functions for the domestic and foreign industries, J_1 and J_2, can be defined as the solutions to the following problems—domestic:

$$(1) \qquad \max_{y_1, x_1} w_{10} G_1(y_1, x_1) - p_1 y_1 - w_1^T x_1 \equiv J_1(p_1, w_{10}, w_1),$$

and foreign:

$$(2) \qquad \max_{y_2, x_2} w_{20}^* G_2(y_2, x_2) - ep_2 y_2 - w_2^{*T} x_2 \equiv J_2(ep_2, w_{20}^*, w_2^*),$$

where e is the exchange rate defined as the foreign currency price of domestic currency.

At this point, two important issues should be noted. First, since the model is partial equilibrium and the exchange rate is a macroeconomic variable, then e can be treated in the model as an exogenous variable. Second, the exchange rate is assumed to affect only the foreign currency price of the export good. For simplicity, the possible effects of the exchange rate on other input prices are ignored.[5]

Assuming that the profit functions defined in (1) and (2) have the usual regularity properties (see Varian 1978) and are differentiable with respect to the input prices, the optimal demand functions for the intermediate good, y_1 and y_2, and for the other inputs, x_1 and x_2, are given by Hotelling's lemma as

$$(3) \qquad -y_1 = \partial J_1(p_1, w_{10}, w_1)/\partial p_1 \equiv H_1(p_1, w_{10}, w_1),$$

$$(4) \qquad -x_1 = \nabla_{w_1} J_1(p_1, w_{10}, w_1),$$

and

$$(5) \qquad -y_2 = \partial J_2(ep_2, w_{20}^*, w_2^*)\partial ep_2 \equiv H_2(ep_2, w_{20}^*, w_2^*),$$

$$(6) \qquad -x_2 = \nabla_{w_2^*} J_2(ep_2, w_{20}^*, w_2^*).$$

Equations (3) and (5) represent the domestic and foreign demand functions for the intermediate good that the monopolist faces, and they can be inserted into the monopolist's profit maximization problem, which is given by:

$$(7) \qquad \max_{p_1, p_2, y_1, y_2} [p_1 y_1 + p_2 y_2 - q^T z: y_1 + y_2 = F(z),$$
$$-y_1 = H_1(p_1, w_{10}, w_1), \ -y_2 = H_2(ep_2, w_{20}^*, w_2^*)]$$

or

$$(8) \qquad \max_{p_1, p_2, y_0} [-p_1 H_1(p_1, w_{10}, w_1)$$
$$- p_2 H_2(ep_2, w_{20}^*, w_2^*) - C(q, y_0): y_0 = y_1 + y_2]$$

or

$$(9) \qquad \max_{p_1, p_2} \{ -p_1 H_1(p_1, w_{10}, w_1) - p_2 H_2(ep_2, w_{20}^*, w_2^*)$$
$$- C[q, -H_1(\cdot) - H_2(\cdot)]: p_1, p_2 \geq 0 \},$$

where $C(q, y_0) \equiv \min_z [q^T z: F(z) = y_0]$ is the cost function that is the dual to the monopolist's production function F. Note that having the cost function depend on total output, y_0, rather than on y_1 and y_2 separately implies that the cost associated with producing and selling a unit of the monopolist's output to domestic and foreign buyers is the same.[6] It is assumed as well that the monopolist is a price taker in markets for the inputs denoted by z and that the cost function has the usual regularity properties (see Varian 1978). However, it need not be assumed that the cost (production) functions of the monopolist exhibit constant returns to scale.

The monopolist's demand for inputs conditional on output y_0 can be obtained by applying Shepherd's lemma and differentiating the cost function with respect to input prices:

$$(10) \qquad z = \nabla_q C(q, y_0).$$

If the demand functions for the intermediate good given by H_1 and H_2 and the cost function are differentiable with respect to p_1 and p_2 and y_0, then the first-order conditions for the monopolist's profit maximization problem in (9) are

$$(11) \qquad p_1 + H_1(p_1, w_{10}, w_1)/[\partial H_1(\cdot)/\partial p_1] - \partial C(q, y_0)/\partial y_0 = 0,$$

$$(12) \qquad p_2 + H_2(ep_2, w^*_{20}, w^*_2)/[e\partial H_2(\cdot)/\partial ep_2] - \partial C(q, y_0)/\partial y_0 = 0.$$

Equations (11) and (12) can be interpreted simply as the condition that marginal revenue be equated across the two markets to the marginal cost of production.

Equations (11) and (12) can be rewritten as

$$(13) \qquad p_1 = \gamma_1(p_1, w_{10}, w_1) + \partial C(q, y_0)/\partial y_0$$

and

$$(14) \qquad p_2 = \gamma_2(ep_2, w^*_{20}, w^*_2) + \partial C(q, y_0)/\partial y_0.$$

Hence, the monopolist's selling prices in the two markets equal the marginal cost of production plus market-specific markups, which are defined as follows:

$$(15) \quad \gamma_1(p_1, w_{10}, w_1) = -H_1(p_1, w_{10}, w_1)/[\partial H_1(p_1, w_{10}, w_1)/\partial p_1]$$
$$= -[\partial J_1(p_1, w_{10}, w_1)/\partial p_1]/[\partial^2 J_1(p_1, w_{10}, w_1)/\partial p_1^2],$$

$$(16) \quad \gamma_2(ep_2, w^*_{20}, w^*_2) = -H_2(ep_2, w^*_{20}, w^*_2)/[e\partial H_2(ep_2, w^*_{20}, w^*_2)/\partial ep_2]$$
$$= -[\partial J_2(ep_2, w^*_{20}w^*_2)/\partial ep_2]/[e\partial^2 J_2(ep_2, w^*_{20}, w^*_2)/\partial (ep_2)^2].$$

The model derived so far represents a complete partial equilibrium model of the demand and supply of the intermediate good y_0. If functional forms are specified for the profit functions, J_1 and J_2, and the cost function, C, and data collected on the variables p_1, p_2, e, w_{10}, w_1, w_{20}^*, and w_2^*, then several interesting empirical results can be obtained.

First, estimates of the values of γ_1 and γ_2 can be determined. In addition, an estimate of the inverse elasticity of demand for y_0 in each market can be obtained from the expressions $\epsilon_1 = \gamma_1/p_1$ and $\epsilon_2 = \gamma_2/p_2$. If $\gamma_1 = \gamma_2 = 0$, that is, the markups are zero, then the monopolist is a price taker in his two output markets since the elasticities of demand are infinite. If γ_1 and γ_2 are estimated to be greater than zero and different, then the monopolist faces different elasticities of demand in the two markets since different markups are being applied to the same marginal cost of production.

Second, the effect of an exchange rate change on the domestic and foreign (export) prices, p_1 and p_2, the level of output, y_0, and the monopolist's demand for inputs can be estimated.[7] Theoretically the effect of the exchange rate change can be determined by totally differentiating (13) and (14) with respect to the exchange rate to obtain (for a complete derivation, see the Appendix):

(17)
$$\frac{dp_1}{de} = \frac{B_{23}}{|D|} [\partial^2 C(q, y_0)/\partial^2 y_0][e\partial^2 J(ep_2, w_{20}^*, w_2^*)/\partial(ep_2)^2]$$

and

(18)
$$\frac{dp_2}{de} = \frac{B_{23}}{|D|} \{1 + B_{11} + [\partial^2 C(q, y_0)/\partial^2 y_0][\partial^2 J_1(p_1, w_{10}, w_1)/\partial p_1^2]\}.$$

The second derivative of the cost function with respect to output can be negative, positive, or zero, depending on whether the monopolist's technology exhibits increasing, decreasing, or constant returns to scale. The second derivative of the profit functions J_1 and J_2 and $|D|$ are unambiguously positive in sign while B_{11} is likely to be positive and B_{23} negative (for more details, see the Appendix). Therefore, the derivatives in (17) and (18) will probably be negative if marginal costs are increasing so that a depreciation of the exporter's currency, a fall in e, will raise the domestic and export prices (expressed in domestic currency) of the intermediate good.

The effect of an exchange rate change on the export price expressed in foreign currency is given by:

(19)
$$\frac{dep_2}{de} = p_2 + e \frac{dp_2}{de}.$$

The sign of this expression is less obvious than the sign of (18). It is more likely to be positive.[8]

Furthermore, the effect of an exchange rate change on the monopolist's level of output is equal to

$$(20) \quad \frac{dy_0}{de} = -\frac{\partial H_1(p_1, w_{10}, w_1)}{\partial p_1}\frac{dp_1}{de} - \frac{\partial H_2(ep_2, w_{20}^*, w_2^*)}{\partial ep_2}\left(p_2 + e\,\frac{dep_2}{de}\right)$$

$$= -\frac{\partial^2 J_1(p_1, w_{10}, w_1)}{\partial p_1^2}\frac{dp_1}{de} - \frac{\partial^2 J_2(ep_2, w_{20}^*, w_2^*)}{\partial(ep_2)^2}\left(p_2 + e\,\frac{dp_2}{de}\right),$$

and the effects on the monopolist's input demands are given by:

$$(21) \quad \frac{dz_j}{de} = \frac{\partial[\partial C(q, y_0)/\partial q_j]}{\partial y_0}\frac{dy_0}{de}, \quad j = 1, \ldots, n.$$

Since theory in the form of regularity conditions and second-order conditions for profit maximization cannot unambiguously determine the signs of the expressions in (17) and (18), the door is left open for empirical estimation to help resolve the issue. Moreover, while the best that theory can do is to determine the signs of the effects of an exchange rate change on the endogenous variables, empirical work can provide an estimate of the magnitude of the effect. Therefore, it is now time to implement the model empirically in order to provide further answers.

6.2   Empirical Implementation

The first step in implementing the theoretical model for the purpose of empirical estimation is to specify functional forms for the monopolist's cost function and for the profit functions of the consuming industries at home and abroad. These functional forms should be flexible in that they should provide second-order Taylor approximations to any arbitrary functions that satisfy the regularity properties. In addition, the functional forms for the profit functions should yield simple expressions for the markup terms γ_1 and γ_2.

Another consideration in specifying the functional forms is the time horizon of the analysis. So far it has been assumed that an exchange rate change does not affect input prices. This assumption is reasonable only if the time horizon of the analysis is relatively short. Therefore, the theoretical model developed earlier that treats all inputs to the production process as variable (which is true only in the long run) needs to be modified to reflect the shorter time horizon of the empirical analysis. This could be accomplished by treating the capital stock (the nth input) as a quasi-fixed factor so that the monopolist's cost function would become a variable cost function and the profit functions of the consuming industries would be restricted or short-run profit functions. While making the resulting empirical model more realistic, this modification does not significantly affect the results derived from the theoretical model.

Given these considerations, the normalized quadratic was chosen from the set of popular flexible functional forms, which also includes the generalized

Leontief and the translog.[9] Therefore, the monopolist's variable cost function is given by

$$
\begin{aligned}
(22) \quad C^r(q^r, y_0, K_0) = {} & a_0 + \sum_{i=2}^{n-1} a_i q_i^r + \frac{1}{2} \sum_{i=2}^{n-1} \sum_{j=2}^{n-1} a_{ij} q_i^r q_j^r + a_y y_0 \\
& + a_K K_0 + \frac{1}{2} a_{yy} y_0^2 + \frac{1}{2} a_{KK} K_0^2 + a_{yK} y_0 K_0 \\
& + \sum_{i=2}^{n-1} a_{yi} y_0 q_i^r + \sum_{i=2}^{n-1} a_{Ki} K_0 q_i^r \; .
\end{aligned}
$$

where $a_{ij} = a_{ji}$ and the superscript r denotes normalized. That is, $C^r = C/q_1$, and $q_i^r = q_i/q_1$, where C is total variable cost and q_1 is the factor price used to normalize the function. Note that constant returns to scale is not imposed on the function, but linear homogeneity of the function in prices is obtained by the normalization. Moreover, this restriction is not nested and thus is not testable.[10]

Similarly, the restricted normalized profit functions for the consuming industries are defined as

$$
\begin{aligned}
(23) \quad J_1^r(p_1^r, w_{10}^r, w_1^r; K_1) = K_1 \Bigg[& d_0 + \sum_{i=2}^{m-1} d_i w_{1i}^r + \frac{1}{2} \sum_{i=2}^{m-1} \sum_{j=2}^{m-1} d_{ij} w_{1i}^r w_{1j}^r \\
& + d_p p_1^r + d_w w_{10}^r + \frac{1}{2} d_{pp} (p_1^r)^2 + \frac{1}{2} d_{ww} (w_{10}^r)^2 \\
& + d_{pw} p_1^r w_{10}^r + \sum_{i=2}^{m-1} d_{pi} p_1^r w_{1i}^r \\
& + \sum_{i=2}^{m-1} d_{wi} w_{10}^r w_{1i}^r \Bigg] ,
\end{aligned}
$$

and

$$
\begin{aligned}
(24) \quad J_2^r(ep_2^r, w_{20}^{*r}, w_2^{*r}; K_2) = K_2 \Bigg[& f_0 + \sum_{i=2}^{m-1} f_i w_{2i}^{*r} + \frac{1}{2} \sum_{i=2}^{m-1} \sum_{j=2}^{m-1} f_{ij} w_{2i}^{*r} w_{2j}^{*r} \\
& + f_p ep_2^r + f_w w_{20}^{*r} + \frac{1}{2} f_{pp} (ep_2^r)^2 + \frac{1}{2} f_{ww} (w_{20}^{*r})^2 \\
& + f_{pw} (ep_2^r)(w_{20}^{*r}) + \sum_{i=2}^{m-1} f_{pi} (ep_2^r)(w_{2i}^{*r}) \\
& + \sum_{i=2}^{m-1} f_{wi} (w_{20}^{*r})(w_{2i}^{*r}) \Bigg] ,
\end{aligned}
$$

where $d_{ij} = d_{ji}$, $f_{ij} = f_{ji}$, $J_1^r = J_1/w_{11}$, and $J_2^r = J_2/w_{21}^*$. Treating the quasi-fixed capital stock as a multiplicative factor imposes constant returns to scale on these functions.

To actually estimate the model, firm-level data on this Canadian export industry are employed along with industry-level data on the Canadian and U.S. final goods industries.[11] It is assumed that three variable inputs—labor, materials, and energy—are used in the production of the intermediate good, and this good, labor, and energy are employed as variable inputs into the final goods industries.

To implement the theoretical model for the Canadian export industry empirically, data on a set of firms rather than on a single monopolist firm are used. Although the Canadian export industry is fairly concentrated with a four-firm concentration ratio of approximately 50 percent, it is not reasonable to assume that the firms in the industry collude to mimic the behavior of a monopolist. Therefore, it would be incorrect simply to sum the data for each firm and treat the aggregate as a single monopolistic firm. Instead, each firm is assumed to face similar output market conditions and employ the same production technology. While the firms are assumed to act competitively in factor markets, the amount of each variable input used in production depends on firm-specific input prices.

Furthermore, the objective of the empirical model is to test not whether the demand curves facing the entire industry are horizontal but whether individual firms set prices above the shadow price of production, which is the marginal variable cost of the last unit of output produced. If each firm is identical and acts as a perfect competitor, then prices should be equal to the shadow price of production regardless of the slope of the industry demand curves. Therefore, since the model focuses on the pricing decision at the firm level, it does provide a valid test of price-taking behavior across markets.[12]

Using the functional forms specified for the variable cost function of the Canadian export industry and for the variable profit functions of the Canadian and U.S. final goods industries—equations (22)–(24)—the empirical model corresponding to equations (10), (13), and (14) can be derived. For each function, the wage rate in the corresponding industry is chosen as the normalizing price. By applying Shepherd's lemma to the cost function, the input demand equations for energy and materials are

$$(25) \quad \frac{\partial(C/q_L)}{\partial(q_M/q_L)} = z_M = a_M + a_{ME}(q_E/q_L) + a_{MM}(q_M/q_L)$$
$$+ a_{KM}K_0 + a_{yM}y_0,$$

$$(26) \quad \frac{\partial(C/q_L)}{\partial(q_E/q_L)} = z_E = a_E + a_{EE}(q_E/q_L) + a_{ME}(q_M/q_L)$$
$$+ a_{KE}K_0 + a_{yE}y_0 .$$

Note that the estimated demand function for labor can be derived as a residual from the other two functions. That is,

$$z_L = (C/q_L) - [(q_E/q_L)z_E + (q_M/q_L)z_M].$$

Using (15), (16), (23), and (24), the expressions for the markup terms are given by

$$(27) \quad \gamma_1 = -\frac{K_1[d_p + d_{pp}(p_1/w_{1L}) + d_{pw}(w_{10}/w_{1L}) + d_{pE}(w_{1E}/w_{1L})]}{K_1[d_{pp}]}$$

$$= -(1/d_{pp})[d_p + d_{pp}(p_1/w_{1L}) + d_{pw}(w_{10}/w_{1L}) + d_{pE}(w_{1E}/w_{1L})]$$

and

$$(28) \quad \gamma_2 = -\frac{K_2[f_p + f_{pp}(ep_2/w_{2L}^*) + f_{pw}(w_{20}^*/w_{2L}^*) + f_{pE}(w_{2E}^*/w_{2L}^*)]}{K_2[ef_{pp}]}$$

$$= -(1/f_{pp})[f_p(1/e) + f_{pp}(p_2/w_{2L}^*) + f_{pw}(w_{20}^*/ew_{2L}^*) + f_{pE}(w_{2E}^*/ew_{2L}^*)].$$

The expression for marginal variable cost is

$$(29) \quad \frac{\partial C}{\partial y_0} = q_L \frac{\partial(C/q_L)}{\partial y_0}$$

$$= q_L[a_y + a_{yM}(q_M/q_L) + a_{yE}(q_E/q_L) + a_{yy}y_0 + a_{yK}K_0].$$

Therefore, the two equations that relate price in each market to marginal cost are

$$(30) \quad p_1 + (p_1/w_{1L}) = -\left(\frac{d_p}{d_{pp}}\right) - \left(\frac{d_{pw}}{d_{pp}}\right)(w_{10}/w_{1L}) - \left(\frac{d_{pE}}{d_{pp}}\right)(w_{1E}/w_{1L})$$

$$+ a_y q_L + a_{yM} q_M + a_{yE} q_E + a_{yy} y_0 q_L + a_{yK} K_0 q_L$$

and

$$(31) \quad p_2 + (p_2/w_{2L}^*) = -\left(\frac{f_p}{f_{pp}}\right)(1/e) - \left(\frac{f_{pw}}{f_{pp}}\right)(w_{20}^*/ew^*_{2L}) - \left(\frac{f_{pE}}{f_{pp}}\right)(w_{2E}^*/ew^*_{2L})$$

$$+ a_y q_L + a_{yM} q_M + a_{yE} q_E + a_{yy} y_0 q_L + a_{yK} K_0 q_L .$$

Note that the relative price terms with a coefficient of one are moved to the left-hand side of each equation.

In addition, the two demand equations given by H_1 and H_2 in the theoretical model can be derived from the profit functions by applying Hotelling's lemma to obtain

$$(32) \quad y_1/K_1 = -d_p - d_{pp}(p_1/w_{1L}) - d_{pw}(w_{10}/w_{1L}) - d_{pE}(w_{1E}/w_{1L})$$

and

(33) $y_2/K_2 = -f_p - f_{pp}(ep_2/w_{2L}^*) - f_{pw}(w_{20}^*/w_{2L}^*) - f_{pE}(w_{2E}^*/w_{2L}^*),$

where the expression on the left-hand side of each equation is demand per unit of capital. The inclusion of these two equations in the empirical model permits the identification of the key parameters d_{pp} and f_{pp}. The identity $y_0 \equiv y_1 + y_2$ is also included in the empirical model.

The final step in implementing the model for estimation is to embed the empirical model in a stochastic framework by adding mean-zero error terms to equations (25), (26), (30), (31), (32), and (33) to capture optimization errors.

6.3 Data

All the data employed in estimating the model are annual and taken from the period 1973–85 (thirteen years). Data prior to 1973 were not readily available on a consistent basis.

The data on the Canadian export industry were taken from the Census of Manufacturers data base. A consistent series of establishments that primarily produce the intermediate good was collected. The establishment-level data were aggregated to the firm level so that data on outputs and inputs are for sixteen firms that account for 90–95 percent of the industry's shipments of the intermediate good. Labor data are the number of hours worked and wages paid for production and related workers. Data on materials consist of quantity and price Divisia indexes for several components. Energy data consist of quantity and price Divisia indexes for coal, natural gas, gasoline, fuel oil, liquid petroleum gases, and electricity used.

Capital stock series at the firm level were constructed using the data collected from the annual capital expenditures survey conducted by Statistics Canada.[13] The capital stock data are midyear net stocks in constant dollars.

Output is the sum of shipments in tons of the intermediate good and other related products. Establishments in the sample were selected on the basis that intermediate good of interest accounted for at least three-quarters of their total shipments.

Separate series are collected by Statistics Canada on prices of the intermediate good for domestic and export sales.[14] The prices of the intermediate good are f.o.b. (freight on board) plant and, therefore, net of any transport costs. U.S. data on quantity and value of imports of the intermediate good from Canada provide an alternate source of export price data. These prices are also net of transport costs.[15]

Consistent data series for the Canadian final goods industry were obtained for wages, industry selling prices, energy input prices, and capital stock. In particular, data used to construct a wage rate for production and related workers and an energy input price index (a Divisia index formed from natural gas, gasoline, fuel oil, and electricity) were taken from the Census of Manufacturers. Capital stock data are midyear net stocks in constant 1971 dollars obtained in unpublished form from the Science, Technology and Capital Stock Division, Statistics Canada. The industry selling price index is the ratio of value added in current dollars to value added in constant dollars.

For the U.S. final goods industry, a wage rate series and energy price index series were taken from the Annual Survey of Manufacturing. The industry selling price series was taken from the U.S. Commerce Department publication *U.S. Industrial Outlook*. Capital stock data are midyear net stocks in constant 1972 dollars obtained in unpublished form from the U.S. Commerce Department.

The exchange rate is the average noon spot rate in U.S. dollars per Canadian dollar.

All the data used in estimation were scaled to take the value of one at the sample mean.

6.4   Estimation and Results

The empirical model represented by equations (25), (26), and (30)–(33) is a simultaneous system with six endogenous variables—input demands, z_M and z_E, intermediate good prices, p_1 and p_2, and intermediate good sales, y_1 and y_2. To estimate this system efficiently so as to impose the across-equation restrictions and allow for contemporaneous correlation of the disturbances across equations, a full-information, maximum likelihood estimation technique was tried. Unfortunately, the nonlinear optimization routine failed to converge despite repeated attempts. Given the size of the system with twenty-one unknown parameters and the limited number of time-series observations on the Canadian and U.S. consuming industries (thirteen years), this failure is not surprising.

In an effort to limit the number of parameters to be estimated at one time and to keep the system as linear as possible, it was decided to estimate the empirical model in two steps. First, equations (25), (26), (30), and (31) were estimated simultaneously using iterated three-stage least squares.[16] Second, equations (32) and (33) were jointly estimated using Zellner's (1962) seemingly unrelated regression technique.

Initially, all the across-equation restrictions were imposed when the first four equations were estimated. These restrictions were strongly rejected by the data using a modified F-test statistic. In particular, the restrictions between the first and the second pairs of equations appeared to be the ones most inconsistent with the data. Therefore, these restrictions were dropped, and only the symmetry restriction between the first two input demand equations and the restrictions on the equivalence of marginal cost across the last two markup equations were maintained.

The results from this estimation are given in table 6.1. In the input demand equations, the coefficients on the own price terms are significantly negative. From these estimates, the cost function is found to be concave in prices at all points in the sample. The coefficient on output is significantly positive in both equations, and the symmetry restriction on the cross-price variable is not rejected by the data at the 1 percent level. In addition, the relatively large values for the Durbin-Watson statistic provide no evidence of model misspecification.

The results for the markup equations are less satisfactory. While many of the estimated coefficients are statistically significant, the low-value Durbin-Watson statistics for both equations indicate serial correlation of the disturbances and possible model misspecification. The restrictions that the marginal cost parameters be the same across the two equations is not rejected at the 1 percent level. However, they are rejected at the 5 percent level, again perhaps indicating some misspecification of the model. The estimated coefficient a_{yy} is positive, which implies that the estimated marginal variable cost function is upward sloping.

It should be noted that, because the complete empirical model is not being estimated, the parameters d_{pp} and f_{pp} cannot be identified in the first step of the estimation procedure. Nevertheless, it is still possible to obtain estimates of the markup terms γ_1 and γ_2. These are given in table 6.2, along with the estimated inverse elasticities of demand.

Table 6.1   **Estimation Results 1: Equations (1)–(4)**

Coefficient	Estimate	Standard Error
Equation (1):[a]		
a_M	.400***	.151
a_{ME}	.044	.034
a_{MM}	−.188***	.052
a_{KM}	.002	.034
a_{yM}	.741***	.131
R^2	.971	
D-W	1.964	
ρ	.012	
Equation (2):[b]		
a_E	.172	.149
a_{ME}	.044	.034
a_{EE}	−.275***	.049
a_{KE}	−.014	.044
a_{yE}	1.074***	.158
R^2	.971	
D-W	1.792	
ρ	.100	

Table 6.1   (continued)

Coefficient	Estimate	Standard Error
Equation (3):[c]		
d_p/d_{pp}	.257***	.078
d_{pw}/d_{pp}	.463***	.081
d_{pE}/d_{pp}	.453***	.071
a_y	−1.018***	.291
a_{yM}	.442***	.086
a_{yE}	−.011	.081
a_{yy}	1.219***	.256
a_{yK}	−.025	.082
R^2	.971	
D-W	1.062	
ρ	.460	
Equation (4):[d]		
f_p/f_{pp}	1.017***	.093
f_{pw}/f_{pp}	−.501***	.091
f_{pE}/f_{pp}	.884***	.062
a_y	−1.018***	.291
a_{yM}	.442***	.086
a_{yE}	−.011	.081
a_{yy}	1.219***	.025
a_{yK}	−.025	.082
R^2	.971	
D-W	.988	
ρ	.498	

Note: Estimation technique is iterated three-stage least squares. Estimation period is 1973–85. Number of observations is 208. R^2's are for the whole four-equation system. Statistical significance is based on asymptotic t-ratios: *** at the 1 percent level; ** at the 5 percent level; and * at the 10 percent level. While the stacked data set consists of 206 observations (thirteen years times sixteen firms), the number of distinct observations on the final goods industries in Canada and the United States is thirteen.
[a]Dependent variable is z_M.
[b]Dependent variable is z_E.
[c]Dependent variable is $p_1(1 + 1/w_{1L})$.
[d]Dependent variable is $p_2(1 + 1/w_{2L}^*)$.

The estimated markups are found to be significantly greater than zero at the 1 percent level in both markets in each year of the sample. More interestingly, the markup on U.S. sales tended to increase over the sample period. This reflects the fact that export prices rose at a faster rate (10.7 percent per annum on the average) than wage rates (10.1 percent) and unit materials costs (9.1 percent). These two components represent 80–85 percent of variable costs in any given year. Only unit energy costs increased at a faster rate (13.2 percent). Markups in both markets fell in the oil price shock years of 1974 and 1979, when unit energy costs jumped by 29 percent and 18 percent, respectively.

Table 6.2   **Estimated Markups and Inverse Elasticities of Demand**

| Year | Markups | | | | Inverse Elasticities of Demand | |
| | Canada | | United States | | Canada | United States |
	γ_1	SE	γ_2	SE		
1973	.348	.043	.363	.083	.890	.877
1974	.260	.047	.317	.082	.536	.612
1975	.234	.049	.262	.084	.409	.402
1976	.161	.047	.280	.081	.257	.417
1977	.159	.051	.294	.089	.235	.370
1978	.193	.054	.372	.094	.272	.416
1979	.179	.053	.326	.096	.223	.321
1980	.149	.053	.370	.098	.161	.325
1981	.209	.060	.399	.102	.201	.308
1982	.260	.062	.504	.105	.230	.372
1983	.383	.062	.638	.104	.353	.499
1984	.342	.061	.557	.107	.343	.392
1985	.267	.058	.529	.111	.267	.340
At sample mean	.242	.054	.401	.095	.256	.401

Note: The markup represents the difference between price and estimated marginal variable cost. It can be interpreted as a percentage only at the sample mean.

The markup on U.S. export sales is greater than the markup on Canadian sales in every year, although this difference is significant only at the 5 percent level in the years 1976, 1978, 1980, and 1983–85. In particular, the difference in markups is relatively large in the years after 1976, when the Canadian dollar depreciated almost continuously against the U.S. dollar. It is clear that during these years firms did not pass the lower value of the Canadian dollar into lower U.S. dollar export prices. They absorbed the exchange rate movement into their profit margins by pricing to market.

Evaluated at the sample mean, both markups are significantly greater than zero, and the U.S. markup is significantly greater than the Canadian markup at the 10 percent level. This supports the hypothesis that Canadian firms had the ability to price discriminate across the two markets.

Also, the fact that the inverse elasticities of demand lie between zero and one in both markets at all points in the sample is consistent with profit-maximizing behavior. Firms with market power are always on the elastic part of the demand curve.

In order to estimate the effect of an exchange rate change on the prices of the intermediate good for domestic and export sales and on output and input demands in the Canadian export industry, it is necessary to obtain estimates of the parameters d_{pp} and f_{pp}. They represent the second-order derivatives of the profit functions, J_1 and J_2, with respect to the price of the intermediate good. As these parameters are not identified in the first step of the estimation procedure, which involved the first four equations in the empirical model, the demand equations for the intermediate good, (32) and (33), need to be estimated.

The results obtained by applying seemingly unrelated regression to these two equations are given in table 6.3. Owing to the small number of degrees of freedom (nine), accurate estimates of the coefficients in the demand equations could not be obtained; most of the coefficients are not statistically significant. In particular, the estimates of the coefficients d_{pp} and f_{pp}, while having the theoretically correct positive sign, are not significantly different from zero. The Durbin-Watson statistics for both equations are in the inconclusive range.

Employing these estimates for d_{pp} and f_{pp} along with earlier estimates, equations (17) and (18) can be evaluated at the sample mean to determine the elasticities of the domestic and export intermediate good prices with respect to an exchange rate change. The estimated elasticity of the domestic price, p_1, with respect to the exchange rate is -0.22 percent, while estimated elasticity for the export price, p_2, is -0.85 percent. Hence, a 1 percent depreciation (appreciation) of the Canadian dollar against the U.S. dollar will cause the domestic price of the intermediate good to rise (fall) by 0.22 percent, while the export price will rise (fall) by 0.85 percent. Under the same circum-

Table 6.3   **Estimation Results 2: Equations (5) and (6)**

Coefficient	Estimate	Standard Error
Equation (5):[a]		
d_p	$-.975*$	.561
d_{pp}	.084	.373
d_{pw}	.015	.277
d_{pE}	$-.124$	.114
R^2	.347	
D-W	1.493	
ρ	.252	
Equation (6):[b]		
f_p	$-1.192***$	.354
f_{pp}	.465	.401
f_{pw}	$-.196$	.485
f_{pE}	.123	.313
R^2	.347	
D-W	1.602	
ρ	.189	

Note: Estimation technique is seemingly unrelated regression. Estimation period is 1973–85. Number of observations is thirteen. The R^2's are for the whole two-equation system. Statistical significance based on asymptotic t-ratios: *** at the 1 percent level; ** at the 5 percent level; and * at the 10 percent level.

[a]Dependent variable is y_1/K_1.

[b]Dependent variable is y_2/K_2.

stances, the U.S. dollar export price will fall (rise) by 0.15 percent. Thus, the U.S. dollar price is not very responsive to an exchange rate change.

Using equation (20), the elasticity of the level of output with respect to the exchange rate change is computed to be -0.051 percent at the sample mean. Hence, a 1 percent depreciation (appreciation) of the Canadian dollar will cause output of the intermediate good to rise (fall) by 0.051 percent. Therefore, the changes in sales in the domestic and U.S. markets partially offset each other, resulting in a relatively small effect on output.

The effect of an exchange rate change on demand for inputs by the Canadian export industry can also be determined by using equation (21) and the regressions results in table 6.1. The elasticity of the demand for materials and energy with respect to the exchange rate computed at the sample mean are -0.038 and -0.055, respectively.[17]

Standard errors for the point estimates of the effects of an exchange rate change are difficult to determine. However, given that the estimates of d_{pp} and f_{pp} are known to be inaccurate, it is likely that the standard errors would be relatively large. Hence, while these point estimates do provide some insight as to the effect of an exchange rate change, they are not likely to be very robust.

6.5   Concluding Remarks

In this paper, a partial equilibrium model of the supply and demand of an exportable intermediate good is theoretically constructed and empirically estimated. The objective of this exercise is to develop a framework in which the effect of an exchange rate change on the industry could be determined so that the recently observed pricing to market behavior of foreign exporters to the United States could be studied. While the model developed in this paper is static, it was still possible to determine whether the export industry being analyzed price discriminates between its domestic and its export markets.

In the case of the major Canadian export industry considered in this paper, price markups over estimated marginal variable cost are found to be statistically greater than zero on sales in both the U.S. export market and the Canadian domestic market. In addition, the markups on U.S. sales were significantly greater than those on Canadian sales for several years in the sample and at the sample mean. This difference in markups tended to increase as the Canadian exchange rate depreciated. Hence, firms in this industry were able to price discriminate between the two markets, and exchange rate changes to a large extent were not passed through into U.S. dollar export prices but were absorbed into the firms' profit margins.

Since firms in the industry possess some degree of market power in each market and marginal costs are not constant, exchange rate changes would not result in one-for-one changes in prices. A 1 percent exchange rate depreciation is estimated to cause a 0.22 percent increase in the domestic ($Canadian) price and a 0.15 percent fall in the export ($U.S.) price.

Although the empirical results provide some support for the model and indicate the existence of pricing to market behavior in this industry, it was difficult to obtain accurate estimates of the effect of the exchange rate on the industry. Finally, it is hoped that the theoretical framework developed in this paper will provide a good basis on which to extend the model to consider dynamic costs of adjustment of quasi-fixed factors. Such an extension will permit a more complete analysis of the pricing to market phenomenon.

Appendix

To determine the effect of an exchange rate change on the model, it is necessary to begin by totally differentiating equations (13) and (14) with respect to the exchange rate:

$$\text{(A1)} \quad \frac{dp_1}{de} = \frac{\partial \gamma_1}{\partial e} + \frac{\partial^2 C(q, y_0)}{\partial y_0^2}\left[-\frac{\partial H_1(\cdot)}{\partial p_1}\frac{dp_1}{de} - \frac{\partial H_2(\cdot)}{\partial ep_2}\frac{\partial ep_2}{\partial p_2}\frac{dp_2}{de} \right],$$

$$\text{(A2)} \quad \frac{dp_2}{de} = \frac{\partial \gamma_2}{\partial e} + \frac{\partial^2 C(q, y_0)}{\partial y_0^2}\left[-\frac{\partial H_1(\cdot)}{\partial p_1}\frac{dp_1}{de} - \frac{\partial H_2(\cdot)}{\partial ep_2}\frac{\partial ep_2}{\partial p_2}\frac{dp_2}{de} \right].$$

Using the expressions for γ_1 and γ_2 given by equations (15) and (16), the following results can be obtained:

$$\text{(A3)} \quad \frac{\partial \gamma_1}{\partial e} = -\left[\frac{1}{\partial^2 J_1(\cdot)/\partial p_1^2}\right]^2 \left\{ \left[\frac{\partial^2 J_1(\cdot)}{\partial p_1^2}\right]^2 \left(\frac{dp_1}{de}\right) - \left[\frac{\partial J_1(\cdot)}{\partial p_1}\right]\left[\frac{\partial^3 J_1(\cdot)}{\partial p_1^3}\right]\left(\frac{dp_1}{de}\right) \right\},$$

$$\text{(A4)} \quad \frac{\partial \gamma_2}{\partial e} = -\left[\frac{1}{e\partial^2 J_2(\cdot)/\partial (ep_2)^2}\right]^2 \left\{ \left[e\frac{\partial^2 J_2(\cdot)}{\partial (ep_2)^2}\right]\left[e\frac{\partial^2 J_2(\cdot)}{\partial (ep_2)^2}\left(\frac{p_2}{e} + \frac{dp_2}{de}\right)\right] \right.$$
$$\left. -\left[\frac{\partial J_2(\cdot)}{\partial (ep_2)}\right]\left[\frac{\partial^2 J_2(\cdot)}{\partial (ep_2)^2} + e^2\frac{\partial^3 J_2(\cdot)}{\partial (ep_2)^3}\left(\frac{p_2}{e} + \frac{dp_2}{de}\right)\right] \right\},$$

which can be simplified and rewritten as

$$\text{(A5)} \quad \frac{\partial \gamma_1}{\partial e} = -\left\{\frac{[J_1''(\cdot)]^2 - J_1'(\cdot)J_1'''(\cdot)}{[J_1''(\cdot)]^2}\right\}\frac{dp_1}{de_1} = -B_{11}\frac{dp_1}{de},$$

$$\frac{\partial \gamma_2}{\partial e} = -\frac{p_2}{e} - \frac{dp_2}{de} + \frac{J_2'(\cdot)}{[eJ_2''(\cdot)]^2}\left[J_2''(\cdot) + e^2J_2'''(\cdot)\left(\frac{p_2}{e} + \frac{dp_2}{de}\right)\right]$$
$$= \frac{J_2'(\cdot)}{e^2J_2''(\cdot)} - \left\{\frac{[J_2''(\cdot)]^2 - J_2'(\cdot)J_2'''(\cdot)}{[J_2''(\cdot)]^2}\right\}\left(\frac{p_2}{e} + \frac{dp_2}{de}\right),$$

$$\text{(A6)} \quad \frac{\partial \gamma_2}{\partial e} = B_{21} - B_{22}\frac{p_2}{e} - B_{22}\frac{dp_2}{de}.$$

From the regularity properties of the profit function, $J_i'(\cdot) \leq 0$ and $J_i'(\cdot) \geq 0$ for $i = 1, 2$. The third derivative of the profit function with respect to an input price can be either negative or positive. If the derived input demand function is linear in its own price, then the derivative would be zero. The usual shape of the demand function is convex to the origin; thus, the third derivative would be a small negative number. Hence, B_{21} is negative, while B_{11} and B_{22} are most likely positive in sign.

Equations (3) and (5) can be used to obtain

(A7)
$$\frac{\partial H_1(\cdot)}{\partial p_1} = \frac{\partial^2 J_1(\cdot)}{\partial p_1^2} = J_1''(\cdot),$$

(A8)
$$\frac{\partial H_2(\cdot)}{\partial ep_2} = \frac{\partial^2 J_2(\cdot)}{\partial (ep_2)^2} = J_2''(\cdot).$$

Substituting (A5)–(A8) in equations (A1) and (A2) and writing them in matrix form gives

(A9)
$$\begin{bmatrix} 1 + B_{11} + C''(\cdot)J_1''(\cdot) & C''(\cdot)eJ_2''(\cdot) \\ C''(\cdot)J_1''(\cdot) & 1 + B_{22} + C''(\cdot)eJ_2''(\cdot) \end{bmatrix} \begin{bmatrix} \dfrac{dp_1}{de} \\ \dfrac{dp_2}{de} \end{bmatrix} = \begin{bmatrix} 0 \\ B_{23} \end{bmatrix},$$

where $C''(\cdot)$ is the second derivative of the cost function with respect to output and $B_{23} = B_{21} - B_{22}(p_2/e)$. Using Cramer's rule, it is straightforward to show that

(A10)
$$\frac{dp_1}{de} = \frac{B_{23}C''(\cdot)eJ_2''(\cdot)}{|D|},$$

(A11)
$$\frac{dp_2}{de} = \frac{B_{23}[1 + B_{11} + C''(\cdot)J_1''(\cdot)]}{|D|},$$

where $|D|$ is the determinant of the square matrix in (A9), and it must be positive for the second-order conditions of the monopolist's profit maximization problem to hold.

Notes

1. Dunn (1970) and Isard (1977) represent earlier references in this area. More recent references include Baldwin (1988), Feenstra (1987), Feinberg (1987), Fisher (1987), Froot and Klemperer (1988), Kiyono (1988), and Knetter (1989).
2. Owing to the data confidentiality requirements of Statistics Canada, the industry being considered cannot be identified.

3. To keep the notation relatively simple, quasi-fixed factors of production, such as the capital stock that is employed in estimating the model, are not explicitly included in the theoretical specification of the production, profit, and cost functions.

4. It is assumed without explicit justification that price arbitrage between the two markets is less than perfect. Typically, transport costs and other transactions costs are large enough for most intermediate goods to prevent effective arbitrage.

5. While this assumption may be justifiable in the context of a static short-run model such as the one estimated in this paper, it is clearly less reasonable the longer the time horizon of the analysis.

6. The cost function represents the cost of manufacturing only. While transport costs are likely to be different in the two markets, the selling prices of the intermediate good that are employed in estimation are f.o.b. (freight on board) plant.

7. Since the model is static rather than dynamic, expectations are also static. Therefore, any exchange rate change is by definition unanticipated and also permanent.

8. Giovannini (1988) finds with his model that dep_2/de is always positive if the exchange rate change is expected to persist.

9. Diewert (1985) points out that the quadratic function has the disadvantage that it is not symmetric in prices. Therefore, the empirical results will be affected by the choice of the normalizing price.

10. A time trend to capture technological change was initially included as an explanatory variable in the cost function and profit functions. However, it added little explanatory power in estimation and was omitted.

11. This intermediate good is used almost exclusively in the final goods industries. It is assumed that the U.S. industry producing the intermediate good behaves like a competitive fringe to the Canadian export industry.

12. Applebaum (1979) also makes this argument when he uses industry-level data for the industry producing the intermediate good. He argues that industry-level data are aggregated over all firms. Therefore, if individual firms are setting prices above marginal cost, then this will also be true in the aggregate.

13. For more details on the construction of firm-level capital stock series, see Schembri and Beaulieu (1988).

14. The domestic and export prices are collected from a survey of major manufacturers' selling prices of a clearly defined commodity sold under the same specified conditions. Therefore, the price data are actual spot prices, not unit values.

15. There are no tariffs on intermediate good imports to the United States.

16. In the iterated three-stage least squares procedure, all the exogenous variables in the model were used as instruments.

17. Since the restrictions across the input demand and markup equations were not imposed in the first step of the estimation procedure, it is not possible to obtain a consistent estimate of the effect on labor demand.

References

Applebaum, E. 1979. Testing price taking behaviour. *Journal of Econometrics* 9(3):283–94.

Applebaum, E., and U. Kohli. 1979. Canada–United States trade: Tests for the small-open-economy hypothesis. *Canadian Journal of Economics* 12(1):1–14.

Baldwin, R. E. 1988. Some empirical evidence on hysteresis in aggregate U.S. import prices. NBER Working Paper no. 2483. Cambridge, Mass.: National Bureau of Economic Research, January.

Diewert, W. E. 1985. The measurement of the economic benefits of infrastructure services. Working Paper no. 85-11. Department of Economics, University of British Columbia.

Dornbusch, R. 1987. Exchange rates and prices. *American Economic Review* 77(1):93–106.

Dunn, R. M. 1970. Flexible exchange rates and oligopoly pricing: A study of Canadian markets. *Journal of Political Economy* 78(1):140–51.

Feenstra, R. 1987. Symmetric pass-through of tariffs and exchange rates under imperfect competition. NBER Working Paper no. 2453. Cambridge, Mass.: National Bureau of Economic Research, December.

Feinberg, R. M. 1987. Recent foreign exchange movements, prices and U.S. trade flows. U.S. International Trade Commission. Typescript.

Fisher, E. 1987. A model of exchange-rate pass through. Board of Governors of the Federal Reserve, International Finance Discussion Paper no. 302.

Froot, K., and P. Klemperer. 1988. Exchange rate pass-through when market share matters. NBER Working Paper no. 2542. Cambridge, Mass.: National Bureau of Economic Research, March.

Giovannini, A. 1988. Exchange rates and traded goods prices. *Journal of International Economics* 24(1/2):45–68.

Isard, P. 1977. How far can we push the law of one price. *American Economic Review* 67(5):942–48.

Kiyono, K. 1988. Yen appreciation and Japan's pass-through structure. Faculty of Economics, Gakushuin University, Japan. Typescript.

Knetter, M. 1989. Price discrimination by U.S. and German exporters. *American Economic Review* 79(1):198–210.

Krugman, P. 1987. Pricing to market when the exchange rate changes. In *Real-financial linkages among open economies,* ed. J. D. Richardson and S. Arndt. Cambridge, Mass.: MIT Press.

Mann, C. 1986. Prices, profit margins and exchange rates. *Federal Reserve Bulletin* 72(6):366–79.

Morrison, C., and E. Berndt. 1981. Short-run labor productivity in a dynamic model. *Journal of Econometrics* 16(3):339–65.

Schembri, L., and E. Beaulieu. 1988. The construction of firm-level capital stocks. Department of Economics, Carleton University. Typescript.

Varian, H. 1978. *Microeconomic analysis.* New York: Norton.

Zellner, A. 1962. An efficient method of estimating seemingly unrelated regressions and tests for aggregation bias. *Journal of the American Statistical Association* 57:348–68

Comment   Alberto Giovannini

This thorough and interesting paper uses a new data set to estimate pricing behavior of internationally trading firms. The main interest of this work is in the unique character of the data, which includes firm-level information on

Alberto Giovannini is associate professor at the Columbia University Graduate School of Business. He is a faculty research fellow of the National Bureau of Economic Research as well as a research fellow of the Centre for Economic Policy Research.

prices and quantities of inputs and outputs. The sixteen firms in this unnamed Canadian industry produce an intermediate industrial good and account for 90–95 percent of the industry's total shipments. We also learn that the industry exports more than three-quarters of its output and that its exports account for more than 50 percent of U.S. consumption.

Interest in international pricing behavior stems from the work of Isard (1977), who demonstrated that, even at a very disaggregated level, relative prices of domestic and export goods in an industry vary dramatically and are sometimes correlated with exchange rates. These results, as Dornbusch (1987) documented, are even stronger when we look at more recent data, including the large swings of the dollar exchange rate since the beginning of 1980. One particularly striking aspect of the recent experience has been the insensitivity of import prices in the United States to fluctuations of the dollar exchange rate. This phenomenon is sometimes referred to as lack of "pass through": a change in the exchange rate, from the firm's viewpoint and other things being equal, represents a shift in demand from the domestic to the foreign market. If the foreign currency price of the export adjusts one for one with the exchange-rate change, then the shift in demand is not associated with any change in relative prices of the two goods, implying a relatively elastic supply curve by trading firms. If, on the other hand, exchange rate changes do not affect the foreign currency prices of exports significantly, then pass through is low, indicating that quantities are unlikely to change in response to changes in relative prices.[1]

The analysis of the relative movements of domestic and export prices is thus especially valuable to determine the elasticity of export supplies to changes in relative prices and provide invaluable information on the nature of the adjustment of trade imbalances to changes in relative prices.[2] Data on domestic and export prices of internationally trading firms are also of great interest to determine the presence of sluggish nominal price adjustment. In the presence of slow nominal price adjustments, which would occur, for example, when pricing decisions are less frequent than exchange rate changes, the correlations between the deviations from the law of one price and the nominal exchange rate depend in a very clear-cut way on the currency of denomination of exports: as is shown in Giovannini (1988a), if exports are denominated in foreign currency terms, in the presence of price stickiness deviations from the law of one price are highly correlated with the nominal exchange rate because the foreign currency price and the domestic currency price do not instantaneously respond to exchange rate innovations. On the other hand, when export prices are denominated in the same currency as domestic prices, then deviations from the law of one price should be uncorrelated with exchange rate innovations.

Although international price discrimination cannot really be studied independently of the issue of the frequency of price adjustments, Schembri concentrates exclusively on the measurement of the degree to which changes in relative demands give rise to changes in relative prices and changes in quantities. He assumes that producers can perfectly discriminate between the domestic and the foreign market and proceeds estimating the relevant parameters of demand and cost functions. Demand functions are obtained assuming that the "downstream" industries at home and abroad are profit maximizers and applying Hotelling's lemma to the postulated profit functions.

The whole analysis is carried out assuming that perfect price discrimination is possible, that is, that the domestic and foreign markets are perfectly isolated from each other. This assumption is questionable. It is likely that, when the U.S. and the Canadian markets are considered, transactions costs, even if high relative to the unit value of the good in question, should provide a natural limitation to the degree of price discrimination allowed to international traders. International price discrimination in the presence of a potential arbitrage industry clearly requires a modification of the model, including a specification of the technology of the incumbent arbitrage industry, which I do not want to pursue. Instead, I want to suggest alternative specifications of the markup equations. As the author shows, the current specification of these equations appears to perform poorly and might be at the root of the rejection of the cross-equation restrictions.

Schembri applies the same set of first-order conditions to each firm in the data set, implying that a "representative firm" exists and that the representative firm's efficiency conditions apply to each firm in the set. Since there are only sixteen firms in this industry, I prefer to take into account the firms' interactions explicitly by considering the markup equations in the case of a Cournot-Nash game. For each firm, let $\bar{Y}$ represent the quantities produced by the rest of the firms in the market. The demand equations, following Schembri's notation, become

(1) $$-(Y_1 + \bar{Y}_1) = H_1(P_1, w_{10}, w_1),$$

(2) $$-(Y_2 + \bar{Y}_2) = H_2(eP_2, w_{20}^*, w_2^*).$$

Define the inverse demand equations Φ and Ψ as follows:

(3) $$\Phi(Y_1 + \bar{Y}_1, w_{10}, w_1) = P_1 ,$$

(4) $$\Psi(Y_2 + \bar{Y}_2, w_{20}^*, w_2^*) = eP_2 ,$$

where $1/\Phi_y = \partial H_1/\partial P_1$ and $1/\Psi_y = \partial H_2/\partial(eP_2)$. Profit maximization implies the two sets of first-order conditions

(5) $$P_1 - Y_1\Phi_y - C_y = 0,$$

(6) $$P_2 - Y_2\Psi_y/e - C_y = 0,$$

where subscripts indicate partial derivatives with respect to output and C stands for the cost function. Expressions (5) and (6) can be directly compared with Schembri's markup equations:

(7) $\qquad P_1 + H_1(P_1, w_{10}, w_1)/(\partial H_1/\partial P_1) + \bar{Y}_1/(\partial H_1/\partial P_1) = C_y$,

(8) $\qquad P_2 + H_2(eP_2, w^*_{20}, w^*_2)/[e\partial H_2/\partial(eP_2)]$
$\qquad\qquad + \bar{Y}_2/[e\partial H_2/\partial(eP_2)] = C_y$.

These equations are formally identical to Schembri's markup equations, except for the two terms representing, for each firm, the level of output supplied by the rest of the market. If firms in this industry are Cournot-Nash oligopolists, the equations estimated by Schembri suffer from an omitted variable problem, which, however, could be easily remedied. Equations (7) and (8) have the added advantage of permitting the estimation of the parameters of demand equations directly, through the coefficient of residual output terms rather than through the estimation of demand equations, for which little data are available.

One important feature of the alternative specification (7) and (8) is that the market price is the same for all firms, an assumption that Schembri is already exploiting since output prices data are not available for all firms. This assumption is acceptable if intrafirm price differences are just the result of sampling error and contain no information about firms' policies.

If intrafirm price differences were systematically related to demand and supply determinants, then an alternative model of product differentiation would be more plausible. In that case, information about other firms' quantities would not enter markup equations. Instead, other firms' prices would enter the equations as additional explanatory variables in the demand functions that each firm faces. These prices would be included in the cost functions of firms in the downstream industry, with coefficients representing the degree of substitutability of the differentiated products in the downstream industry's production function.

Notes

1. The interpretation of the results from these partial equilibrium pass-through equations has often been fallacious. Partial pass through at the firm level does not imply that, in the aggregate, changes in the nominal exchange rate that originate from purely nominal disturbances should not be reflected one to one in changes in nominal prices. For a discussion, see Giovannini (1988b).

2. For cross-industry evidence on exchange rate pass through, see Feinberg (1986) and Feenstra (1987).

References

Dornbusch, R. 1987. Exchange rates and prices. *American Economic Review* 77(1):93–106.

Feenstra, R. C. 1987. Symmetric pass-through of exchange rates under imperfect competition: An empirical test. University of California, Davis. Typescript.

Feinberg, R. M. 1986. The interaction of foreign exchange and market power effects on German domestic prices. *Journal of Industrial Economics* 35(1):61–70.

Giovannini, A. 1988a. Exchange rates and traded goods prices. *Journal of International Economics* 24, no. 1 (March):45–68.

———. 1988b. The macroeconomics of exchange-rate and price-level interactions: Empirical evidence on West Germany. NBER Working Paper no. 2544. Cambridge, Mass.: National Bureau of Economic Research, March.

Isard, P. 1977. How far can we push the "law of one price"? *American Economic Review* 67(4):942–48.

Comment   Catherine J. Morrison

My comments will be divided into four sections. First, I will emphasize the important contributions that are made in the paper. Then, I will focus, second, on some of the problems I see with the model and its implementation and, third, on the interpretation difficulties that result. Finally, I will highlight the important implications of Lawrence Schembri's analysis.

Important Contributions

The questions that Schembri is considering are very interesting, and the general approach that he uses to address these issues is up to the task. The model is related to research that I am currently working on, so I both agree with his focus and commiserate with him about the difficulties in interpretation and implementation of such a model.

In particular, I believe that the structural approach to modeling the industry using production theory provides important and theoretically consistent implications about the full range of firm behavior and what it responds to. Depending on which characteristics of an industry are important, various types of firm decision variables can be incorporated and their effects on firm behavior explored through construction of performance indicators and elasticities. These types of models have had wide use in the production theory literature by researchers such as Elie Appelbaum, Mel Fuss, Ernst Berndt, Erwin Diewert, Robert Pindyck, Julio Rotemberg, myself, and a host of others. Related work along these lines in the macro area follows the lead of Robert Hall and, with a more industrial organization focus, includes Domiwitz, Hubbard and Peterson, and Timothy Bresnahan.

The major indicator of interest in the current study is the index of price over marginal cost, or the markup indicator. The elasticities that are important are primarily exchange rate elasticities, although others clearly could be computed. Given the full structural model, a large number of interrelated firm responses, both for the export industry and the consuming industries, can be

Catherine J. Morrison is associate professor of economics at Tufts University and a research associate at the National Bureau of Economic Research.

modeled. This is critical for consideration of important questions such as the effect of fluctuating exchange rates; what mechanisms cause us not to observe a direct proportional adjustment such as one would expect from a rescaling of prices? The ability to "explain" occurrences using this model is the advantage of Schembri's approach over the nonparametric or nonstructural time-series types of models. I should also note that there could also be other characteristics of a particular industry such as inventory holding, advertising, and monopsonistic effects that could potentially be incorporated into this type of framework and could be illuminating.

Schembri incorporates exchange rate responses into the basic structural production theory model and appends demand equations for the output of the "monopolistic" firm explicitly structured as input demand equations for domestic and "foreign" (U.S.) firms. This is a more complete consideration of differing market power across markets than I have seen in such a structural model; it provides much potential for interpretation. Note, however, that just including the *existence* of markups adds an extra dimension to the adjustments that a firm can make to cushion the effects of exogenous changes. This would allow some assessment of how changes in the exchange rate may fail to act like a pure price scale effect for the importing industry even in the absence of explicit modeling of exchange rate behavior.

On the empirical side, the data set appears to be excellent for looking at the questions posed. The data are at an establishment level aggregated to the firm, in an industry that is relatively homogeneous with a small number of firms, that produces "almost exclusively" for Canadian and U.S. consumption, and that exports much of its output. The advantages of this data set will help interpretation significantly once justifiable results are developed.

The frustration that arises from the data is that it is hard to analyze the results when one does not know which industry we are talking about. This may not be a solvable problem, although, elaborating as far as Statistics Canada will possibly allow, to mention, for example, whether this is a durable good industry or, perhaps, a natural resource industry would help.

What Are Some of the Problems?

Although I like the focus of the paper, serious difficulties—most of which I sympathize with—arise in implementation of the model. One of the most important theoretically may be the problem of interpreting results from a "monopoly" framework when the industry of interest is an oligopoly and it is therefore unlikely that marginal revenue (MR) and marginal costs (MC) are equated in the aggregate. The problem is whether anything effective can be done about this. Aggregation conditions are difficult to deal with explicitly, although they could possibly be used to rationalize a "representative firm" type of approach. Another way to go would be to assume some kind of tacit collusion, depending on whether the particular industry justified this. Alternatively, perhaps some limited type of conjectural variation framework could be developed to provide structure.

Overall, however, the use of the theory of the firm to obtain implications about the industry is problematic. This is recognized early in the paper when it is clarified that, as Elie Appelbaum has stated, if the results suggest that price (P) is not equal to marginal cost in the aggregate, we can conclude only that each individual firm does not set $P = MC$ and that therefore some market power exists. In the results section of this paper, however, this care is discarded and interpretation is conducted as if the industry were monopolistic. Similarly, it is difficult rigorously to justify nonconstant returns to scale in the (export) industry because aggregation conditions will not be met in general. These types of aggregation problems are difficult to deal with, but at least interpretation of the results should be carried out with care.

It might also be useful to consider the implications of the functional forms used for the analysis. It has often been noted that the normalized quadratic form causes asymmetry of the demand equations for inputs that is not invariant to which input is used for normalization. This could be a serious problem, particularly when labor, which is likely relatively fixed in the short run, is used as the normalizing input. The main advantage of the quadratic form is the fact that second derivatives are simply parameters. However, since this property does not seem to be that important for the current model, other functional forms may be more appropriate. It should also be noted that the labor demand expression is not estimated in this study, which leaves the demand system incomplete. This cannot be accomplished in the current framework, however, because consistent estimates of all cost function parameters are not generated. In addition, the demand functions for the "monopolistically" produced good are also part of a system; ignoring the rest of the consuming firm's input demand structure leaves the demand functions facing the export industry somewhat incomplete. I do not think that this is worthwhile incorporating since this may be pursuing "completeness" of the model a bit too far. However, it may be worth taking into account. Finally, technological change is not included as an argument of the function.

Other difficulties arise when the analysis is suddenly expressed in terms of short-run functions at the point where functional forms are specified. It is stated that this shift does not significantly affect the results derived from the theoretical model very much, which is true. However, specification originally in terms of the short-run analysis would be desirable to make the empirical analysis more directly applicable to the model development. Also, constructing a short-run instead of long-run model as a basis for analysis implies additional questions about interpretation. For example, are we interested in short-run or long-run markups? Also, is it possible to develop a representation of the long run in this framework since capital in all industries considered must adjust to a steady state and the interactions to this "general equilibrium" may be difficult to tie down? It is important to address these issues.

Another problem is one of omission rather than commission. Schembri emphasizes in the introduction the role of dynamic adjustment and expectations that has been outlined by Krugman and Giovannini, and yet these characteristics are not included in either the theoretical or the empirical model. The current study is a good first cut to look at the questions identified, but, if these behavioral characteristics are so important, they should be included for the results to make sense. Exchange rate "surprises" in terms of exogenous shocks and responses are capable of being modeled in the current framework, but, since only static optimization is incorporated, the pattern of responses over time is ignored. At the very least, the focus on dynamic adjustment and expectations should be reduced in the introduction, and the emphasis should be on what contributions *are* made with the static model in the paper. A related but less critical problem is that the second half of the "complete explanation" of "pricing to market" phenomenon discussed in the introduction, the ability to set different prices across markets, does not receive much consideration or support in the interpretation of the empirical results.

Difficulties in Interpretation

This brings me to another dilemma; because of problems with the model and its implementation, interpretation of the results and providing justifiable conclusions become tricky at best.

The first dilemma is that the results are based on a very short data series, only thirteen years. However, the (perhaps related) problems with convergence that stimulated Schembri to estimate the model both in two parts and with not all symmetry conditions imposed raise even more questions. The problem is that the results for the second part differ substantially from those of the first part; the first coefficient I checked, for example, d_{pw}/d_{pp}, is estimated as .473 in the first part and .278 in the second. Although this is less of a difference than in previous versions of the paper, if these results are merged to make any implications, which they are for construction of the exchange rate elasticities, the results are seriously suspect. The rejection of symmetry conditions is also a problem because, when they are not imposed, the interpretation of the results is ambiguous; the integrated model breaks down, and aggregation conditions, for example, no longer stand.

At the very least, the effect of these inconsistencies should be clarified. It may be possible to determine, for example, how different the results would be if all the parameter estimates from the second stage were used rather than just appending the additional parameter estimates to the original set of estimates or if the "symmetry-imposed" estimates of parameters such as a_{yE} (or those from the other equation) were used. These tests would be crude, but they would provide some indication of sensitivity. Alternatively, and more ideally of course, some method of joint optimization should be pursued.

An additional interpretational difficulty arises with the exchange rate elasticities because there is so much endogeneity in the model that the elasticity computations may be suspect. I assume the reason p_1 is affected by the exchange rate even though it does not directly depend on e is that e

changes cause production to change, which, in turn, affects marginal cost. This mechanism is outlined to some extent in the Appendix, which is the computation that appears to motivate the elasticity calculation and is also discussed a bit earlier in the paper. It would, however, be useful to have the intuition of the elasticity construction spelled out more because it is not completely clear what is being held fixed as all the adjustments are made.

This uncertainty about the measurement of the elasticities is a serious problem for interpretation of the results. The implied output change, for example, is so small compared to the price change, especially in the light of the large effect that seems to come from the markup—it appears to attenuate 85 percent of the expected response of the U.S. price to an exchange rate change. I cannot see why this large effect should be directly counteracted by an opposite change in the Canadian market. It also seems that input demand increases with an exchange rate change even though output decreases. If I am interpreting this correctly, I think that there are some problems here with consistency.

An additional relatively minor interpretation problem arises from recent treatments of the purchasing power parity literature by Mel Fuss and his colleagues at the University of Toronto, who have worked extensively on how to adjust prices when comparing industries in different countries. They find, I believe, that we should not expect purchasing power parity to hold, which could be important for interpretation of the current results.

Theoretical and Policy Implications and Conclusions

The model and results from Schembri's study are potentially very useful. In terms of the production theory framework, the model of an industry with market power producing for another industry, and the potential discriminating monopolist stories that can be assessed in this framework are intriguing. In terms of the international ramifications, I do not know of any other treatment of exchange rate fluctuations that allows alternative decisions of firms to be explicitly characterized in a structural model. The potential insights about the deviations of exchange rate effects from those that would be expected from a strict purchasing power parity focus are fascinating and wide ranging. Since dramatic changes in exchange rates between such countries as Japan and the United States have resulted in significantly smaller changes in U.S. prices, and since this in turn has muted the effects of exchange rate changes on the balance of trade that would be expected, this type of explanation is provocative.

The model also provides a first cut at even more elaborate models, including dynamic effects and other characteristics of firms in a particular industry that may provide buffers to macro adjustments. I think that this is an important line of research. An extension to dynamic analysis will be particularly important for interpretation of the results. I am doing a study along these lines that suggests that incorporating slow adjustment for capital is particularly important and that including fixity of labor also has a significant effect, particularly if nonconstant returns to scale is incorporated. Ultimately, constructing a justifiable model of the expectations process will also provide important insights. Including these extensions allows one more carefully to interpret the indexes and elasticities and to facilitate more complete model specification.

7

U.S.-Canada Bilateral Tariff Elimination: The Role of Product Differentiation and Market Structure

Drusilla K. Brown and Robert M. Stern

Recent empirical literature evaluating the trade and welfare effects of the proposed U.S.-Canada free trade area (FTA) has emphasized the significant gains associated with tariff removal on trade in differentiated products. In this connection, there are two welfare conclusions concerning U.S.-Canada bilateral tariff elimination that tend to dominate the public discussion of the trade initiative. The first conclusion emphasized by the proponents of a U.S.-Canada FTA relates to the mutual gains from capturing scale economies and increased product variety that access to each other's market will make possible. Moreover, the influx of tariff-free imports will improve the competitive environment for firms selling domestically, with the result that these firms must either exit or reduce cost. Free trade, then, is expected to rationalize the production process by increasing output per firm and lowering average total cost.

The predicted gains from liberalization draw heavily from the literature that compares autarky and free trade (e.g., Krugman 1979; and Markusen 1981). However, from a theoretical perspective, the question of whether there are gains from liberalization is distinct from the question of whether there are gains from trade. U.S. and Canadian firms already enjoy substantial access to each other's markets. Post–Tokyo Round bilateral tariffs on U.S.-Canada trade are quite low, averaging less than 2 percent. Furthermore, Canadian firms are subjected to the efficiency-stimulating experience of competing with U.S. firms in the U.S. market. Whether small tariff changes lead to rationalization depends on certain characteristics of the input markets, as

Drusilla K. Brown is assistant professor of economics at Tufts University Robert M. Stern is professor of economics at the University of Michigan and Brandeis University.

Financial assistance was provided in part by a grant from the Ford Foundation to support a program of research in trade policy at the University of Michigan. The authors would like to thank Chris Jackson for his assistance in assembling and editing data.

217

Flam and Helpman (1987) have shown, as well as the procompetitive effects emphasized in the gains-from-trade literature.

Second, the emphasis on trade in differentiated products in evaluating liberalization leads to the conclusion that increased trade will be primarily intraindustry. Interindustry resource reallocation necessary under an FTA is therefore presumed to be minimal. On the other hand, the policy debate has tended to downplay the terms-of-trade changes typically associated with tariffs, resource movements due to interindustry trade, or the second-best nature of bilateral tariff reductions.

Aside from the theoretical welfare issues, there are some basic modeling choices that arise in evaluating the bilateral tariff elimination using computable general equilibrium techniques. In particular, U.S.-Canada bilateral trade flows that are the subject of tariff removal must be identifiable.

There are four basic approaches to this problem. First, there is the textbook model that examines the case in which each good is homogeneous across firms and countries. The implication of this framework is that some bilateral trade flows will cease with bilateral tariff elimination. Typically, the smaller country in the FTA will trade within the FTA only.

In order to avoid this particular pattern of trade in which some bilateral trade flows disappear, it is common to adopt some form of product or market differentiation. One popular approach has been to assume that products are differentiated by place of production, embodied in the Armington (1969) assumptions.[1] Alternatively, there are two other modeling approaches that draw on the behavior of imperfectly competitive firms. The first is to assume that there is product differentiation at the firm level rather than at the national level. The second alternative is to assume that all firms supply a homogeneous product but that national markets are segmented, as in Venables (1985). Thus, firms make separate price and supply decisions for each national market based on the perceived elasticity of demand.

The purpose of this paper is to analyze some important issues that arise in the modeling of bilateral tariff removal and to assess these issues computationally in the context of the U.S.-Canada FTA. Our paper is structured as follows. The differentiated products models are discussed in the following section, and the theoretical relation between tariff liberalization and firm output is developed. We also comment on the demand structure adopted in some previous modeling efforts. In particular we will discuss the practice of assuming both firm and national product differentiation and the implications for the debate concerning intra- versus interindustry trade, rationalization of the production process, and the gains from trade.

In section 7.2, we present a market segmentation model and discuss the likely welfare implications of bilateral tariff removal. The issues raised are then illustrated using a computational model designed to analyze U.S.-Canada bilateral tariff removal. The model is discussed in section 7.3, and computational results are presented in section 7.4. Conclusions follow.

7.1   The Differentiated Products Models

The earliest versions of the differentiated products models involved differentiating by country of origin using the Armington assumptions. "Love of variety" in the utility function guarantees that all bilateral trade flows will continue following the formation of the preferential trading club as long as industries are not eliminated in any country. Models of this type tend to assume that production is characterized by constant returns to scale and that firms are perfectly competitive.

There is an important difficulty, however, with the national product differentiation (NPD) model insofar as it means that each country will have a monopoly in the supply of its own characteristic variety.[2] Consequently, optimal tariffs tend to be large, even for small countries. Terms-of-trade changes, rather than efficiency gains, therefore dominate the welfare predictions of NPD models.

National product differentiation is the approach adopted by Brown and Stern (1987), who find that Canada's welfare declines by 0.3 percent as the result of bilateral tariff removal. This result appears to emerge because removal of the relatively high tariffs currently in place in Canada leads to deterioration in the terms of trade. On the other hand, Hamilton and Whalley (1985) consider nontariff barrier (NTB) removal as well as bilateral tariff removal and find that Canada enjoys a 0.7 percent increase of GDP from the formation of an FTA, presumably because of the relatively high NTBs in the United States.

An alternative is to differentiate products at the firm level, using the Dixit-Stiglitz-Spence form of the utility function. Love of variety will again guarantee the existence of all bilateral trade flows since no two firms in the world sell the same variety. In this model, firms are typically assumed to have downward-sloping average total cost curves and to be monopolistically competitive.

Harris (1984) developed the imperfectly competitive approach, computationally, incorporating a variety of different assumptions concerning a firm's price-setting behavior. The Harris approach yielded startling results. Multilateral pre–Tokyo Round tariff removal was shown to increase Canada's welfare by up to 9 percent of GDP, depending on the precise assumptions concerning firm behavior. Increasing firm output, thereby reducing average total cost, is a key source of welfare gain in the imperfectly competitive computational trade models. Subsequent revisions of tariff data and parameters of the model, however, place the welfare gain for Canada in the Harris model closer to 2.5 percent of GDP.[3]

In this section, we will first describe a typical monopolistically competitive (MC) trade model and evaluate the effects of tariff liberalization on firm output. The NPD model and the MC model are then compared in terms of the implications of a tariff for the terms of trade and intra- versus interindustry trade.

Assume a model consisting of n traded goods that are produced by m countries. Good j produced by each firm in each of the m countries is aggregated using a linearly homogeneous aggregation function to form a composite good j. Following Spence (1976) and Dixit and Stiglitz (1977), modelers have typically chosen the constant elasticity of substitution (CES) function to aggregate different varieties into a single aggregate. The conditional demand in country i for the product of a representative firm in country r that produces good j for a CES aggregation function is

$$(1) \qquad D_{ij}^r = \frac{E_{ij}(P_{ij}^r)^{-\sigma}}{\displaystyle\sum_{s=1}^{m} n_{sj}(P_{ij}^s)^{1-\sigma}},$$

where P_{ij}^r is the price paid in country i for good j produced by a representative firm in country r, E_{ij} is expenditure in country i on the aggregate good j, n_{sj} is the number of firms in industry j in country s, and $\sigma > 1$ is the elasticity of substitution among the different varieties.

Firms set price as a markup over marginal cost according to

$$(2) \qquad P_{rj}^* = MC_{rj}(1 + 1/\eta_{rj})^{-1},$$

where P_{rj}^* is the price received by a representative producer of j in country r, $\eta_{rj} < -1$ is the firm's perceived elasticity of demand, and MC_{rj} is marginal cost. The firm's perceived elasticity of demand is a sales-weighted average of the elasticities of demand in each national market. The elasticity of demand in country i for the product of a representative firm in country r is obtained from equation (1) above to be

$$(3) \qquad \eta_{rj}^i = -\sigma + (\sigma - 1)\frac{P_{ij}^r D_{ij}^r}{E_{ij}},$$

or

$$(3') \qquad \eta_{rj}^i = -\sigma + (\sigma - 1)\frac{\theta_{ij}^r}{n_{rj}},$$

where θ_{ij}^r is country r's share of the market in country i for good j.

The firm's production function requires a fixed input of capital plus variable capital and labor inputs that are characterized by constant returns to scale. Thus, the average total cost (ATC) curve is downward sloping, and marginal cost is constant. Entry occurs until profits are eliminated, requiring the firm's price to equal ATC:

$$(4) \qquad P_{rj}^* = P_r^K\left(\frac{K^F}{q_{rj}} + a_j^K\right) + w_r \, a_j^L \,,$$

where P_r^K is the price of capital in country r, w_r is the return to labor, a_j^K is the variable capital unit input requirement in industry j, a_j^L is the unit labor requirement, K^F is the fixed capital requirement, and q_{rj} is output of a typical firm in industry j in country r.

Capital and labor are assumed to be mobile between sectors. The return to each factor is determined to equate demand to a fixed supply.

Finally, tariff policy serves to link the price received by the seller to the price paid by the buyer. Thus,

$$(5) \qquad P_{ij}^r = P_{rj}^*(1 + t_{ij}^r),$$

where t_{ij}^r is the ad valorem tariff that country i imposes on imports of good j from country r.

7.1.1 Rationalization

We now examine the conditions under which tariff liberalization will lead to rationalization of production in this model. That is, will a tariff reduction increase output per firm and lower ATC? There are several considerations that determine the effect of liberalization on rationalization, such as differing factor intensities across industries and the effect of liberalization of the elasticity of demand.

Turning first to the production side, suppose that there are two industries and that industry 1's fixed capital input requirement is zero. Throughout this exercise, we will hold the shape of the demand curve fixed so as to focus on technological determinants of firm output.

Equilibrium in the labor market requires that

$$(6) \qquad L = a_1^L Q_1 + a_2^L n_2 q_2 ,$$

where L is the endowment of labor, Q_1 is the output of industry 1, and $n_2 q_2$ is output of industry 2. Proportionate differentiation yields

$$(6') \qquad \lambda_{L1}\hat{Q}_1 + \lambda_{L2}(\hat{q}_2 + \hat{n}_2) = \delta_L(\hat{w} - \hat{P}^K),$$

where $\delta_L = \lambda_{L1}\theta_{K1}\sigma_1 + \lambda_{L2}\theta_{K2}^V\sigma_2$, λ_{fj} is industry j's share of the employment of factor f, θ_{fj} is factor f's share of total cost in industry j, θ_{fj}^V is variable factor f's share of variable cost in industry j, and σ_j is the elasticity of substitution between capital and labor in industry j.

Similarly, capital market equilibrium requires

$$(7) \qquad K = a_1^K Q_1 + a_2^K n_2 q_2 + n_2 K^F,$$

which, when proportionately differentiated, yields

$$(7') \qquad \lambda_{K1}\hat{Q}_1 + \lambda_{K2}^V(\hat{q}_2 + \hat{n}_2) + \lambda_{K2}^F\hat{n}_2 = -\delta_K(\hat{w} - \hat{P}^K),$$

where $\delta_K = \lambda_{K1}\theta_{L1}\sigma_1 + \lambda_{K2}^V\theta_{L2}^V\sigma_2$, λ_{K2}^V is variable capital in industry 2's share of capital employment, λ_{K2}^F is fixed capital in industry 2's share of capital employment, and $\lambda_{K2}^V + \lambda_{K2}^F = \lambda_{K2}$ is industry 2's share of capital employment.

A tariff reduction will lower demand for the domestically produced good, yielding negative profits for domestic firms. The question is whether output per firm in industry 2 will rise or fall as firms exit. Suppose first that q_2 is held constant as n_2 falls so that firms neither rationalize nor derationalize. The markup pricing rule used by firms requires that the percentage change in price be equal to the percentage change in marginal cost if the elasticity of demand is held constant. Therefore,

$$(8) \qquad \hat{P}_2 = \theta_{L2}^V \hat{w} + \theta_{K2}^V \hat{P}^K .$$

On the other hand, the zero-profit condition requires that the percentage change in price be equal to the percent change in ATC. Therefore,

$$(9) \qquad \hat{P}_2 = \theta_{L2} \hat{w} + \theta_{K2} \hat{P}^K - \theta_{K2}^F \hat{q}_2 .$$

Now, as industry 2 contracts and industry 1 expands, relative factor prices must also be adjusting. As a result, equations (8) and (9) cannot be satisfied simultaneously if output per firm is held constant. This conclusion follows from the assumption that capital is the only fixed factor, which implies that labor's share of variable cost must be greater than labor's share of total cost and that capital's share of variable cost must be smaller than capital's share of total cost.

The necessary change in firm output will depend on the relative factor intensity ranking of the two industries. It can be demonstrated using equations (6′) and (7′) that, if industry 2 is the capital-intensive industry ranked according to its variable inputs, then $\hat{w} - \hat{P}^K > 0$ as resources are transferred from industry 2 to industry 1. On the other hand, if industry 2 is the labor-intensive industry, then $\hat{w} - \hat{P}^K < 0$. That is,

$$\hat{w} \gtrless \hat{P}^K \quad as \quad \lambda_{L1}\lambda_{K2}^V \gtrless \lambda_{K1}\lambda_{L2} .$$

For the case in which industry 2 is relatively labor intensive, so that $\hat{w} - \hat{P}^K < 0$, marginal cost has fallen relative to ATC, requiring output per firm to rise. However, if industry 2 is relatively capital intensive, then marginal cost has risen relative to ATC, requiring output per firm to fall.

As a general rule, if an industry's intensively used factor has a greater share in variable cost than in total cost, then a policy that lowers price will also lead to rationalization. On the other hand, if an industry's intensive factor has a smaller share in variable cost than in total cost, then derationalization will occur.[4] It should also be noted that, if technological considerations are leading to rationalization of the domestic industry, derationalization will be occurring in the foreign industry.

There are, of course, several demand side considerations that will also help determine firm output. An increase in the absolute value of the firm's perceived elasticity of demand will lower the markup over marginal cost, and firm output will therefore rise. To the extent that liberalization increases the number of firms in the industry worldwide, reducing individual firm market share, the second term on the right-hand side of equation (3) will become smaller, and the absolute value of the elasticity will therefore rise.

On the other hand, as noted by Horstmann and Markusen (1986), ad valorem tariff reductions tend to steepen the demand curve facing the foreign firm, lowering the elasticity of demand and lowering output per firm. This point can be seen by differentiating equation (3) with respect to t_{ij}^r, using equation (5).

7.1.2   Tariff Liberalization and the Terms of Trade

It is reasonable to presume that a tariff reduction on imports of the monopolistically competitive good 2 will tend to lower the price received by domestic producers, P_2^d, relative to the price paid for imports, P_2^m, thus worsening the terms of trade for the liberalizing country. The terms of trade for the competitive good will also deteriorate. The tariff reduction will shift production in the home country toward good 1 and away from good 2. Thus, P_1/P_2^d will rise. If the home country is a net exporter of good 2 and an importer of good 1, then the increase in P_1/P_2^d constitutes a fall in the price of exports. The tariff reduction will also shift production in the foreign country toward good 2 and away from good 1. Thus, P_1/P_2^m will fall. If the home country is a net importer of good 2 and an exporter of good 1, then the fall in P_1/P_2^m also constitutes a deterioration in the home country's terms of trade.

The welfare implications of the relative price changes for the home country should nonetheless be smaller than in the more conventional Armington model, in which goods are differentiated at the national level and individual firms are price takers. This will be the case for two reasons.

First, the powerful terms-of-trade gain from a tariff in the NPD model stems from the fact that firms, as price takers, do not internalize the market power attendant on national product differentiation. Thus, a tariff that reduces national supply to the world market exploits monopoly power ignored by the firms. However, if product differentiation exists at the firm level rather than at the national level, there is little market power associated with product differentiation that can be perceived by the government that is not already exercised by the firm.

Second, the number of differentiated products in an NPD model equals the number of countries. On the other hand, the number of products in an MC model is significantly larger and equal to the sum over the number of firms in each country. By increasing the number of products, the market power of the seller of an individual product is reduced, leaving less room to increase welfare by reducing supply.

The terms-of-trade loss of the home country may be further mitigated if rationalization occurs in the foreign country. An increase in output per firm is associated with a reduction in the markup over marginal cost, offsetting some of the original increase in price by foreign firms.

7.1.3 Increasing Returns to Scale and National Product Differentiation

Implementation of the differentiated products model computationally does not require national product differentiation. Nonetheless, the tendency has been to preserve both national and firm product differentiation. In this context, a third level is added to the utility function. Expenditure on imports is allocated among competing sources following the decision concerning allocation between an import aggregate and a domestic aggregate. For example, Wigle (1988) adopts this approach and finds that bilateral tariff removal would reduce welfare in Canada by 0.1 percent of GDP.

National product differentiation is not necessary to explain cross-hauling in models with firm product differentiation. It may nonetheless seem plausible to retain a preference for the domestically produced good in the utility function. However, if perfect aggregation is used to form separate domestic and import aggregates, then domestic firms are insulated from changes in the composition of the import aggregate with the consequence of introducing a new equilibrating mechanism that has questionable economic content.

Adding a third stage to the budgeting process will have three implications for the computational results. First, the model will be predisposed toward the conclusion that free trade will stimulate intraindustry trade, thus minimizing the necessary intersectoral adjustment. To see this point, consider the extreme case in which consumers distinguish between the import and the domestic variety of good j, D_j, but all firms within a country produce perfect substitutes. That is,

$$(10) \qquad D_j = [(D_j^d)^\rho + (D_j^m)^\rho]^{1/\rho},$$

where the domestic variety, D_j^d, and the imported variety, D_j^m, are given by

$$(11) \qquad D_j^d = \sum_{i=1}^{ndj} X_{ij}^d$$

and

$$D_j^m = \sum_{i=1}^{nmj} X_{ij}^m,$$

where n_{df} is the number of domestic firms, n_{mj} is the number of foreign firms in industry j, and X_i denotes the output of the ith firm. This is the case analyzed by Horstmann and Markusen (1986).[5] A key assumption in this framework is that the number of firms in the domestic industry does not affect demand facing an individual foreign firm, nor does the number of firms in the foreign industry affect the demand facing an individual domestic firm.

A tariff on imports will stimulate demand for the domestic variety and reduce demand for the foreign variety, leaving domestic firms with positive profits and foreign firms with negative profits. To restore the zero-profit condition, entry occurs domestically while foreign firms exit. Since domestic firm demand does not depend on the number of foreign firms, entry in the domestic industry reduces individual firm demand until profits are once again zero. The opposite occurs for foreign firms. The essential equilibrating mechanism here is that local entry dissipates positive profits by dividing the market among a larger number of firms, thereby reducing firm output and raising average fixed cost. Indeed, Horstmann and Markusen conclude that the tariff change has no effect on domestic firm output.[6]

In comparison, consider the model outlined above, in which consumers distinguish between the output of different firms but not between imports and the domestic good. In this case, the level of firm demand depends not on whether there is local entry or exit but rather on whether there is global entry or exit. If the increase in the number of domestic firms is smaller than the fall in the number of foreign firms, then all firms in the industry, both domestic and foreign, will experience an increase in demand. As a result, positive profits for domestic firms will increase even further.

Entry in the domestic industry restores the zero-profit condition by raising the return to the factor used intensively in the expanding sector, which raises total cost. The effect of local entry on firm demand, which occurs in the Horstmann-Markusen model, is absent here. Thus, restoring the zero-profit condition depends entirely on intersectoral factor movements.

The second implication of adding a third stage to the budgeting process is that reducing the change in factor prices necessary to restore equilibrium will also weaken the forces leading to rationalization or derationalization associated with differing factor intensities. The third implication is that reintroducing national product differentiation increases national market power that is not perceived by firms, thus raising the optimal tariff.

7.1.4   Summary

There are a few lessons that we can draw in comparing the likely welfare and trade conclusions of each approach for a U.S.-Canada bilateral tariff elimination that will be relevant for the computational results presented below. Welfare conclusions from a model assuming perfect competition and national product differentiation will be dominated by changes in the terms of trade. The average level of tariffs currently in place in Canada is somewhat higher than in the United States. This implies that tariff elimination will tend to worsen Canada's terms of trade, resulting in a welfare loss. In addition, the intersectoral trade pattern will not be particularly affected by tariff liberalization. Rather, increased trade will be primarily intraindustry.

In contrast, if industries are monopolistically competitive, then product differentiation is removed to the firm, and firms incorporate market power associated with product differentation into their pricing decisions. Therefore, welfare-reducing changes in the terms of trade as the result of liberalization will be confined primarily to large countries and are not likely to play a dominant role in the welfare conclusions of bilateral tariff removal. Consequently, welfare gains for Canada are more likely than in the NPD model. Further, more distinctive changes in the intersectoral pattern of specialization will emerge in view of the fact that each variety of a good is not nationally specific. Production can be relocated in the country where the cost of production is lowest.

Rationalization of the production process will depend on the general equilibrium effects of tariff liberalization on the return to capital, which in turn depends on the relative factor-intensity ranking of industries. If the protected sector is labor intensive and liberalization therefore causes the return to capital to rise, output per firm will tend to rise. However, if the protected sector is capital intensive, then the return to capital is likely to fall. Consequently, firm output may fall as well.

7.2 A Market Segmentation Model

Another alternative to modeling bilateral tariff elimination is to assume that all firms sell a homogeneous product but that national markets are segmented. Thus, all firms selling to a single national market must charge the same price, but price may vary across countries. This approach has not been used previously in the context of U.S.-Canada bilateral tariff removal but has been applied to the European Community by Smith and Venables (1988). Here we extend the model of Venables (1985) to three countries.

The market demand in country j is

$$(12) \qquad D_j = S_j(D - p_j), \quad j = 1, 2, 3,$$

where p_j is the price paid by consumers in country j and S_j is a parameter indicating the size of market j. Firms are assumed to behave as Cournot followers, so that the perceived demand is the market demand net of supply by other firms. Therefore, a typical firm in country i perceives the demand for its exports to country j to be

$$(13) \qquad x_i^j = S_j(D - p_j) - Q_j, \quad j \neq i$$

where Q_j is supply by other firms, and demand in the local market to be

$$(14) \qquad y_i = S_i(D - p_i) - Q_i.$$

As above, each firm in country i faces a fixed cost, f_i, and constant marginal cost, c_i, yielding profits of

$$(15) \qquad \pi_i = \sum_{j \neq i} (p_j - c_i - t_j)x_i^j + (p_i - c_i)y_i - f_i ,$$

where t_j is the tariff imposed by country j on imports. The first-order conditions for profit maximization are

(16)
$$x_i^j = S_j(p_j - c_i - t_j) \quad i \neq j$$

and

(17)
$$y_i = S_i(p_i - c_i).$$

Free entry guarantees that profits will be zero, which, when making use of the first-order conditions for profit maximization, equations (16) and (17), implies that

(18)
$$\sum_{j \neq i} (p_j - c_i - t_j)^2 S_j + (p_i - c_i)^2 S_i - f_i = 0.$$

Consider now the effect of a tariff change by country 2 on imports from country 1. Totally differentiating equation (18) for each i yields

(19)
$$\begin{bmatrix} y_1 & x_1^2 & x_1^3 \\ x_2^1 & y_2 & x_2^3 \\ x_3^1 & x_3^2 & y_3 \end{bmatrix} \begin{bmatrix} dp_1 \\ dp_2 \\ dp_3 \end{bmatrix} = \begin{bmatrix} x_1^2 \, dt_2 \\ 0 \\ 0 \end{bmatrix}.$$

Solving for the equilibrium price changes yields

(20)
$$\begin{bmatrix} dp_1 \\ dp_2 \\ dp_3 \end{bmatrix} = \frac{-x_1^2 dt_2}{A} \begin{bmatrix} -y_2 y_3 + x_3^2 x_2^3 \\ y_3 x_2^1 - x_1^1 x_2^3 \\ y_2 x_3^1 - x_2^1 x_3^2 \end{bmatrix},$$

where $A = y_1(y_2 y_3 - x_3^2 x_2^3) - x_1^2(y_3 x_2^1 - x_1^1 x_2^3) - x_1^3(y_2 x_3^1 - x_2^1 x_3^2)$.

If A is positive[7] and $c_i < c_j + t_i$, then it can be shown that $dp_1/dt_2 > 0$. The restriction on marginal cost implies that a typical domestic firm sells more to the domestic market than a typical foreign firm. In this case, the tariff imposed by country 2 raises the price paid by consumers in country 1, thus lowering welfare in country 1. If, in addition, $y_3 x_2^1 > x_3^1 x_2^3$, then it follows that $dp_2/dt_2 < 0$. The tariff lowers the price to consumers in country 2, raising welfare in country 2.[8]

The effect of a tariff imposed by country 2 in this model is to lower the price net of tariff that country 1 firms receive for their exports to country 2. In order to restore the zero-profit condition, country 1 firms must increase price in other markets, such as the domestic. However, the higher price in country 1's market raises profitability for country 2 firms, leading to a reduction in price on sales to domestic consumers. The price increase to country 1 consumers lowers welfare in country 1, and the price reduction in country 2 raises consumer welfare in country 2.

This outcome, of course, is not inevitable. Negative profits for country 1 firms are eliminated by raising the price in countries in which country 1 firms have a relatively large market share. The change in relative price, then, will depend closely on the pattern of trade and preexisting market share.

In the U.S.-Canada case, the volume of trade between the United States and Canada is large, while trade between Canada and the rest of the world is comparatively small. A tariff reduction by Canada will raise the profitability of U.S. firms. A price reduction in the United States that lowers profits of U.S. firms and a price increase in Canada and the rest of the world that offsets the price reduction in the U.S. market are likely.

7.3   The Computational Model

Sections 7.1 and 7.2 leave us with a set of propositions concerning the implications of modeling choices that we would like to illustrate computationally. There are three variants of the model. The perfect competition (PC) version is characterized by national product differentiation, perfect competition, and constant returns to scale. The monopolistic competition (MC) version differs in that product differentiation exists only at the firm level, there are increasing returns to scale, and firms set price as a markup over marginal cost. In the market segmentation (MS) version, there are economies of scale as well, but each product is homogeneous across firms and countries. Firms behave as Cournot followers and perceive national markets as segmented.[9]

Canada, the United States, and a group of thirty-two other countries are modeled explicitly, and the rest of the world constitutes an abbreviated fourth region. Our sectoral coverage includes twenty-two tradable product categories based on three-digit ISIC industries and seven nontradable categories based on one-digit ISIC industries.[10]

In all three models, consumers initially allocate final demand and producers allocate intermediate demand across sectors without regard to the location of production. Bilateral trade flows are identified in the PC model by assuming that consumers and producers aggregate the variety produced by each country using a CES aggregation function. Thus, the demand in country i for the output of country r's production of good j, conditional on expenditure on the aggregate good j, E_{ij}, is

$$(21) \qquad D_{ij}^r = \frac{E_{ij}(P_{ij}^r)^{-\sigma}}{\sum_{s=1}^{m}(P_{ij}^s)^{1-\sigma}},$$

where P_{ij}^r is the price consumers in i pay for good j produced in country r. This price differs from the price received by the seller in country r by any tariffs imposed by country i.

Bilateral trade flows in the MC model are similarly identified, though product differentiation exists at the firm level only. Monopolistically competitive firms set price as a markup over marginal cost according to equation (2), and the firm's perceived elasticity of demand is given by equation (3).

In the MS model, consumers do not distinguish between the output of various firms or countries. Rather, firms perceive national markets as segmented. The firm set price and supply in each market to maximize firm profits. That is,

$$\max_{\{P^l_{rj},\ldots,P^m_{rj}\}} \sum_{i=1}^{m} D^r_{ij}(P^i_{rj} - MC_{rj}) - FC_{rj},$$

where MC and FC are marginal and fixed costs and P^i_{rj} is the price a typical firm in country r receives for sales in country i. This price differs from the price paid by consumers in country i by any tariffs imposed. Firms behave as Cournot followers. Therefore, the firm's perceived demand, D^r_{ij}, is the market demand in country i for good j, D_{ij}, less output by other firms, Q. The underlying utility function determining industry demand is Cobb-Douglas. Under this assumption, it can be shown that the supply to country i by a representative firm in country r is

(22)
$$S^i_{rj} = D_{ij}\frac{(P^i_{rj} - MC_{rj})}{P^i_{rj}}.$$

The production function in all three models requires intermediate and primary inputs. Intermediate inputs and a primary input aggregate are employed in fixed proportion to output. The primary input aggregate is a CES function of capital and labor employed. Capital and labor demand are determined by minimizing the cost of attaining the level of the primary input aggregate required by the upper level of the production function. In addition to variable capital and labor inputs, a fixed input of capital is necessary in the MC and MS models.

Capital and labor are mobile between sectors but not countries. The return to capital is determined to equate demand to a fixed supply of capital. The return to labor is held constant. National income is adjusted to maintain total employment at the base level.

Freedom of entry is assumed, and, therefore, firm profits are zero. This implies that PC firms must set price equal to marginal cost. MC firms must set price equal to ATC, and MS firms must set average price equal to ATC.

Equilibrium prices are determined in global markets to equate supply and demand. In the PC model, one price is determined for each national variety of each good. In the MC model, one price is determined for each firm. However, firms within each country face identical costs and technology, and demand is symmetric. Therefore, all firms within an industry and country charge the same price. In the MS model, one price is determined for each national market. Thus, all firms selling in a single market must charge the same price.

The base year for data on production, employment, and trade for the United States, Canada, and other countries and the rest of the world is 1976.

Input-output coefficients for the production function were derived from the U.S. input-output table for 1972 and the Canadian table for 1976.

The key parameters in the base period for the MC model are obtained in the following manner.[11] The firm's perceived demand in the base period is calculated according to equation (3), assuming that the elasticity of substitution among varieties of each good is 15.0.

Once the elasticity of demand is determined, it is straightforward to calculate the variable input share of total cost. The variable cost share is equal to the ratio of marginal cost and average total cost, θ^{VC} = MC/ATC. Since profits are zero, average total cost is equal to price. The ratio of marginal cost and price is determined by the markup pricing rule in equation (2). Therefore, $\theta^{VC} = 1 + 1/\eta$.

The share of total capital that is variable is implied by the variable cost share, capital's primary input cost share, θ^K, and the primary input share of total cost, b_0. Capital is assumed to be the only fixed factor. Therefore, the share of capital that is fixed is equal to the ratio of fixed cost's share of total cost to capital's share of total cost. That is,

$$(23) \qquad \frac{1 - \theta^{VC}}{\theta^K b_0} = \frac{P^K K^F / \text{TC}}{P^K (K^F + K^V) / \text{TC}} = \frac{K^F}{K^F + K^V}.$$

The distribution of primary input cost between capital and labor is available from industry data, and primary input share of total cost is obtainable from input-output data.

The relation between fixed capital's share of total capital and the elasticity of substitution in the aggregation function places restrictions on the size of the elasticity of substitution. A small value for σ can imply a fixed capital share that does not lie between zero and one. Setting $\sigma = 15$ was the smallest value for this parameter consistent with the restrictions on the fixed capital share.

Structural equations of the MS model also imply base period values for the parameters. The markup over marginal cost, $(P - \text{MC})/\text{MC}$, for each of the three national markets is derived from equation (22) to be

$$(24) \qquad M_r^i = \frac{\theta_i^r / n_r}{1 - \theta_i^r / n_r},$$

where M_r^i is the markup over marginal cost by producers in country r on their sales to country i and θ_i^r is country r's share of the market in country i.

This procedure tended to lead to very small markups for many industries, which caused instability in the computational model. Therefore, the markups are bounded from below by 5 percent. Utility functions other than Cobb-Douglas may produce larger markups. However, it may also be the case that this model is unsuitable for modeling sectors that are not highly concentrated.

The variable cost share for the MS model can be obtained in a manner similar to the method employed with the MC model. Variable cost share is equal to the ratio of marginal cost to average cost. The zero-profit condition implies that the average price received by the firm for its sales in each market must equal ATC. Therefore,

$$(25) \qquad \theta_r^{\text{VC}} = \frac{\text{MC}_r}{\sum\limits_i \delta_r^i p_r^i} \,,$$

where δ_r^i is the share of country r's output that is sold to country i. Equation (22) can be used to find that

$$(26) \qquad \theta_r^{\text{VC}} = \left[\sum_i \frac{\delta_r^i}{1 - \theta_i^r/n_r}\right]^{-1}.$$

7.4 Computational Results of U.S.-Canada Bilateral Tariff Elimination

The models described in section 7.3 have been used to analyze computationally the effects of bilateral tariff removal by the United States and Canada. Our purpose here is to illustrate the implications of various modeling choices for the trade and welfare conclusions of U.S.-Canada bilateral tariff removal. The model was run three times, employing each of the three different market structures in all industries: perfect competition, monopolistic competition, and market segmentation. It is of course more plausible to assume that market structure will vary across industries. Results reflecting our best judgment concerning the proper market structure for each industry can be found in Brown and Stern (1989).

Tariffs removed are those prevailing in both countries subsequent to full implementation of the Tokyo Round tariff reductions, which was completed in 1987. The last column of each of tables 7.2 and 7.3 below list the bilateral trade weighted ad valorem tariff equivalents on U.S.-Canada trade. Notice that U.S. tariffs on Canadian exports are somewhat lower than Canadian tariffs on the United States. Nevertheless, U.S. tariffs on Canadian exports on some products such as clothing and footwear remain quite high.

The results for imports, exports, the exchange rate, terms of trade, and welfare are summarized in table 7.1. Panel A of table 7.1 reports the change in trade and welfare under perfect competition. U.S. and Canadian trade increases by close to $7 billion, while rest-of-world trade falls by nearly $2 billion. The welfare and terms-of-trade changes are similar to those obtained elsewhere using such a model,[12] and the role of national product differentiation is clearly evident. The comparatively deep tariff reductions by Canada worsen its terms of trade by 0.7 percent, leading to a trivial decline in welfare. U.S. terms of trade, on the other hand, improve by 0.3 percent, raising U.S. welfare by $781 million on the basis of 1976 trade. Rest-of-world welfare declines as well.

Table 7.1   Summary Results of a U.S.-Canada Free Trade Area: Changes in Country
                   Imports, Exports, Exchange Rates, Terms of Trade, and Welfare (trade
                   and welfare in millions of U.S. dollars)

Country	Imports[a]	Exports[a]	Exchange Rate[b]	Terms-of-Trade Percentage Change	Equivalent Variation
A. Perfect Competition: National Product Differentiation:					
United States	6,981.3	6,643.4	.0	.3	780.9
Other	−1,758.1	−1,611.2	.2	−.1	−145.4
Canada	6,254.8	6,546.8	.6	−.7	−28.5
B. Monopolistic Competition: Firm Product Differentiation:					
United States	9,194.2	9,051.7	.0	.1	476.1
Other	−1,882.1	−1,762.7	.1	−.1	−116.1
Canada	9,366.3	9,557.0	−1.0	−.5	2,304.0
C. Market Segmentation Model: Homogeneous Products:					
United States	12,947.9	12,624.5	−.0	.2	−1,175.3
Other	−1,547.3	−1,620.2	−.0	−.1	−240.0
Canada	10,668.0	10,754.2	.0	−.3	−1,389.1
D. Sensitivity Analysis: Perfect Competition:[c]					
United States	14,689.2	14,372.4	−.0	.2	657.1
Other	−2,991.2	−2,871.0	.2	−.1	−267.8
Canada	13,190.4	13,462.4	.6	−.7	−163.9
E. Sensitivity Analysis: Monopolistic Competition:[c]					
United States	19,107.9	19,024.4	.0	.1	−1,002.8
Other	−3,181.4	−3,101.0	.0	−.0	−55.9
Canada	18,875.5	18,890.3	−1.4	−.3	2,797.2

[a]Dollar value of change in trade volume.
[b](+) indicates depreciation of currency.
[c]Elasticity of substitution between varieties increased above base run.

The outcome is somewhat different if industry structure is taken to be
monopolistically competitive. These results are presented in panel B of table
7.1. U.S. and Canadian trade increases by about $9 billion. The U.S.
terms-of-trade gain is now only one-third as large (0.1 percent), and Canada's
terms-of-trade loss is about 30 percent smaller (−0.5 percent). This result
was expected. The move from products differentiated at the national level to
products differentiated at the firm level significantly increases the number of
products, thereby increasing the elasticity of demand for each individual
variety. In addition, rationalization occurs in the United States as a result of
liberalization, forcing U.S. firms to reduce the markup over marginal cost.

The U.S. welfare gain is accordingly reduced to $476 million, but Canada's
welfare gain rises to $2.3 billion, which is 1.2 percent of Canadian GDP in
1976. There are several possible explanations for the welfare improvement for
Canada. First, a smaller deterioration in Canada's terms of trade will reduce
the welfare loss. Second, as discussed above, internalizing market power by
differentiating products at the firm level, rather than at the national level,
lowers Canada's optimal tariff. Thus, despite the deterioration in the terms of

trade, Canadian welfare still rises owing to efficiency gains. Third, Canada may be gaining from rationalizing production.

In order to illustrate the sensitivity of the model to the choice of the elasticity of substitution, the PC and MC versions of the model were rerun after increasing the elasticity of substitution. Values for this parameter ranged from seventeen to forty-five across industries, compared to fifteen in the base run. These results are summarized in panels D and E of table 7.1.

In the case of perfect competition, the most notable effect of increasing the elasticity of substitution is to increase the change in the volume of trade. The effects on the terms of trade and welfare are trivial. This is not the case, however, if firms are monopolistically competitive. The terms-of-trade changes are further weakened as the elasticity of substitution increases. In particular, Canada's terms of trade deteriorate by only 0.3 percent, as compared to 0.5 percent in the base run and 0.7 percent under national product differentiation. Canada's welfare gain rises to 1.4 percent of GDP.

Panel C of table 7.1 summarizes the effects of liberalization in the MS model. The trade effect is significantly larger than for the other two market structures, with U.S. and Canadian trade increasing by about $11–$13 billion. The terms-of-trade effects are similar to those obtained in the MC model, but welfare for all three country groups declines. It should be noted at the outset that the MS model is a poor approximation of firm behavior in unconcentrated industries. Results presented for this version of the model should therefore be considered illustrative only. Little weight should be attached accordingly to the aggregate measures such as the terms of trade and welfare.

7.4.1   Sectoral Results: Perfect Competition and Monopolistic Competition

Sectoral results for each experiment are presented in tables 7.2–7.7. Tables 7.2 and 7.3 report the percentage change in exports, imports, bilateral trade, output, capital employment, the return to capital, and labor employment due to bilateral liberalization under perfect competition for the United States and Canada, respectively. Tables 7.4 and 7.5 report similar values for the MC model. The percentage changes in the number of firms and in the firm's perceived elasticity of demand are also included.

The most notable feature of the PC model is the strong tendency toward increased intraindustry trade. Bilateral trade increases in virtually every sector. The only exception is that Canadian imports of transportation equipment from the United States fall by 3.2 percent. Total trade for both countries generally increases as well. U.S. imports increase in every sector, and Canada's imports decline only in petroleum products and transportation equipment.

Employment effects are equally small. The largest decline in employment in the United States is 1.3 percent in nonferrous metals. Significantly more

Table 7.2 Sectoral Effects on the United States of U.S.-Canada Free Trade, Tariffs Only, Post–Tokyo Round: Perfect Competition (percentage change)

Sector	Exports	Imports from: World	Canada	Output	Capital	Rental Rate	Employment	Tariff on Canada Exports
Agriculture	−.2	4.2	30.9	−.3	−.3	−.1	−.4	1.6
Food	7.0	7.5	64.4	−.0	.0	−.1	−.1	3.8
Textiles	30.7	5.8	125.0	3.4	3.4	−.1	3.3	7.2
Clothing	47.8	3.8	255.8	.6	.7	−.1	.6	18.4
Leather products	2.7	4.8	49.7	−.3	−.3	−.1	−.4	2.5
Footwear	80.5	3.0	141.3	−.1	.0	−.1	−.1	9.0
Wood products	2.0	8.7	12.4	−.7	−.7	−.1	−.8	.2
Furniture, fixtures	77.4	31.8	80.0	.2	.3	−.1	.2	4.6
Paper products	11.6	10.2	10.9	.1	.2	−.1	.1	.0
Printing, publishing	2.2	5.2	15.0	.0	.1	−.1	.0	.3
Chemicals	9.4	7.4	23.5	1.0	1.1	−.1	1.0	.6
Petroleum products	−.9	1.2	6.4	−.6	−.5	−.1	−.7	.0
Rubber products	22.5	13.2	62.3	−.2	−.11	−.1	−.2	3.2
Nonmetal mineral products	11.2	5.5	14.7	.2	.2	−.1	.2	.3
Glass products	22.0	18.9	93.1	.6	.6	−.1	.5	5.7
Iron & steel	8.7	6.9	48.4	−.3	−.3	−.1	−.4	2.7
Nonferrous metals	4.6	7.4	19.3	−1.3	−1.2	−.1	−1.3	.5
Metal products	25.1	14.2	69.7	.4	.4	−.1	.4	4.0
Nonelectrical machinery	4.2	13.2	45.1	−.2	−.1	−.1	−.2	2.2
Electrical machinery	11.3	5.9	81.3	.7	.7	−.1	.7	4.5
Transport equipment	−2.1	5.7	10.8	−1.1	−1.1	−.1	−1.1	.0
Miscellaneous manufacturers	5.4	4.5	29.2	.1	.1	−.1	.0	.9
Mining & quarrying				−.4	−.3	−.1	−.4	
Utilities				.0	.0	−.1	−.1	
Construction				.0	.1	−.1	−.0	
Wholesale trade				.0	.1	−.1	−.1	
Transportation				.0	.1	−.1	−.0	
Financial services				.0	.0	−.1	−.1	
Personal services				−.0	.0	−.1	−.0	

Table 7.3 Sectoral Effects on Canada of U.S.-Canada Free Trade, Tariffs Only, Post–Tokyo Round: Perfect Competition (percentage change)

Sector	Exports	Imports from: World	Imports from: United States	Output	Capital	Rental Rate	Employment	Tariff on U.S. Exports
Agriculture	8.0	13.3	23.6	.5	.5	.4	.8	2.2
Food	31.8	22.2	65.4	-.3	-.5	.4	-.1	5.4
Textiles	34.7	67.9	165.5	-25.1	-25.4	.4	-25.0	16.9
Clothing	99.9	15.3	260.7	-1.5	-2.0	.4	-1.3	23.7
Leather products	22.9	4.5	27.8	17.3	16.9	.4	17.4	4.0
Footwear	99.1	4.6	245.7	4.4	4.0	.4	4.5	21.5
Wood products	11.2	17.7	24.2	3.4	3.2	.4	3.5	2.5
Furniture, fixtures	79.0	99.7	160.6	.8	.5	.4	.9	14.3
Paper products	9.8	68.1	74.3	.9	.7	.4	1.0	6.6
Printing, publishing	13.8	3.9	6.4	.9	.6	.4	1.0	1.1
Chemicals	20.8	48.9	72.9	-13.3	-13.7	.4	-13.1	7.9
Petroleum products	6.1	-.7	3.4	5.7	5.1	.4	6.4	.4
Rubber products	58.7	36.6	76.4	3.6	1.9	.4	4.0	7.3
Nonmetal mineral products	9.5	24.6	46.8	-.4	-.7	.4	-.2	4.4
Glass products	73.8	40.4	60.6	-6.5	-6.9	.4	-6.4	6.9
Iron & steel	33.9	26.8	63.3	5.7	5.6	.4	5.8	5.1
Nonferrous metals	14.0	4.3	25.8	18.7	18.6	.4	18.8	3.3
Metal products	45.2	66.2	97.3	-4.6	-4.8	.4	-4.5	8.6
Nonelectrical machinery	34.5	12.2	22.9	7.3	6.8	.4	7.5	4.6
Electrical machinery	47.4	40.9	75.1	-6.5	-6.6	.4	-6.4	7.5
Transport equipment	10.0	-3.0	-3.2	9.1	9.0	.4	9.2	.0
Miscellaneous manufacturers	27.1	12.4	38.6	3.4	3.0	.4	3.6	5.0
Mining & quarrying				3.5	3.3	.4	4.0	
Utilities				-.4	-.7	.4	.3	
Construction				-.1	-.4	.4	.1	
Wholesale trade				-.3	-1.0	.4	.0	
Transportation				-.1	-.6	.4	.1	
Financial services				-.3	-.5	.4	.2	
Personal services				-.5	-.8	.4	-.3	

Table 7.4 Sectoral Effects on the United States of U.S.-Canada Free Trade, Tariffs Only, Post–Tokyo Round: Monopolistic Competition (percentage change)

Sector	Exports	Imports from: World	Imports from: Canada	Output	No. of Firms United States	No. of Firms World	Elasticity	Capital	Rental Rate	Employment
Agriculture	.4	3.2	17.7	-.1	-.1	-.2	.0	-.1	.1	-.0
Food	8.8	5.7	50.5	.0	-.1	-.1	.0	-.1	.1	.0
Textiles	43.7	-1.0	72.0	5.0	4.8	4.6	.1	4.8	.1	5.0
Clothing	52.1	1.9	234.2	.9	.7	.6	.0	.8	.1	.9
Leather products	2.7	5.8	72.2	-.5	-.6	.3	.0	-.7	.1	-.5
Footwear	84.1	1.9	131.6	.2	-.1	-.1	.2	-.0	.1	.2
Wood products	6.6	-5.8	-9.2	1.5	.7	.2	.7	1.1	.1	1.5
Furniture, fixtures	85.9	24.5	63.4	.5	-.8	-1.0	1.1	-.6	.1	.5
Paper products	19.4	-21.3	-23.3	3.5	2.0	.8	1.3	2.5	.1	3.5
Printing, publishing	11.6	-.2	-6.7	.2	.0	.0	.1	.0	.1	.2
Chemicals	19.6	-11.5	-48.3	3.9	1.0	.5	2.6	2.8	.1	3.9
Petroleum products	1.6	-1.0	-12.0	.7	.5	.0	.1	.5	.1	.7
Rubber products	27.6	12.4	63.8	-.7	-.8	-.4	.0	-.8	.1	-.6
Nonmetal mineral products	17.7	-1.3	-8.9	.7	.6	.5	.0	.6	.1	.7
Glass products	32.6	10.6	57.9	1.1	1.0	.8	.0	1.0	.1	1.1
Iron & steel	9.3	7.8	63.8	-1.6	-1.7	-1.5	.0	-1.8	.1	-1.6
Nonferrous metals	5.2	28.4	76.9	-6.5	-6.6	-2.9	.0	-6.6	.1	-6.5
Metal products	30.6	9.8	52.6	-.1	-.2	-.2	.0	-.2	.1	-.1
Nonelectrical machinery	7.4	5.8	22.6	.7	.6	.2	.0	.6	.1	.7
Electrical machinery	15.9	2.5	60.1	1.2	-.2	-.3	1.2	.1	.1	1.2
Transport equipment	-11.0	44.6	96.0	-7.6	-15.8	-11.3	7.5	-13.1	.1	-7.5
Miscellaneous manufactures	10.0	-.3	-1.3	2.0	2.3	1.1	-.4	2.1	.1	2.0
Mining & quarrying				.1	.1		.0	.1	.1	.2
Utilities				.0	-.0		-.0	-.0	.1	.1
Construction				-.1	-.1		-.0	-.1	.1	-.1
Wholesale trade				-.1	-.2		-.0	-.2	.1	-.1
Transportation				.0	-.1		-.0	-.1	.1	.0
Financial services				-.0	-.0		-.0	-.1	.1	.0
Personal services				-.1	-.2		-.0	-.2	.1	-.1

Table 7.5 Sectoral Effects on Canada of U.S.-Canada Free Trade, Tariffs Only, Post–Tokyo Round: Monopolistic Competition (percentage change)

Sector	Imports from: World	Imports from: United States	Exports	Output	No. of Firms Canada	No. of Firms World	Elasticity	Capital	Rental Rate	Employment
Agriculture	22.1	32.4	−1.2	−4.8	−4.6	−4.2	−.1	−4.5	−1.1	−5.4
Food	34.7	78.1	20.8	−1.8	−1.8	−1.7	.2	−.9	−1.1	−2.0
Textiles	112.3	212.9	5.1	−32.5	−33.6	−24.6	.5	−32.8	−1.1	−32.6
Clothing	31.9	279.0	86.5	−5.1	−6.0	−4.8	.4	−4.5	−1.1	−5.1
Leather products	1.7	25.4	42.8	37.2	36.1	4.0	1.0	37.4	−1.1	37.2
Footwear	12.2	254.4	91.6	2.8	.9	.6	1.3	3.2	−1.1	2.7
Wood products	34.8	41.7	−10.4	−9.0	−6.5	−5.5	−2.2	−6.8	−1.1	−9.1
Furniture, fixtures	116.2	177.6	62.4	−1.2	−13.1	−11.7	11.1	−9.1	−1.1	−1.3
Paper products	93.9	100.4	−22.6	−20.4	−19.3	−17.4	−.9	−19.4	−1.1	−20.5
Printing, publishing	20.0	22.7	−7.2	−4.9	−3.0	−2.6	−1.4	−3.0	−1.1	−5.1
Chemicals	91.0	116.1	−50.4	−52.4	−38.2	−27.4	−13.1	−44.0	−1.1	−52.7
Petroleum products	12.1	17.2	−12.0	−9.6	−9.9	−2.5	.5	−6.9	−1.1	−9.7
Rubber products	52.1	92.2	60.2	18.7	18.1	13.9	.5	23.1	−1.1	18.4
Nonmetal mineral products	44.0	66.6	−11.8	−10.6	−10.4	−8.2	−.0	−9.7	−1.1	−10.9
Glass products	65.8	86.5	39.1	−20.1	−22.3	−14.0	2.1	−20.2	−1.1	−20.3
Iron & steel	33.5	69.7	48.3	27.4	27.0	22.6	.6	27.5	−1.1	27.4
Nonferrous metals	24.6	44.7	68.0	68.1	67.7	−4.1	.2	68.2	−1.1	68.1
Metal products	85.3	116.6	32.7	−3.0	−3.8	−3.3	.8	−2.8	−1.1	−3.0
Nonelectrical machinery	21.1	32.2	15.1	−9.6	−13.1	−3.1	3.1	−11.2	−1.1	−9.7
Electrical machinery	58.6	93.6	31.5	−10.4	−16.7	−12.7	5.4	−15.1	−1.1	−10.5
Transport equipment	−20.7	−21.4	89.4	85.1	48.6	18.3	33.2	50.1	−1.1	85.1
Miscellaneous manufactures	27.5	55.0	−3.2	−18.8	−33.5	−12.8	13.3	−27.4	−1.1	−18.9
Mining & quarrying				−2.2	−2.0		−.1	−1.6	−1.1	−3.3
Utilities				−1.5	−1.0		−.1	−.4	−1.1	−2.9
Construction				.7	.8		.1	1.6	−1.1	.4
Wholesale trade				.9	1.4		.2	3.0	−1.1	.4
Transportation				.6	1.0		.1	2.0	−1.1	.3
Financial services				1.1	1.3		.1	1.9	−1.1	.1
Personal services				.3	.9		.1	1.2	−1.1	−.1

labor adjustment is required in Canada. For example, employment in textiles falls by 25.0 percent.

In comparison, the interindustry effect of liberalization is much more pronounced under monopolistic competition. While liberalization causes U.S. imports from Canada to rise in every sector in the PC model, U.S. imports from Canada in the MC model fall in wood products (-9.2 percent), paper products (-23.3 percent), printing and publishing (-6.7 percent), chemicals (-48.3 percent), petroleum products (-12.0 percent), nonmetallic mineral products (-8.9 percent), and miscellaneous manufactures (-1.3 percent).

Interindustry specialization in production, particularly for Canada, follows a similar pattern. Under the MC model, output in Canada declines in sixteen of the twenty-two tradable sectors, as compared to eight sectors that decline in the PC model. The expanding sectors are leather products (37.2 percent), footwear (2.8 percent), rubber products (18.7 percent), iron and steel (27.4 percent), nonferrous metals (68.1 percent), and transportation equipment (85.1 percent). On the other hand, U.S. output declines in several of these sectors, such as leather products (-0.5 percent), rubber products (-0.7 percent), iron and steel (-1.6 percent), nonferrous metals (-6.5 percent), and transportation equipment (-7.6 percent).

The degree to which firms rationalize or derationalize can be determined by comparing industry output to the number of firms. If the percentage change in industry output exceeds the percentage change in the number of firms, then output per firm must have risen. In the case of the United States, rationalization occurs in every sector except miscellaneous manufactures. In that industry, output rises by 2.0 percent, but the number of firms increases by 2.3 percent.

This is not a particularly surprising result. The return to capital in the United States rises by 0.1 percent, causing ATC to increase. Firms return to the zero-profit position by increasing output.

On the demand side, the reduction in Canada's tariffs was expected to reduce the perceived demand elasticity of U.S. firms, while the fall in the U.S. tariff should have raised the firm's perceived elasticity of demand. Overall, the demand elasticity increased, reducing markup overall marginal cost and further raising firm output. Miscellaneous manufactures is the only industry in the United States for which the firm's perceived elasticity of demand falls. The increased market power attendant to a fall in elasticity induces profit-maximizing firms to reduce output and increase the markup of price over marginal cost. Thus, as noted above, output per firm in the industry also falls.

Rationalization effects for Canada are mixed. The comparatively deep tariff reductions by Canada would have been expected to increase the elasticity of demand and increase firm output. However, the return to capital fell in Canada by 1.1 percent, which tends to lower firm output. Rationalization occurred in fifteen of the twenty-two tradable industries in Canada, but derationalization occurred in all the nontradable industries.

The tradable industries in which firm output declined are agriculture, wood products, paper products, printing and publishing, chemicals, and nonmetallic mineral products. These tend to be the industries in which Canadian tariffs are already quite low. (Canadian average tariffs on U.S. exports are 2.2 percent on agricultural products, 2.5 percent on wood products, 1.1 percent on printing and pubishing, and 4.4 percent on nonmetallic mineral products.) Consequently, tariff reductions did little to increase the perceived elasticity of demand of Canadian firms.

We conclude, then, that the relatively large increase in welfare for Canada may in part be due to realized economies of scale. However, the U.S. welfare gain is distinctly smaller even though rationalization occurs much more consistently across all U.S. industries. Therefore, it is likely that intersectoral specialization is playing an important role as well.

7.4.2 Sector Results: Market Segmentation

Sectoral results for U.S.-Canada bilateral tariff removal in the MS model are presented in table 7.6 for the United States and table 7.7 for Canada. The special characteristics of the MS model are most readily apparent when examining the production and price changes in the United States. The reduction in Canadian tariffs on U.S. exports raises the after-tariff price received by U.S. exporters, thus increasing firm profits. The zero-profit condition is restored by a reduction in the price received for sales to the domestic market. As can be seen from column 7 of table 7.6, the price paid by U.S. consumers for tradable goods generally declines. The only exceptions are leather products, iron and steel, and transportation equipment.

In addition, entry occurs in most U.S. industries. The number of U.S. firms declines only in leather products (-42.2 percent), petroleum products (-4.4 percent), rubber products (-0.4 percent), iron and steel (-1.8 percent), metal products (-0.1 percent), and transportation equipment (-18.0 percent).

The tariff reductions by the United States increase the profits of Canadian firms as well. However, the adjustment is dominated by intersectoral resource shifts. Interestingly, sectoral specialization in Canada in the MS model occurs in many of the same industries as in the MC model. Output in Canada increases in only six tradable sectors: leather products, footwear, petroleum products, rubber products, nonelectrical machinery, and transport equipment. Owing to increased specialization in Canada, U.S. imports from Canada decline in several sectors, such as wood products (-17.2 percent), paper products (-43.1 percent), printing and publishing (-6.0 percent), chemicals (-62.9 percent), nonmetallic mineral products (-5.1 percent), nonferrous metals (-185.9 percent), and miscellaneous manufactures (-68.1 percent). On the other hand, Canada's imports from the United States increase in all categories except leather products (-73.2 percent) and transportation equipment (-42.2 percent).

Table 7.6   Sectoral Effects on the United States of U.S.-Canada Free Trade, Tariffs Only, Post–Tokyo Round: Market Segmentation (percentage change)

Sector	Exports	Imports from: World	Canada	Output	U.S. Firms	Price	Marginal Cost	Capital	Rental Rate	Employment
Agriculture	5.3	.6	13.2	1.2	1.0	-.0	-.0	1.1	.1	1.3
Food	15.3	4.5	59.6	.2	.1	-.0	-.0	.0	.1	.2
Textiles	67.9	-7.1	81.6	8.1	6.9	-.5	-.2	7.2	.1	8.1
Clothing	77.3	-4.2	303.0	2.5	2.1	-.3	-.2	2.3	.1	2.5
Leather products	-45.8	92.9	1150.9	-42.1	-42.2	.2	-.0	-42.3	.1	-42.1
Footwear	104.4	-1.4	219.4	1.4	1.4	-.1	-.0	1.2	.1	1.4
Wood products	12.1	-11.8	-17.2	2.9	2.4	-.1	-.0	2.8	.1	3.0
Furniture, fixtures	114.5	27.4	76.6	.4	.5	-.2	-.1	.4	.1	.4
Paper products	31.9	-39.6	-43.1	6.2	5.3	-.2	-.1	5.5	.1	6.3
Printing, publishing	17.0	-2.0	-6.0	.4	.3	-.0	-.0	.3	.1	.4
Chemicals	30.8	-17.3	-62.9	6.3	5.5	-.3	-.0	5.8	.1	6.3
Petroleum products	-1.1	10.4	72.2	-4.5	-4.4	.0	.0	-4.6	.1	-4.3
Rubber products	45.3	11.1	69.1	-.8	-.4	-.1	-.1	-.8	.1	-.8
Nonmetal mineral products	24.2	-2.3	-5.1	.8	.9	-.0	.0	.7	.1	.8
Glass products	39.3	12.4	81.7	.6	.9	-.1	-.0	.6	.1	.6
Iron & steel	12.2	3.1	40.9	-3.0	-1.8	.1	.0	-2.2	.1	-3.0
Nonferrous metals	21.2	-67.0	-185.9	14.7	10.8	-.1	-.0	14.1	.1	14.7
Metal products	42.4	9.8	64.7	-.9	-.1	-.0	.0	-.5	.1	-.9
Nonelectrical machinery	10.2	10.8	48.4	.5	.6	-.1	-.0	.5	.1	.5
Electrical machinery	24.5	.2	72.6	1.8	2.0	-.1	-.0	1.9	.1	1.8
Transport equipment	-28.6	88.3	185.6	-17.6	-18.0	.3	.0	-17.9	.1	-17.6
Miscellaneous manufactures	25.0	-11.8	-68.1	7.4	7.2	-.2	-.0	7.3	.1	7.5
Mining & quarrying				-2.0	-.2	.1	.1	-2.0	.1	-1.9
Utilities				.1	.0	.1	.1	.0	.1	.2
Construction				-.2	-.0	-.0	-.0	-.2	.1	-.1
Wholesale trade				-.2	-.0	.0	.0	-.4	.1	-.1
Transportation				-.1	-.0	.0	-.0	-.2	.1	-.0
Financial services				-.1	-.0	.1	.1	-.1	.1	.0
Personal services				-.2	-.0	.0	.0	-.3	.1	-.2

Table 7.7   Sectoral Effects on Canada of U.S.-Canada Free Trade, Tariffs Only, Post–Tokyo Round: Market Segmentation (percentage change)

Sector	Exports	Imports from: World	Imports from: United States	Output	Canada Firms	Price	Marginal Cost	Capital	Rental Rate	Employment
Agriculture	-11.5	38.7	55.3	-11.2	-7.8	.9	.5	-11.0	1.3	-10.5
Food	20.7	49.9	110.5	-4.2	-4.0	.5	.5	-5.2	1.3	-4.1
Textiles	-16.3	160.1	297.6	-39.8	-46.8	-.6	-.1	-46.1	1.3	-39.7
Clothing	111.0	42.1	378.1	-10.9	-11.3	-.4	-.4	-13.0	1.3	-10.9
Leather products	1,116.8	-93.6	-73.2	1,098.2	1,094.5	-7.6	-.3	1,095.4	1.3	1,098.3
Footwear	170.0	-21.6	304.8	20.6	15.6	-2.6	-2.0	15.3	1.3	20.7
Wood products	-18.0	48.8	58.7	-15.4	-13.9	.7	.4	-15.8	1.3	-15.3
Furniture, fixtures	75.4	151.1	233.7	-5.4	-9.2	-.9	-.0	-9.3	1.3	-5.4
Paper products	-42.3	134.6	143.5	-34.9	-31.8	1.4	.5	-34.7	1.3	-34.7
Printing, publishing	-6.6	26.4	30.5	-4.1	-4.5	.5	.4	-5.6	1.3	-4.1
Chemicals	-64.9	127.1	161.6	-72.5	-64.2	1.4	.4	-69.4	1.3	-72.1
Petroleum products	72.2	-5.4	17.2	75.3	72.0	-.2	.1	72.4	1.3	77.0
Rubber products	64.8	84.8	140.7	35.3	14.0	-1.9	.2	16.3	1.3	35.8
Nonmetal mineral products	-8.1	52.0	83.2	-7.9	-10.5	-.3	.0	-10.5	1.3	-7.6
Glass products	57.4	72.1	99.4	-14.1	-23.4	-1.9	.0	-20.8	1.3	-13.9
Iron & steel	23.9	34.5	82.8	-19.3	-11.7	.3	-.0	-12.5	1.3	-19.3
Nonferrous metals	-191.6	21.4	50.1	-191.9	-195.0	.5	.2	-192.6	1.3	-191.8
Metal products	37.9	113.9	156.2	-4.0	-8.9	-.4	.1	-7.5	1.3	-3.9
Nonelectrical machinery	37.6	22.6	37.6	5.3	2.5	-2.8	-.2	1.2	1.3	5.5
Electrical machinery	35.0	80.0	127.7	-14.7	-19.0	-.9	-.4	-18.1	1.3	-14.6
Transport equipment	185.3	-40.3	-42.2	170.6	153.3	-4.3	-1.4	156.8	1.3	170.7
Miscellaneous manufactures	-70.0	60.5	100.2	-76.7	-78.7	-.2	.2	-78.7	1.3	-76.3
Mining & quarrying				33.1	14.1	-.0	.7	31.3	1.3	34.6
Utilities				-3.3	-1.9	.8	.6	-4.3	1.3	-1.6
Construction				-.9	-1.0	.2	.1	-2.0	1.3	-.5
Wholesale trade				-.4	-.7	.3	.3	-3.0	1.3	.1
Transportation				.1	-.5	.1	.1	-1.7	1.3	.5
Financial services				1.2	.2	.5	.6	.1	1.3	2.4
Personal services				-1.8	-1.3	.5	.4	-2.6	1.3	-1.3

Exit accompanies the decline in output in most Canadian industries. The number of Canadian firms increases only in leather products (1,094.5 percent), footwear (15.6 percent), petroleum products (72.0 percent), rubber products (14.0 percent), nonelectrical machineray (2.5 percent), and transportation equipment (153.3 percent).

Though the MS and MC models yield similar intersectoral results, they differ in one important respect. Rationalization is much more prevalent for Canadian firms and much less prevalent for U.S. firms in the MS model than in the MC model. A comparison of the percentage change in industry output and number of firms in Canada shows that output per firm rises in sixteen of the twenty-two tradable sectors. This result is similar to that obtained with the MC model. However, rationalization also occurs in five of the seven nontradable sectors, whereas all the nontradable Canadian industries derationalized in the MC model.

In the United States, derationalization occurs in furniture and fixtures, petroleum products, rubber products, nonmetallic mineral products, glass products, iron and steel, metal products, nonelectrical machinery, and electrical machinery. In comparison, all U.S. industries increase output per firm in the MC model, except miscellaneous manufactures. In the nontradable industries, six of seven sectors derationalize in the MS model, compared to none in the MC model.

The relative return to capital in Canada increases by 1.3 percent, raising firm fixed costs. In order to maintain zero profits, firm output in Canada tends to rise. The return to capital in the U.S. increases as well, but by a much smaller 0.1 percent. This result suggests that the rationalization effects in the model may be quite sensitive to the method used for calculating the variable cost share, though demand side considerations are also affecting firm behavior.

7.5 Summary and Conclusions

Our purpose in this paper has been to review the important modeling issues involved in analyzing the economic effects of bilateral tariff removal between the United States and Canada. The major modeling issues identified include (1) improving modeling techniques for identifying the bilateral trade that will be subject to tariff removal, (2) whether liberalization would lead firms to increase output and capture scale economies in production, (3) whether the gains from the agreement would stem from increased intraindustry or interindustry trade, and (4) whether terms-of-trade effects or efficiency gains would dominate the welfare outcome of liberalization.

Three classes of models were identified as suitable for studying bilateral tariff removal. These are models in which products are differentiated at the national level, models in which products are differentiated at the firm level, and models in which markets are segmented at the national level.

In all three cases, markets may be imperfectly competitive as the result of increasing returns to scale in production. Reaping economies of scale provides an additional source of potential gain from trade liberalization, which is thought to be especially important in the Canadian case because of the small size of its national market. The determination of the scale of production for each firm in an MC market was shown theoretically to depend on the factor-intensity ranking of the industries most heavily protected. If liberalization raises the return to capital, thereby increasing ATC relative to marginal cost, firm output must rise to satisfy the zero-profit and maximum-profit conditions. The opposite occurs if the return to capital falls. Though the power of rationalization effects may depend on country size, the direction does not.

Previous studies of the U.S.-Canada FTA have exhibited a strong tendency toward the conclusions that increased trade will be primarily intraindustry, that rationalization will occur in most Canadian industries, but that Canada's terms of trade will deteriorate. These results where shown in section 7.1 to be influenced by the assumption of national product differentiation. In particular, national product differentiation and strong terms-of-trade effects appear to lie behind most negative welfare conclusions found for Canada.

Differentiating products by place of production is a convenient and popular procedure for identifying bilateral trade flows. However, the development of computational models with imperfectly competitive firms offers an attractive alternative. We have not provided empirical evidence that product differentiation is more likely to exist at the firm level than at the national level. However, given the artificial nature of the assumption of national product differentiation and its strong welfare, trade, and terms-of-trade implications, it should be used sparingly and only on the condition that this assumption is convincingly justified in each case. This is especially the case in view of the fact that differentiating products at the firm level sidesteps many of the problems associated with differentiation at the national level.

The theoretical results were illustrated using a general equilibrium computational model. Three market structures were adopted: perfect competition with national product differentiation; monopolistic competition with firm product differentiation; and a national market segmentation model with homogeneous products.

The computational results from the MC model *without* national product differentiation indicate that rationalization depends on the change in the return to capital, with the United States more likely to experience rationalization than Canada. Strong interindustry specialization occurs, particularly in Canada, with output in Canada declining in sixteen of the twenty-two tradable sectors and exports declining in eight tradable sectors. Intersectoral specialization gains are in part responsible for an increase in Canadian welfare by 1.2 percent of GDP, despite the deterioration in Canada's terms of trade. The U.S. welfare gain is also positive but smaller in absolute terms.

Notes

1. The Armington assumptions are that the utility function is weakly separable in goods and that the function used to aggregate the import and the domestically produced good is linearly homogeneous. That is, the utility function can be written as a function of the n goods, $U = U(X_1,...,X_n)$, and each good is an aggregate of the domestic and imported varieties, $X_i = f(X_i^H, X_i^M)$. These are simply the assumptions necessary for perfect aggregation as demonstrated by Green (1964).

2. National product differentiation and the terms of trade effects of a tariff are discussed in detail in Hamilton and Whalley (1983) and Brown (1987).

3. For a summary and analysis of the various studies of the U.S.-Canada FTA, see Brown and Stern (1989).

4. Flam and Helpman (1987, p. 87) explore a similar model but cast their results somewhat differently. They conclude that the utilization rate in industry 2 depends on whether the absolute value of the elasticity of supply of 2 with respect to the price of 1 is larger or smaller than the absolute value of the elasticity of research and development with respect to the price of 1.

5. Horstmann and Markusen make the additional assumption that there is a single factor of production.

6. This strong result depends on two assumptions. First, there is only one factor of production. As a result, the industry can expand without changing relative factor prices. This implies that the slope of the ATC curve does not change during the adjustment. Second, the demand for the domestic good is assumed to shift in a parallel fashion in response to changes in the price of imports. Thus, the slope of the demand curve is also unaffected. Together, these two assumptions imply that the point of tangency between the ATC curve and domestic demand will always occur at the same level of output.

7. Sufficient conditions for $A > 0$ are that all countries of the model are identical and that all countries impose a positive tariff. This implies that $y_i = y_j$, $x_i^i = x_i^k$, and $y_i > x_j^i$. An alternative is that $y_i > x_i^i + x_i^k$ and that $y_i > x_j^i$. That is, a typical firm sells more domestically than it exports, and a domestic firm sells more to the domestic market than a foreign firm.

8. This condition requires that a country 3 firm's sales to the domestic market add more to profits than exports to country 1 as compared to a typical firm in country 2. As a result, an increase in p_1 and a fall in p_3 that hold country 3 firm profits at zero will imply positive profits for country 2 firms. Thus, dp_2 must be less than zero.

9. For the proportionately differentiated equations of the model, see the appendix to Brown and Stern (1989).

10. The thirty-two countries are sixteen industrialized countries (Australia, Austria, Belgium-Luxembourg, Denmark, the Federal Republic of Germany, Finland, France, Ireland, Italy, Japan, the Netherlands, New Zealand, Norway, Sweden, Switzerland, and the United Kingdom) and sixteen newly industrializing countries (Argentina, Brazil, Chile, Colombia, Greece, Hong Kong, India, Israel, Mexico, Portugal, Singapore, South Korea, Spain, Taiwan, Turkey, and Yugoslavia).

11. Values for these parameters can be obtained from the authors on request.

12. See Brown and Stern (1987) and Boadway and Treddenick (1978).

References

Armington, P. S. 1969. A theory of demand for products distinguished by place of production. *International Monetary Fund Staff Papers* 16:159–76.

Boadway, R., and J. Treddenick. 1978. A general equilibrium computation of the effects of the Canadian tariff structure. *Canadian Journal of Economics* 11(3):424–46.

Brown, D. K. 1987. Tariffs, the terms of trade and national product differentiation. *Journal of Policy Modeling* 9(3):503–26.

Brown, D. K., and R. M. Stern. 1987. A modeling perspective. In *Perspectives on a U.S.-Canadian free trade agreement*, ed. R. M. Stern, P. H. Trezise, and J. Whalley, 155–82. Washington, D.C.: Brookings Institution.

———. 1989. Computable general equilibrium estimates of the gains from U.S.-Canadian trade liberalization. In *Economic aspects of regional trading arrangements*, ed. T. Hyclak and D. Greenaway. London: Wheatsheaf Books.

Dixit, A., and J. E. Stiglitz. 1977. Monopolistic competition and optimum product diversity. *American Economic Review* 67(3):297–308.

Flam, H., and E. Helpman. 1987. Industrial policy under monopolistic competition. *Journal of International Economics* 22(1–2):79–102.

Green, H. A. J. 1964. *Aggregation in economic analysis: An introductory survey.* Princeton, N.J.: Princeton University Press.

Hamilton, B., and J. Whalley. 1983. Optimal tariff calculations in alternative trade models and some possible implications for current world trading arrangements. *Journal of International Economics* 15(3–4):323–48.

———. 1985. Geographically discriminatory trade arrangements. *Review of Economics and Statistics* 67(3):446–55.

Harris, R. 1984. Applied general equilibrium analysis of small open economies with scale economies and imperfect competition. *American Economic Review* 74(5):1016–32.

Horridge, M. 1987. Increasing returns to scale and the long run effects of a tariff reform. Preliminary Working Paper no. OP-62. IMPACT Research Centre, University of Melbourne and Industries Assistance Commission.

Horstmann, I. J., and J. R. Markusen. 1986. Up the average cost curve: Inefficiententry and the new protectionism. *Journal of International Economics* 20(3–4):225–47.

Krugman, P. R. 1979. Increasing returns, monopolistic competition, and international trade. *Journal of International Economics* 9(4):469–79.

Markusen, J. R. 1981. Trade and gains from trade with imperfect competition. *Journal of International Economics* 11(4):531–51.

Nguyen, T. T., and R. M. Wigle. 1987. Imperfect competition and world trade: An applied general equilibrium analysis. University of Western Ontario. Mimeo.

Smith, A., and A. Venables. 1988. Completing the internal market in the European Community: Some industry simulations. Discussion Paper no. 233. London: Centre for Economic Policy Research.

Spence, M. E. 1976. Production selection, fixed costs, and monopolistic competition. *Review of Economic Studies* 43(2):217–36.

Venables, A. J. 1985. Trade and trade policy with imperfect competition: The case of identical products and free entry. *Journal of International Economics* 19(1–2):1–20.

Wigle, R. M. 1988. General equilibrium evaluation of Canada-U.S. trade liberalization in a global context. *Canadian Economic Journal* 20(3):539–64.

Comment   Robert W. Staiger

I found the paper by Brown and Stern to be extremely interesting. The authors consider a timely topic and use the opportunity to produce some suggestive numbers on the likely magnitude of the gains from the U.S.-Canada free trade agreement as well as to tackle some important methodological issues in computable general equilibrium (CGE) modeling in the presence of noncompetitive markets. The authors compare the gains from trade liberalization between the United States and Canada under three model scenarios corresponding to three different characterizations of market structure: that markets are competitive but the Armington assumption holds, that markets are monopolistically competitive, and that markets are segmented. As might be expected from the work of Harris (1984), and as the authors illustrate here, market structure can have a profound effect on the nature and magnitude of the gains from trade liberalization.

The results described by the authors under the three market structure alternatives are suggestive of the contributions to the overall gains from trade liberalization that each kind of industry will make. Nevertheless, no single market structure will characterize all industries, and the assumption made by the authors that all industries are either perfectly competitive, monopolistically competitive, or segmented must be viewed as artificial. Thus, while I find the quantitative results intriguing, for this and other reasons outlined below I interpret the main contribution of the paper as methodological rather than empirical.

In this regard, I found the discussion of the monopolistically competitive model most interesting but, at the same time, least transparent. I will therefore focus my comments on what I view as the paper's main methodological insight with regard to the monopolistically competitive model: that is, the link between protection and output per firm in the monopolistically competitive sector, or the issue of "rationalization." After summarizing the authors' methodological points, I will then comment on their attempt to implement these insights in the CGE modeling experiment of the paper.

Rationalization

In my view, the main contribution of the paper involves formalizing the general equilibrium relation between "rationalization" and changes in factor prices that accompany a change in the level of protection in a two-factor setting. Here, I will attempt to summarize the main argument.

The free-entry (symmetric) equilibrium conditions for a monopolistically competitive industry are given by the profit-maximizing markup equation and the free-entry zero-profit condition

Robert W. Staiger is assistant professor of economics at Stanford University and a faculty research fellow of the National Bureau of Economic Research.

(1)
$$\frac{P - C_q(r, w, q)}{P} = 1/\eta \, ,$$

(2)
$$P = C(r, w, q)/q,$$

where firm subscripts can be dropped owing to symmetry and where P, $C(\cdot)$, and $C_q(\cdot)$ are price, total cost, and marginal cost, respectively, of the monopolistically competitive good, r and w are rental and wage rates, q is the output level of a representative firm in the industry, and η is the elasticity of demand as perceived by the firm with the sign reversed. Expressions (1) and (2) can be combined to yield

(3)
$$1 - \frac{1}{\eta} = \frac{C_q(r, w, q)}{C(r, w, q)/q} \, .$$

Under the assumption of constant marginal costs, (3) can be rewritten as

(4)
$$1 - \frac{1}{\eta} = \frac{C_q(\omega)}{C(\omega, q)/q} \equiv \theta(\omega, q),$$

where ω is the wage-to-rental ratio w/r. The variable $\theta(\omega, q)$ is the elasticity of cost with respect to output, the inverse of which is used as an index of scale economies by Helpman and Krugman (1985).

Expression (4) implicitly defines equilibrium output per firm as a function of ω and η, or

(5)
$$q = q(\omega, \eta).$$

Totally differentiating (5) with respect to the tariff τ yields

(6)
$$\frac{dq}{d\tau} = \frac{\delta q}{\delta \omega} \frac{d\omega}{d\tau} + \frac{\delta q}{\delta \eta} \frac{d\eta}{d\tau}.$$

Note from (6) that, if the demand elasticity is unaltered, a change in the level of protection will affect the equilibrium level of output for the representative firm in the sector only through its effect on the wage-rental ratio ω. It is this production side link between trade liberalization and rationalization that is in my view the primary methodological contribution of the paper.

To focus on this link between changes in protection and output per firm in the monopolistically competitive sector, I will assume throughout that demand elasticity is held constant. To see how output per firm varies with relative factor prices when the elasticity of demand is held constant, totally differentiate (4) to get

(7)
$$\frac{\delta q}{\delta \omega} = \frac{-\delta\theta/\delta\omega}{\delta\theta/\delta q} .$$

Therefore, with the elasticity of demand held constant, the general equilibrium effect of a change in the level of protection on output per firm in the monopolistically competitive sector is given by

$$(8) \qquad \frac{dq}{d\tau} = \frac{\delta q}{\delta \omega} \frac{d\omega}{d\tau} = \frac{-\delta\theta/\delta\omega}{\delta\theta/\delta q} \frac{d\omega}{d\tau}.$$

Direct calculation and substitution of equilibrium condition (4) allows (8) to be rewritten as

$$(9) \qquad \frac{dq}{d\tau} = - [q\eta(\varphi - \psi)]\frac{d\omega}{d\tau}$$

where φ and ψ are the elasticities of marginal and total cost, respectively, with respect to the wage-rental rate.

With the assumption of constant marginal cost, total cost can be written as

$$(10) \qquad C(\omega, q) = F(\omega) + qC_q(\omega, q),$$

where $F(\omega)$ is fixed cost for a representative firm. Using (10), an expression for $(\varphi - \psi)$ can be derived as

$$(11) \qquad \varphi - \psi = (1 - \theta)\left(\varphi - \frac{\delta F}{\delta \omega}\frac{\omega}{F}\right).$$

Hence, $\varphi - \psi$ will be positive if and only if fixed costs are more capital intensive than variable costs. Expression (9) then implies that, provided this factor intensity condition is met,

$$(12) \qquad \text{sign}\left(\frac{dq}{d\tau}\right) = - \text{sign}\left(\frac{d\omega}{d\tau}\right).$$

In words, abstracting from demand side effects, the monopolistically competitive sector will undergo "rationalization" when trade is liberalized if and only if liberalization reduces the wage-rental ration in the country.

Figure 7C.1 illustrates this relation. The variable θ is measured on the vertical axis, while output is measured on the horizontal axis. The positively sloped solid curve measures θ as a function of output holding factor prices fixed at ω_0. This curve will have a positive slope provided we maintain the assumption of constant marginal cost. A solid horizontal line has been plotted through $1 - 1/\eta$, and its intersection with the θ curve determines the equilibrium output level given factor prices ω_0. Firm profits would be negative if output were below q_0, leading to exit and a rise in output per remaining firm. Output above q_0 would result in positive firm profits and a fall in output per firm as entry of new firms occurs.

An increase in the wage-rental ratio will shift the θ curve vertically upward provided that fixed costs are more capital intensive than variable costs. At the original level of output, firms now make positive profits owing to the

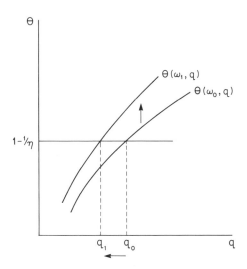

Fig. 7C.1   Rationalization and the wage-rental ratio

diminished magnitude of fixed relative to variable costs. This induces entry and lowers output per firm.

The production side relation between liberalization and rationalization is surprising both in its simplicity and in its apparent generality. Aside from the free-entry equilibrium conditions for monopolistic competition, the relation requires only that marginal costs be constant and that fixed costs be more capital intensive than variable costs. Of course, as the authors point out, demand side consideration also enter, and changes in demand elasticities associated with liberalization will factor into the rationalization process. But I think the authors have isolated an interesting and potentially important link between trade liberalization and rationalization.

Implementation

The power of the theoretical predictions outlined above can be readily appreciated once we turn to implementation. To quantify the bracketed term in the relation in (9), surprisingly little information need be gathered. In particular, under the assumption that capital is the only fixed factor, the authors require only measures of labor's primary input cost share, the primary input share of total cost, firm output, and the elasticity of demand faced by firms in the monopolistically competitive sector. Data on the first three variables are readily available. However, data on demand elasticities are difficult to come by and are absolutely crucial: demand elasticities play a central role in the production side relation emphasized by the authors, not to mention the direct effect that changes in demand elasticities will have on rationalization in response to trade liberalization.

For this reason, the quality of the results of the CGE experiments that the authors undertake in an attempt to quantify these relations will depend heavily on the quality of their estimates of demand elasticities for the monopolistically competitive sectors. Unfortunately, the authors come very close to simply assuming a value for the demand elasticities of the model with little in the way of discussion to support their chosen values. In the light of the central importance of the demand elasticities in determining the degree of rationalization in their model, this comes close to assuming the quantitative effects that are the focus of the paper. As such, I would have more confidence in drawing general lessons from the CGE modeling results of this paper if better estimates of the crucial demand elasticities could be found.

References

Harris, Richard. 1984. Applied general equilibrium analysis of small open economies and imperfect competition. *American Economic Review* 74(December):1016–32.
Helpman, Elhanan, and Paul R. Krugman. 1985. *Market structure and foreign trade.* Cambridge, Mass.: MIT Press.

Comment   John Whalley

I very much enjoyed this paper by Brown and Stern, which struck me as both well written and interesting. What the paper does is to use three different numerical general equilibrium models to look at tariff cuts between Canada and the United States using 1976 data. These are a perfectly competitive model, a monopolistically competitive model, and a market segmentation model.

The conclusion is that the model matters for the evaluation of tariff cuts. The early material in the paper gives clear intuition as to how various model features interact. For instance, with an assumption of product differentiation at the national level plus product differentiation by firm, it is clear that there are small rationalization effects resulting from tariff cuts. In turn, rationalization effects depend most on factor intensity differences across industries.

I have two points to make about the paper. One concerns the applicability of the paper to the recent Canada-U.S. free trade agreement and the other the results and implications of the analysis.

John Whalley is director for the Centre for the Study of International Economic Relations and professor of economics at the University of Western Ontario. He also currently holds the William G. Davis chair for international economics and is a research associate of the National Bureau of Economic Research.

First, however, I will present some comments about Canada-U.S. trade and the applicability of this analysis to the current free trade agreement. The Canada-U.S. free trade agreement is, of course, much more than the tariff cuts that are considered in this paper and, in turn, apply to 1988 rather than 1976 tariffs. The agreement has twenty-one chapters and is longer than the whole of the General Agreement on Tariffs and Trade (GATT). It has complex chapters on dispute settlement, energy, investment, agriculture, procurement, services, financial services, and standards. As a result, it is important to keep in mind that the paper is only tangentially related to the issues that are at the heart of the Canada-U.S. free trade agreement.

Indeed, from the point of view of the Canadians, who were the demanders for this agreement, the main objective was security of access rather than improvements in access per se. From the Canadian side, tariffs were not that big an issue. In the aggregate, approximately 80 percent of Canadian exports are already duty free, although there are remaining spikes in the U.S. tariff wall, particularly in the textiles area. Indeed, the tariff reductions are by no means complete since in the textile area these are restricted by a tariff quota.

As a result, when evaluating the agreement, it is important to keep in mind that such issues as the security value to Canada from hoped-for improvements on dispute settlement applying to countervailing and antidumping duties are in no way attacked through this modeling effort. Equally, from a U.S. point of view, the security value of access to Canadian energy supplies is not quantified, nor is the removal of investment restrictions.

In addition, it is important to keep in mind the nature of Canada-U.S. trade and how that also qualifies the analysis in this paper. A large fraction— my impression is as large as 60–70 percent of Canada-U.S. trade in manufacturers—is trade that is internal to integrated firms across the border. Thus, much of the analysis in the paper hinging on national product differentiation no longer applies. In turn, around 50 percent of Canadian exports to the United States are in the form of nonmanufactured exports. Also, 30 percent of trade takes place in autos and parts under the coverage of the auto pact, again covering vertically integrated firms on both sides of the border. Thus, to apply this modeling framework in an overly mechanical way to Canada-U.S. trade might be somewhat misleading.

Also, in analyzing rationalization effects, it seems to me that this paper has to confront the Canada-U.S. productivity differences that were at the heart of the earlier Harris analysis. This showed large effects from Canada-U.S. free trade, resulting from the collusive behavior in his work. The old view in Canada, from the 1950s, was that average costs in manufacturing were about 30 percent higher in Canada than in the United States and that production runs were shorter. As a result, there were more product lines per plant. These differentials tended to fall in the 1960s and 1970s as tariffs fell. These were the stylized facts that Harris was attempting to deal with in his work on Canada-U.S. trade but that in the framework in which Brown and Stern present are perhaps less transparent.

With these comments about the applicability of the modeling to both current Canada-U.S. trade and the agreement, it is perhaps worth moving on to some comments about the results and their implications. First comes the issue of the size and the sign of the welfare effects and how these change as model selection changes. In the constant returns-to-scale case, the authors find that, owing to an adverse terms-of-trade effect, Canada loses as a result of bilateral tariff elimination. This, in turn, reflects the differential level of initial tariffs. Although Canada is the smaller country and therefore might be expected to gain, because they have the higher level of initial protection they therefore lose.

In the monopolistically competitive model, they find, in contrast, that Canada gains by about 1.2 percent of GNP. And, in the market structure case, although the welfare effects are not emphasized, there is a loss of around 0.6 percent of GNP.

Rather than emphasize only the sign difference, it is important to compare these results to those of other studies, such as Harris. Harris's earlier models produced welfare effects for Canada as large as 10 percent of GNP because of large rationalization effects. Harris's treatment of collusion and implicit limit pricing under his treatment of the Eastman-Stykolt hypothesis has been discussed at some length in the literature. But the point to keep in mind is that the variation in results among the model approaches used by Brown and Stern is small compared to the larger differences relative to Harris.

Second, there is an issue of whether the authors' results are more parameter dependent than structure dependent. For instance, perceived elasticities in the monopolistically competitive model are not endogenous, nor are the markup rates. There are sensitivity analyses in the paper, and these indicate limited sensitivity of findings, but the question as to parameter or structural dependence remains as central in evaluating their results.

Third are some issues as to the plausibility of some of the detailed industry results in their analysis. For instance, in their table 7.5, there is an 85 percent increase in the output of transport equipment in Canada as a result of joint elimination of tariffs. This occurs even though there is free trade between Canada and the United States under the auto pact and is, therefore, somewhat doubtful. Also, there is a 32 percent reduction in output of textiles in Canada. It has long been held to be the case in Canada that the textile industry would be one of the main beneficiaries of a comprehensive Canada-U.S. trade agreement because of the improved access to the large U.S. market behind the quota wall against all developing countries through the multifiber arrangement provisions. Thus, a 32 percent reduction in output of textiles in Canada when the U.S. industry has fought so hard to maintain tariff protection against Canadian textiles in the actual negotiations seems somewhat implausible.

Fourth, there are some features of the model that are perhaps a little misleading. The entry assumptions are perhaps inadequately defended. The implication seems to be that all firms in the monopolistically competitive case are of equal size. This is too strong since a typical structure is to have a small number of large firms and a larger number of small firms.

There are also issues concerning the modeling of Canada-U.S. barriers themselves and how they are to be interpreted vis- à-vis price dispersion data. My understanding, for instance, is that there are data in Europe that show that as part of the current integration exercise in Europe there is more dispersion among prices in national domestic markets in products where it is known that there are no significant country barriers than in those products where major barriers exist. This suggests that it may well be differences in market structure across the two borders that are more important than price differentials induced by restrictions.

In the final analysis, the question that I ask myself is whether this analysis has convinced me of major propositions that are important for the analysis of Canada-U.S. trade. The major contribution clearly lies in the insights the paper has generated rather than the precise results. Market structure makes a difference for the welfare analysis of trade policy. We can build many different models with different results. Unfortunately, however, there are other potential market structures that have not been taken into account in this analysis. Also, it is not obvious that one necessarily wants the same market structure for all industries, and the results are always parameter dependent— markups, the treatment of scale economies, and perceived elasticities all matter. Brown and Stern have given us an excellent paper, one that takes us well on our way, but more analysis is clearly needed.

Contributors

Harry P. Bowen
Graduate School of Business Administration
New York University
100 Trinity Place, Room 810
New York, NY 10006

Drusilla K. Brown
Department of Economics
Tufts University
Medford, MA 02155

Elias Dinopoulos
Department of Economics
University of Florida
Gainesville, FL 32611

Robert Driskill
Department of Economics
410 Arps Hall
Ohio State University
1945 North High Street
Columbus, OH 43210-1172

Barry Eichengreen
Department of Economics
University of California
250 Barrows Hall
Berkeley, CA 94720

Robert C. Feenstra
Department of Economics
University of California
Davis, CA 95616

Raquel Fernandez
Department of Economics
Boston University
270 Bay State Road
Boston, MA 02215

Ronald D. Fischer
Department of Economics
114 Rouss Hall
University of Virginia
Charlottesville, VA 22901

Kenneth A. Froot
National Bureau of Economic Research
1050 Massachusetts Avenue
Cambridge, MA 02138

Alberto Giovannini
622 Uris Hall
Graduate School of Business
Columbia University
New York, NY 10027

Lawrence H. Goulder
Department of Economics
Harvard University
Littauer 212
Cambridge, MA 02138

Lawrence F. Katz
National Bureau of Economic Research
1050 Massachusetts Avenue
Cambridge, MA 02138

James Levinsohn
Department of Economics
University of Michigan
Ann Arbor, MI 48109

Keith E. Maskus
International Economic Studies Center
Campus Box 256
University of Colorado
Boulder, CO 80309-0256

Stephen McCafferty
Department of Economics
410 Arps Hall
Ohio State University
1945 North High Street
Columbus, OH 43210-1172

Catherine J. Morrison
Department of Economics
Tufts University
Medford, MA 02155

Edward John Ray
Department of Economics
Ohio State University
410B Arps Hall
1945 North High Street
Columbus, OH 43210-1172

David W. Roland-Holst
Department of Economics
Mills College
Oakland, CA 94613

Gary R. Saxonhouse
Department of Economics
611 Tappan Street, Room 213
The University of Michigan
Ann Arbor, MI 48109

Lawrence Schembri
Department of Economics
Loeb Building
Carleton University
Ottawa, Ontario K1S 5B6
Canada

Robert W. Staiger
Department of Economics
Stanford University
Stanford, CA 94305

Robert M. Stern
Department of Economics
University of Michigan
Ann Arbor, MI 48109

Lawrence H. Summers
National Bureau of Economic Research
1050 Massachusetts Avenue
Cambridge, MA 02138

Laura D'Andrea Tyson
BRIE
University of California
2234 Piedmont Avenue
Berkeley, CA 94027

John Whalley
Department of Economics
Social Science Centre
University of Western Ontario
London, Ontario N6A 5C2
Canada

Wing Thye Woo
Department of Economics
University of California
Davis, CA 95616

Author Index

Subject Index

Airbus Industrie, 102–3
Armington assumptions, 218–19, 223, 244n.1
Assets: household decisions for allocation of, 15–16, 37, 45; substitutability of, 7, 11, 16–18
Automobile industry, 102–3
Average total cost (ATC), 220–22

Bertrand conjecture equilibrium, 133, 138–39

Canada: direct investment in U.S. by, 53–58, 70; export industry pricing in, 187–88, 194–96, 197–203; and free trade agreement with U.S., 217–18, 250–53
Capital: flow of, 45; mobility or immobility of, 7, 26–33, 39, 45, 47
CES. *See* Constant elasticity of substitution (CES) function
CGE. *See* Computable general equilibrium (CGE) model
Comparative advantage, 146, 154. *See also* Factor endowments
Competitiveness, international, 6–7
Computable general equilibrium (CGE) model, 5–6, 7–22, 46–47
Computational model, to analyze effects of trade liberalization, 228–42
Conjecture variations equilibrium. *See* Nash-Cournot noncooperative equilibrium

Conjecture(s). *See* Bertrand conjecture equilibrium; Consistent conjecture; Cournot conjectures
Consistent conjecture, 133, 138
Constant elasticity of substitution (CES) function, 16, 18, 220
Consumption: of manufactures in Japan, 145–46; tax to promote savings, 26–30; treatment in CGE model of, 18, 34, 37
Contract costs, effect on foreign direct investment decisions of, 58–62. *See also* Licensing
Cournot conjectures, 138
Cournot followers, 226–28
Current Population Surveys (CPS), 88–92

Data sources, 22–25, 196–97
Demand elasticities, 247, 249–50
Derationalization of production, 242
Differentiated products models, 219–26, 242–43. *See also* Derationalization of production; Rationalization of production
Dixit-Stiglitz-Spence utility function, 219–20
Duopoly, international: analysis using output adjustment costs, 125–37

Elasticity of substitution, 37
Equilibria, intra- and intertemporal, 20–22. *See also* Expectations
European Community (EC), direct investment in U.S. by, 53–58, 70
Excess demand, 39–40